HELL ON THE EDGE
OF HEAVEN

"Help me," a faint voice said. It sounded like a little girl.

Venturing outside, Ida walked the one hundred feet or so to the end of her cinder driveway. "Where are you?" Ida called out. "Keep calling. I'm coming."

"Help me."

Ida picked up her pace and walked to the top of the rock trail. It led to a popular fishing spot, a secluded lava-rock cliff that overlooked the ocean.

Ida heard sobbing. She followed the sobs along the trail, peering into the jungle of dense, prickly shrubs that grew alongside it. About halfway down she stopped dead in her tracks. A battered young woman lay on her back in the bushes like a discarded piece of rubbish. Her head faced the ocean and her body was partially covered with branches and shrubbery.

Her long hair was so soaked in blood that Ida could hardly tell it was blond.

"Who did this to you?" Ida asked.

"Help me up," the woman begged, extending her hand toward Ida . . .

MURDER IN PARADISE

A Christmas in Hawaii Turns to Tragedy

CHRIS LOOS AND RICK CASTBERG

AVON BOOKS
An Imprint of HarperCollinsPublishers

Murder in Paradise is a journalistic account of the actual murder investigation of Frank Pauline Jr., Albert Ian Schweitzer, and Shawn Schweitzer for the 1991 killing of Dana Ireland in Hawaii. The events recounted in this book are true. The personalities, events, actions, and conversations portrayed in this book have been constructed using court records, police reports, personal interviews, newspaper reports, and personal papers. The names of certain individuals referred to in this work have been changed to protect their privacy. In any such event, the use of the name of an actual individual is entirely coincidental.

AVON BOOKS
An Imprint of HarperCollins*Publishers*
10 East 53rd Street
New York, New York 10022-5299

First Avon Books paperback printing: August 2003

Avon Trademark Reg. U.S. Pat. Off. and in Other Countries, Marca Registrada, Hecho en U.S.A.
HarperCollins® is a registered trademark of HarperCollins Publishers Inc.

Printed in the U.S.A.

10 9 8 7 6 5 4 3 2

In memory of Dana Ireland, who treasured life.

MURDER
IN
PARADISE

Chapter 1

Ida Smith called her small wooden house a fishing shack. It was anything but fancy. The windows were screened but had no glass, which was not unusual for this part of Hawaii. What distinguished this house from others in the area was the stunning ocean view across the dirt road in front. As she watched the waves, Ida began preparing dinner. It was Christmas Eve and she was in high spirits.

Ida's neighborhood, Waa Waa, is one of many sparsely populated subdivisions in Puna, a district of the Big Island as different from Waikiki Beach as the Adirondacks are from Manhattan. The absence of basic services—telephones, electricity, even county-supplied water—enhances the tranquility that draws people to Puna from the U.S. mainland, not as tourists but as residents.

The water flowing from Ida's kitchen faucet came from rainwater diverted from her roof to a backyard reservoir and then pumped into the house. The rainfall at Hilo airport this year, at 151 inches, was more than 23 inches above average.

The National Weather Service had predicted showers, but they had never materialized.

Over the hum of the pump, Ida heard something she thought was a truck gunning its engine. Perhaps the driver was trying to maneuver out of the gravel fishing trail across the way. Vehicles without four-wheel drive often got stuck there.

Ida was a large woman, 56 years old. She busied herself in the kitchen for another five or ten minutes before a high-pitched noise attracted her attention. At first she hardly noticed it over the crashing surf. It sounded like the call of the hawks that soar above Puna's *ohia* forests. On second thought, it was more like the screaming of children at play. Maybe the part-time neighbors in the house next door were having a Christmas party. She put down her vegetables and listened. It was about 4:45.

"Help me," a faint voice said. It sounded like a little girl.

Venturing outside, Ida walked the 100 feet or so to the end of her cinder driveway and then turned right and headed for the house next door. It looked deserted.

"Help me." The voice definitely wasn't coming from the neighbor's house.

"Where are you? Keep calling. I'm coming," Ida called back. *Maybe someone had an accident on the fishing trail*, she thought.

"Help me. Help me. I'm over here."

Ida picked up her pace and walked to the top of the rock trail, about 100 yards from her property.

The trail led to a popular fishing spot, a secluded lava-rock cliff that overlooked the ocean.

Ida heard sobbing. She scanned the length of the 100-foot trail, but saw no one. "I'm coming. I'm coming," she said, puzzled. She followed the sobs along the trail, peering into the jungle of dense, prickly shrubs that grew alongside it.

About halfway down Ida stopped dead in her tracks and gasped. Off to the right, a battered young woman lay on her back in the bushes like a discarded piece of rubbish. Her head faced the ocean and her body was partially covered with branches and shrubbery. Ida moved closer. What she saw made her shudder. The woman's long hair was so soaked in blood that Ida could hardly tell it was blond. The woman's left shoe was missing, her denim shorts were pulled down below her knees, and her halter top was pushed up to her neck, exposing a lean, light-skinned torso covered with bruises and scratches. Her right arm had a deep cut. A large, U-shaped gash on her head exposed part of her skull. Blood flowed from between her legs and her left breast had teeth marks around the nipple.

Ida's heart raced. Her palms were clammy and she was breathing hard. "Oh, my God. Who did this to you?" she asked.

The shivering woman muttered something through torn lips. "Help me up," she begged, extending her hand toward Ida.

Hoping to take the woman to her house so she could drive her to the hospital, Ida grasped her hand. The woman shrieked with pain. Ida backed off. The blood was attracting flies.

"Do you know where you are?" Ida asked the bloody woman.

"No, sir," she said, clearly confused, and then muttered something else.

"What, honey?"

"Help me take 'em off," she said, pointing to the shorts binding her ankles.

Ida carefully removed the shorts and the lone athletic shoe, trying not to touch the legs that were scraped raw as if they'd been dragged on a rough surface. She placed the shoes and shorts on the trail two feet away from where the young woman lay. The woman began screaming and flailing her arms.

Ida took a deep breath and tried to figure out how to get help.

"I'll be right back," she said. "I need to run up to my house to get a blanket. I'll be right back."

"No!" the woman screamed. "Stay."

"Okay," Ida said. She gingerly took the woman's hand. "Let's pray."

Ida recited a special prayer she reserved for dire emergencies. After a few minutes, the woman stopped screaming.

"What's your name?" Ida asked.

"Dana."

"Don't worry, Dana," Ida said. "Everything's going to be all right."

She ran home for a sheet and a quilt, since she had no medical supplies at home and knew it was unwise for a bystander to move an injured person without medical help available. Her house had no telephone so she had no way to call for help; the houses were few and far between in this remote neighborhood, a hodgepodge of shacks and designer homes occupied by people who shared a common love for the isolation of the jungle. She rushed back to the trail and spread the bedding over Dana. The high temperature today had been 82 degrees, but this was winter, so the mercury would drop to 65 degrees before morning.

The sky glowed a spectacular shade of lavender—a nice touch on Christmas Eve. Elsewhere in Puna people took time to gaze at it. But all it meant to Ida was that nightfall was coming. She returned home to get her Chevy Suburban, driving it down her driveway, across the road, and onto the trail. She parked it with the headlights shining on Dana. While waiting for someone to come along, she took Dana's hand and prayed with her again.

A short time later, Ida heard a car on the road above. She left Dana and ran up the trail, yelling and waving her arms. In the car was Hazel Allan, who was headed to her house five minutes away.

"Help!" Ida said. "There's a woman in the bushes. She's been raped. She's in very bad shape. She needs help."

Shaken, Hazel promised she would call the police when she got home. Hawaii County didn't yet have an emergency 911 system. Emergency phone calls had to be placed separately to the police and fire departments by dialing the appropriate seven-digit numbers. It wasn't policy for a police dispatcher to notify a fire department dispatcher automatically but Hazel, like most residents, wasn't aware of that.

When she got home she dialed the police emergency number from a mobile phone she kept in her house. That call was logged in at 5:47 P.M. Hazel repeated what Ida had told her and gave directions to the site.

"You go down Kahakai from Pahoa to Government Beach Road and then take the Government Beach Road. Her van is parked on the side of the road," she said. "It's like a blue Wagoneer, and it's less than two miles down the Beach Road, and it's before the Waa Waa Subdivision turnoff, which doesn't have a sign. It doesn't have a road post, name, or anything, but it's less than two miles."

Assuming police were familiar with the unpaved road, Hazel didn't think it necessary to describe its condition. Like many Puna roads, Beach Road was narrow and uneven, covered only with crushed lava rock for most of its length. Dense jungle hugged both sides, forming a dark, narrow passage that looked like a scene from a *Tarzan* movie. In some spots, cars had to pull off to the side to let oncoming traffic pass.

Hawaii County residents love the wide open spaces and natural beauty of their island, but they pay the price by living with fewer government services than more populated areas do. Hawaii

County is almost exactly the same size as Los Angeles County but has only 1.5 percent of its population, and thus a much smaller tax base.

After police took Hazel's call, a dispatcher radioed Sergeant Gabriel Malani, who was investigating a bicycle accident five miles from Dana's Waa Waa location. There, police had found a crushed bike but no sign of a young woman named Dana Ireland who'd been riding it. The dispatcher informed Malani of a possible rape victim in a blue Jeep Wagoneer in Waa Waa. Sergeant Malani connected the two incidents and assigned Officer Harold Pinnow to the scene. Police didn't know the extent of Dana's injuries other than Hazel Allan's description that she was in bad shape.

Shortly after Hazel left to call the police, another car passed. Ida flagged it down.

"You don't have any weapons, do you?" she asked.

The woman and three men in the car thought she was crazy until she told them about Dana. Not sure whom she could trust, Ida insisted that the men stay in the car but took the woman down the trail with her. When the woman returned to the car, tears were streaming down her face. The men jumped out and rushed down to try to help Dana. One of them wore a Santa Claus hat adorned with battery-operated Christmas lights. It was a bizarre contrast to the bloody woman moaning in the bushes.

Ida ran back home for another quilt while one

of the men, Brian, sped off with the woman, Ronlen, to find a phone and to locate a nearby nurse friend of his. Ida no longer was wary of the strangers because they showed such concern for Dana. It was now about six o'clock and nearly dark.

Geri, the nurse, returned to the scene with Brian while her husband ran next door to call the police. Geri inspected Dana's injuries and decided it was safe to move her. She supervised the others as they carried Dana from the bushes to a level area on the rock trail and then eased her onto the ground.

Geri's first priority was to treat Dana for shock. With help from the others, she elevated Dana's feet and re-covered her with Ida's blankets. Dana drifted in and out of consciousness. Most of the time she was incoherent. At one point, she muttered something about "Mike Ingham." Another time she said something about getting into a fight with her boyfriend at the beach.

Geri held a gauze pad to Dana's head, trying to stop the bleeding. "We've got to get her some help, quick."

"Just give me the keys and I'll drive home," Dana said.

At 6:07 P.M. police received the call from Geri's husband. The dispatcher told him that officers were already on the way and then called the fire department, using a direct hot line.

"This is Don, dispatch. We need an ambulance.

Kahakai Boulevard, take a right on Government Beach Road, female sex assault victim."

"So it's going to be how far when you get onto Government Beach Road?" the Fire Department dispatcher asked.

"It should be right after you get on Government Beach Road." He neglected to mention that 20 minutes earlier Hazel Allen had told police the location was about two miles farther on Beach Road.

At 6:09 P.M. the dispatcher radioed the fire engine stationed in Pahoa, nine miles away, and the ambulance stationed in Keaau, another nine miles beyond Pahoa, telling their crews about the report of a sex assault victim. He directed them to go all the way down Kahakai Boulevard and then turn right on Government Beach Road. The Pahoa ambulance normally would have been sent, but it was out of the area dropping off a patient at Hilo Hospital.

At 6:13 the fire dispatcher called police dispatch for more information about the victim and her location. The police dispatcher said the victim was in a blue Renegade, changed it to a blue Wagoneer, and then said the victim actually was on the side of the road.

"She's conscious, but she's been badly beaten," he said. This information was immediately relayed to the crews on the fire engine and ambulance.

Twelve minutes later, the firefighters reported that they made a right turn from Kahakai Boulevard onto Beach Road but saw no sign of the Wag-oneer. By now, Officer Harold Pinnow had already arrived at Dana's side, but the police dispatcher still hadn't given the correct location to the fire dispatcher.

It wasn't possible for police to speak directly with the fire department by radio. As is common in most jurisdictions, fire and police departments are assigned different radio frequencies. All communications from units in the field had to go through their respective dispatchers, who then spoke to each other over a hot line. The procedure was time-consuming and subject to error.

At 6:35 the ambulance crew reported that they were in the area searching for the victim. Actually, they were almost two miles away. A minute later the fire engine crew radioed that they had walked in about 100 yards from the end of the pavement, where the dirt road began, and had met people in a car who said police and the injured woman were about two miles down Beach Road. Because of the road's condition, however, the firefighters doubted that the engine could make it to the scene. They asked their dispatcher to confirm the location with police. The police dispatcher said the victim was 2.2 miles from the pavement.

"Our truck can't go in there," said the fire dispatcher.

"Your truck can't go in there?" the police dispatcher asked. "They got a police car back in there."

"Can a police car bring 'em out? She's too messed up?"

"Apparently, she was pretty badly—somebody ran her off the road with a car," the police dispatcher explained.

"Somebody ran her off the road?"

"So besides being beat up, from that, she was raped on top of it all."

"I'll have to get back to you," the fire dispatcher said.

Despite assurances by Officer Pinnow that the fire units could safely make it to his location, the fire captain was reluctant to send either the engine or the ambulance. Instead, he asked for Rescue 2, a van that carries equipment for extricating victims from crushed vehicles or inaccessible terrain. The van—which cannot transport victims—would take at least 40 minutes to reach the scene from Hilo, some 30 miles away, and would be of little use once it arrived. Fire officials finally decided to let the ambulance go as far toward Dana's location as possible without risking damage to the vehicle. At 6:50—25 minutes after the ambulance first arrived at the end of Kahakai Boulevard and more than two hours after Ida first found Dana—the ambulance reached her.

Dana was in serious condition. She was conscious but disoriented and very pale as well as combative, possibly a sign of a serious head injury. Although Dana was no longer bleeding, her wounds and pallor suggested that she had lost a lot of blood. Paramedic Johnson Kahili inserted two intravenous lines and put a cervical collar around Dana's neck in case she had suffered neck or spinal injuries. The paramedic couldn't feel a pulse; only his heart monitor revealed that Dana had one. He suspected that his patient had been run over but could detect no internal injuries on initial examination. He didn't know about the crushed bike found five miles from where Dana had been dumped.

It took the paramedic and an EMT almost 15 minutes to stabilize Dana before they loaded her into the ambulance and headed for the hospital. The paramedic radioed fire dispatch at 7:13 P.M. and told them that the ambulance was en route to Hilo Hospital. He said the patient was in serious but not critical condition.

At 7:40 P.M., the paramedic tending to Dana called Hilo Hospital from the ambulance radio and spoke with the emergency room physician. The doctor approved of the treatment administered so far, asked for a blood sugar reading, and told the ambulance crew to administer Narcan, a substance used to counter the influence of any narcotic drugs that might be affecting a patient. Although nothing indicated that Dana had ingested drugs, the use of Narcan is common practice in cases like this where paramedics don't know the patient's history or how she sustained her injuries.

The ambulance arrived at Hilo Hospital at 7:56 P.M. Paramedics rushed Dana directly into the emergency room. A little more than three hours had passed since Ida Smith first heard her cries for help. It was a little more than two hours since police were notified that Dana had been found and a few minutes shy of that since the fire department had first dispatched its units.

The emergency room doctor, Dr. Nigel Palmer, ordered X rays, O-negative blood, and massive doses of fluids for Dana, who was suffering from extremely low blood pressure and severe shock. Meanwhile, Dr. Ruben Casile scrubbed for emergency surgery to check for internal bleeding.

At 8:45 P.M., Dana was taken into the operating room, where Dr. Casile labored to stop the internal bleeding he found during the exploratory surgery. She had extensive damage in her pelvic area; a fractured pelvic bone had pierced her bladder. The doctor sutured the torn body parts, thoroughly explored her abdomen, and then cleaned it out and sewed it shut. Dr. Casile then turned his attention to cleaning and suturing Dana's head wound.

Dana remained in shock. At 10:35 she was wheeled into the intensive care unit where she was further treated for low blood pressure. She didn't respond. Her heartbeat remained abnormally slow and irregular. The hospital staff tried their best to stabilize Dana's condition. After it became clear that there was nothing more they could do, they conducted a sex assault examination.

Despite the hospital's best efforts, Dana Ireland died seven minutes after midnight Christmas morning. Dr. Casile signed the death certificate at 12:25 A.M.

A nurse tried to make the corpse presentable so her family, gathered in the waiting room, could see her one last time. She didn't want the family to see their loved one covered by a bloody sheet. Because of all the infused fluids, Dana's body had swollen from 104 pounds to 152 pounds. Every time the nurse wiped Dana's body, bloody fluids oozed out of the many raw spots on her skin. After 45 minutes, the nurse gave up.

Chapter 2

The state of Nevada was the first in the nation to use the gas chamber for an execution on February 8, 1924. Chinese-born Gee Jong was strapped to a chair while an executioner pumped lethal fumes into an airtight chamber. The condemned murderer struggled for his life and then gave up the ghost.

That same day, on the other side of the country, a baby boy came into the world. John Austin Ireland, of Carnegie, Pennsylvania, had two sisters waiting to meet him. His mother would be dead by the time John was five, but not before she gave birth to two more boys.

The family moved often, living in various towns in Ohio, Pennsylvania, and West Virginia. It was the Depression, and both John's paternal grandfather and his father, a railroad worker, lost their jobs. His aunt was the only employed person in the family, earning 90 dollars a month. John didn't think much of it at the time, because he knew very few people with jobs.

John's paternal grandmother took care of John and his four siblings until she developed stomach cancer. Then John and his brother Bob went to an orphanage while his other brother and his two sisters lived with various relatives. After a while, John and Bob were transferred to another orphanage. At times their only food came from donations from the Heinz Company.

At age 13, John moved into his third orphanage and Bob went to live with their aunt. During those days, John desperately missed Bob and would walk five or six miles to visit him. John stayed in the orphanage until just before his seventeenth birthday, when a cousin on his mother's side was appointed his legal guardian. Despite his hardship, John managed to graduate from high school in Wierton, West Virginia, just over the border from Pittsburgh.

This was during World War II, so as soon as John turned 18, he enlisted in the Navy. After basic training, he went to gunnery school and then trained people on the 90 mm antiaircraft gun. He was shipped out to Attu, an island in the Aleutians, just after the U.S. took it back from Japan. From there he went to the destroyer *Lawrence* and finally to the battleship *New Jersey*, the flagship of the fleet in Japan, where he stayed until just before Christmas 1945.

In January 1946, John's Navy service ended. He went to work with open-hearth furnaces in a steel mill, and then attended West Virginia University until he enlisted in the Army in September 1947. There, he designed and managed computer information systems. His assignments took him to

Japan, Korea, Germany, and many bases in the United States. Along the way, he attended college, majoring in political science; but, because his career kept him on the move, he never earned a degree.

Louise Crank was born on May 31, 1924, in Shipman, Virginia. She was the fourth in a family of eight children. She lived in her family home until she was 18, when she and her younger sister Lorraine moved to Washington, D.C. At first the sisters shared an apartment, but eventually each sister got her own place. Louise lived in Alexandria, Virginia, and worked at the Pentagon as a typist/stenographer.

In 1952, while Louise was visiting Lorraine's apartment, she met John Ireland, who was by now a second lieutenant in the Army. A day or two later John called Louise to ask her out on a date. It wasn't long before they became boyfriend and girlfriend.

One night, when John was taking Louise home from a date, he handed her a diamond ring and asked her to try it on for size.

"So I put it on," Louise said decades later. "I don't know whether you call that being engaged or what, but I kept it and we got married not too long after that."

The wedding at Fort Belvoir, Virginia, on October 9, 1953, was modest, with a small reception afterward for close friends and family. John and

Louise moved into a one-bedroom apartment in Alexandria. Louise continued working at the Pentagon until April 1955, when she was six months pregnant.

On July 30, 1955, Louise gave birth to a girl she and John called Sandy. "She was a good-looking little kid, spunky," John said. When Sandy was only 15 months old, the Army sent John to Germany for three years and his wife and baby went with him. His next assignment took the family to San Antonio, Texas.

After that, John was transferred to Korea. This time, Louise and Sandy stayed with Louise's mother in Shipman, Virginia.

John's tour got cut short by two weeks when doctors discovered a large tumor in six-year-old Sandy's liver. John returned home in time for Sandy's surgery at Walter Reed Army Hospital in Washington, D.C. The tumor was benign, but the surgeon had to perform a tricky operation and remove more than half of Sandy's liver. The Irelands bought a four-bedroom house, surrounded by oak, walnut, and poplar trees, on a third of an acre in Springfield, Virginia. The house was situated in a quiet residential neighborhood with nicely landscaped yards. It was the ideal place to raise a child.

Sandy was an outgoing child with lots of friends. John and Louise loved to travel, and they took Sandy with them on vacations. Her favorite places were beach destinations; she loved playing in the ocean.

When Sandy was almost 13, Louise was working in the garden; her neighbor, Gerta Kilday, the wife of a U.S. ambassador, was building a patio in the yard next door.

"Gerta, you know, I think I'm gaining weight. And I missed my period," Louise said over the fence.

"Oh my God," said Gerta. "You're pregnant."

"That's impossible," replied the 44-year-old Louise. But when she went to see her doctor, he confirmed Gerta's diagnosis.

"It can't be true," Louise told him. "Look, something is wrong. It must be a tumor. It must be something, but I'm not pregnant." She hadn't even told John about Gerta's suspicions and only had mentioned the doctor's appointment in passing.

When John arrived home from work that evening, he found Louise sipping bourbon. John did a double-take, as Louise rarely drank, especially alone.

"What's wrong?" John asked. "Was everything okay with your doctor's visit?"

Louise stared straight ahead.

"He says I'm pregnant."

"What?"

"I'm pregnant."

John grabbed the bourbon and took a swig straight from the bottle. "Who the hell's going to cut the grass this summer?" he joked.

Once the initial shock was over, John and Louise looked forward to having another child. Sandy was almost a teenager and it would be nice for her to have a young sibling. Sandy, who was perfectly happy being an only child, wasn't quite so thrilled with the idea herself, but the Irelands' midlife surprise turned out to be the best thing that ever happened to them. Sandy liked having a younger sister much more than she thought she would, partly because her parents let her name the baby.

Dana Marie Ireland was a sweet, shy little girl who carried a blanket everywhere she went. The Kilday boys next door nicknamed her "Magoo" after John tried to convince Dana that her middle initial stood for the cartoon character, Mr. Magoo. Sandy, who was a bookworm, loved reading to her little sister. When Dana was four, Sandy took her to the Springfield Mall where Dana saw a caged bird. "That's so sad," she said. "That bird should be free."

The day Dana started kindergarten at Keene Mill Elementary School, Sandy left for college at the Florida Institute of Technology, where she would earn a two-year degree. While she was there, some friends told her about the University of Hawaii at Hilo on the Big Island. Because of her love for nature, surfing, and the ocean, she thought it sounded great. It was cheaper for John and Louise to let Sandy go to UH Hilo than back to Florida, so they agreed to send her there.

Sandy returned from Florida to Springfield for the summer before going to Hilo. Dana was thrilled to see her. She constantly asked her big sister to take her to places that had trees or animals. When it was time for Sandy to go to her new college, Dana was too young to have any concept of how far away Hawaii was; she just knew her big sister was going away again.

At first Sandy didn't like Hawaii much. She missed Florida's beaches and had trouble adjusting to all the Hilo rain. But over time, island life grew on her, and she loved to surf. At the university, she earned a degree in biology. She also worked at Mauna Loa Observatory. After sharing a house with two girlfriends, she spent a few months living in a van with her boyfriend, who had followed her to Hawaii from Florida. In 1984 she met her future husband, Jim Ingham, on a surfing trip to Indonesia.

While Sandy was becoming an adult in Hawaii, Louise and John were enjoying their child at home. By now, John was a retired Army captain and was managing a large computer center for the Army near the Pentagon. In his free time, he, Louise, and Dana played cards together; when Sandy came home during school breaks, the family took trips together. Other times, John and Louise took Dana to visit Sandy in Hawaii.

In the summer of 1980, the 11-year-old Dana wrote in her diary about one of those visits. "I just got back from Hawaii after spending a month over there," she wrote. "I hated to leave it, mostly because of my sister. I love her very much, and like to be around her a lot. I would like to live with her."

Around that time, John was helping coach Dana's soccer games. Dana continued playing for years. She was so good at it that the high school soccer coach wanted her to try out for his team, but she said she wouldn't do it unless he let her girlfriends try out, too. The coach wasn't interested in her friends, so Dana kept playing for the youth league after school.

Louise was protective of her younger child and, being a stay-at-home mom, spent a lot of time with her. As Dana grew up, the two were practically inseparable. Dana laughed at her mother's better jokes and playfully made fun of her when a joke fell flat. Dana and Louise loved to shop and go for walks together, even during Dana's teenage years.

Although Dana was shy, she did meet a few lifelong friends in school. Jennifer Shepherd, who Dana met in kindergarten, lived a quarter-mile away. As kids, they went sledding, swimming, and bicycling together. In high school, both girls had long blond hair. They would go to Dana's house and highlight each other's locks. Sometimes they dressed alike and told people they were sisters.

Valerie Oliver was Dana's next-door neighbor for about six months while she was in sixth grade, but her friendship with Dana lasted much longer. In high school they double-dated at the senior prom. Dana's date was her senior-year boyfriend, Mike Dickerson, who adored her. Dana was elegant in her prom dress with her hair up, but she looked awkward wearing high heels. She was really much more comfortable in jeans and athletic shoes—and every bit as beautiful. She loved nature and animals more than glitz and glamour.

Dana got good grades, but she didn't enjoy the campus social scene. Mike helped her pick out a mountain bike and they rode together. When Mike decided to go to Radford College after graduation, Dana followed him there. She lived in the dorm next to his, but she wasn't happy. She was homesick.

Dana didn't socialize much at Radford, either. Mike liked to party, so Dana would urge him to go to parties without her. Dana rarely drank. Once she had two wine coolers at the beach with Mike and got sick. She was happier when the two of them went for walks, to the movies, or out for ice cream.

Dana often spoke to Mike about going to Hawaii to be with Sandy. She told him how much she enjoyed snorkeling, bodyboarding, and wading in the tide pools. She said she wanted to study dolphins. But she was unsure about her future.

"She didn't really know what she wanted—she'd tell you that," Mike said. "But we were young and we didn't talk about that a whole lot. I loved her and wanted to be with her. I didn't really care where she was."

As it turned out, Mike and Dana broke up when Dana decided to move back home and finish college at George Mason University in Fairfax, Virginia. Mike gave her a cat named Boots. She also had a dog named Nicky, and as a child she'd raised hamsters.

Before Dana returned to Springfield, she sent Mike a card with this note:

> *Mike—I just wanted to let you know I love you and I am going to miss you a bunch. You are very special to me and I will never forget all the great times we have spent. Thanks for sticking by me and staying my friend. Don't be sad when I leave, just look at it as a long vacation until I see you again.*
>
> *Love always,*
> *Dana.*

Even after Dana returned to Springfield, Mike remained her closest friend, the person to whom she confided her deepest secrets. When he went home during breaks, she would invite him to join her and her friends for a movie or a hike.

The summer after Radford, Dana got a job as a lifeguard at Danbury Forest Pool in Springfield. Another lifeguard there, Heather Preast, took an instant liking to Dana. "She was the most beautiful person I've ever known," Heather said. "Not only on the outside, but on the inside as well. Very caring. She did not have an enemy. I mean, if anybody didn't like her, it was because she was one of those girls that just had it all, and she wasn't conceited about her beauty. She was never vain. It was a very natural beauty that she had, because a lot of it came from within her."

After the summer ended, both women went to work at a health club, Nauti Body, while Dana continued her college education at George Mason University. Nauti Body was in a tall building, and sometimes birds would smash into its big glass windows and die. Because of her love for animals, Dana insisted that Heather help her bury the dead birds.

While working at the health club, Dana, who was five-foot-four, began to exercise faithfully, and her weight dropped from 117 pounds to 104 pounds. On weekends, Heather and Dana would sometimes ride their bikes 50 miles in one day. Other times, Dana would go on all-day hikes on Old Rag Mountain with Valerie Dexter, who described her as "an aerobics fitness queen." Dana sometimes got carsick on the winding road leading to the mountain, but that never deterred her.

She regularly sent letters to Mike Dickerson at Radford.

Hi (she wrote one weekend). *It's Saturday night and I don't think I am going to do anything except watch TV and lift weights and do my sit-ups and pushups.*

Boots went to the doctor today. It was awful they had to shave his neck. Blood was everywhere. He is real sick now. It is probably from the shots. His eyelids are closed but his eyes are open. It looks real gross.

Today Lynn Martin and I went shopping. She has changed so much and she got real fat. 120 pounds she told me, and she is shorter than I am. Yeesh!

The weather is so awesome. I wish you were here so we could go riding. I have no one to ride with. Tomorrow I am going to ride my bike and lay in the sun.

I might come down for Halloween. So you better have something awesome for us to do. Well, I am sorry this letter is so boring but that's how life is without ya!!!

Miss you lots,
Dana

At Nauti Body, Dana met Jeff Stiles, a former basketball star from Dana's high school, West Springfield High. Jeff, who was three years older than Dana, was about to become her first serious boyfriend. He was six-foot-six and handsome and spent a lot of time at the gym. They both loved to work out; it showed. With Dana's innocent beauty and Jeff's size and good looks, they made a striking couple.

Mike Dickerson had admired Jeff in high school, but he was devastated when Dana started dating him. "He was really tall and he was awesome," Mike said. "I thought he was the greatest player. So, I liked him then. And then when he started going with Dana, I hated him."

Despite her close friendships with her peers, Dana still spent a lot of time with her mother. Now that Dana was in her twenties, she and Louise were more like two adult friends than a mother and daughter. Dana often told Louise that having a child late in life was what kept her young. Louise bragged to her friends that Dana never lied to her, didn't use drugs or alcohol, and was always home before midnight.

Even with a new boyfriend and the wholesome fun on weekends, Dana managed to make the honor roll all through college. When she earned her degree in physical education in 1991, her father gave her a camera as a graduation gift. That August, Dana took the camera with her on a vacation to Hilton Head with Heather Preast's family. While there, she spent a lot of time talking about her plans to go to Hawaii in the fall to visit Sandy.

Sandy and Jim worked out of their home, where they had a large palm nursery. Dana thought that was a terrific life and was looking forward to helping them out at the nursery. Dana idolized her older sister and envied her life. She didn't know how long she would stay in Hawaii, but she promised Heather she would return to Virginia to be maid of honor at her wedding the following July.

The day Dana packed for Hawaii, the leaves on the maple tree outside her bedroom window had already started turning yellow and orange and red. As Louise helped Dana stuff the suitcase full of items more suitable for summer than fall, Dana teased her mother about the big fuss she was making. It was as if Louise never expected her baby to return home. Despite the kidding, there was no question then that Dana loved Hawaii and looked forward to being in the tropical state she had first visited at age nine. Years after that original trip, she had written in her diary that when she died, she wanted to be buried in Hawaii, because it was a beautiful and peaceful place.

The night before Dana left, Heather, who was a devout Christian, gave her a Bible. Dana had no formal religious upbringing but was beginning to explore her spirituality.

"Here," Heather said. "This is for you to read and tell me what you think. We can talk about it over the phone and write about it in letters." When Heather hugged Dana goodbye, she had tears in her eyes.

"Gosh," Dana said. "You act like you're never going to see me again."

"Well," Heather replied, "I have this awful feeling I won't."

Chapter 3

When John and Louise Ireland left Springfield, Virginia, for a vacation on the Big Island of Hawaii, they had no idea they would spend Christmas grieving. All they knew was that they would soon see their daughters, Sandy, 36, and Dana, 22. It was December 10, 1991, and cold in Virginia, but a warm reunion was about to take place in Hawaii.

The close Ireland family had endured its first separation since Sandy'd moved to Hawaii when Dana was just seven. Now, John and Louise looked forward to seeing both girls. Christmas on Hawaii's Big Island promised to be one of their best ever.

John and Louise landed first in Honolulu, on the island of Oahu, to catch a connecting flight to the Big Island. The final leg of their trip covered 200 miles and lasted about 50 minutes. Their flight path took them past downtown Honolulu, Waikiki Beach, and Diamond Head Crater. As they flew south toward Hilo, John and Louise looked out the window at the islands of Molokai, Lanai, and Maui.

John, 67, had a full head of shockingly white

hair. He was slightly shorter than average but had a commanding presence. His piercing blue eyes telegraphed his serious nature. Although John had been a career Army man, the tattoos on his upper arms betrayed his early Navy days.

John had retired in 1985. Now he had the leisure and money to travel and spend time with his daughters. When Dana was a child, the Irelands took frequent vacations, often going to island destinations like Puerto Rico and the Virgin Islands. Those early experiences created a passion for the sea in Sandy and Dana that ultimately drew them both to Hawaii.

Sandy and Jim lived in Kapoho Farmlots, in the rural and sparsely populated Puna district. John and Louise had arranged to rent a house near Sandy and Jim's place, on Kapoho Kai Drive in the Kapoho Vacationland subdivision. Dana would stay there with them.

John looked out of the airplane as it approached the Big Island from the north. He saw the volcanic peaks of Mauna Kea and Mauna Loa poking through the white clouds. The aircraft descended and followed the Hamakua Coast—with its fields of sugarcane, waterfalls, and scattered small communities—before landing at Hilo International Airport.

When John and Louise rode down the escalator to claim their baggage, they scanned the waiting area, looking for Dana.

"Where the devil is she?" John asked.

"She's around," Louise reassured him. Louise was petite with short hair that hung in white ringlets. Her eyes, as blue as John's, had a playful twinkle that complemented her devilish grin.

Louise and John turned right at the bottom of the escalator and walked a few yards to where travelers pushed past one another to grab bags from a moving carousel. The sweet scent of tropical blossoms permeated the moist air.

Suddenly, Dana's face appeared in the crowd. Her blue eyes sparkled and her long, blond hair danced in the trade winds that blew through the waiting area. John, weary from his day of travel, regained his vigor when he saw Dana. Louise beamed. Dana was slim, attractive, and athletic, but her natural intelligence and gentle kindness were what people noticed more than her outer beauty.

Dana ran to her parents, hugged them, and apologized for being late. She explained that she had parked in a three-minute zone and that when she returned to check on the car, she had discovered a parking ticket. Although at first annoyed, she was glad to be in the company of her parents and soon forgot about the ticket. John and Louise were equally delighted to be with Dana. John doted on both his girls, and Louise and Dana were so devoted to each other that a neighbor had once remarked that she had never known any other mother and daughter that close.

After graduating from college, Dana had told all her friends that she wanted to go to Hawaii to be with Sandy, but beyond that, she was still deciding what to do with her life. Among other possibilities, she was considering joining the Peace Corps or becoming a physical therapist. Although her short-term plans were to spend time with Sandy and to look for a job, her parents secretly hoped she would return to Virginia to live with them. They had even financed the construction of an extra room in Sandy and Jim's house for Dana's use whenever she visited.

John had reserved a rental car. However, Dana insisted on driving her parents home in Sandy's rusty Toyota station wagon, so John agreed to pick up the rental car another day. It took the family almost an hour to drive from the airport to Kapoho. The ride took them southeast toward Kilauea Volcano, where lava had been flowing for almost nine years, and then southwest to the Puna coast.

The route led Dana and her parents past *ohia* forests and abandoned sugarcane, coconut palms and wild orchids, ferns and other exotic flora. They passed through a tropical canopy of Albizzia trees, groves of papaya plants, and lava fields. Along the way they saw wild mynah birds and an occasional mongoose, local creatures that some Hawaii residents consider pests. But Dana appreciated them. She loved animals and other living things. Her college hiking companions would recall the time Dana saw a caterpillar crossing her path. She had gently picked it up and moved it out of the way so no other hiker would trample on it.

Before reaching the coast, Dana turned right on Highway 137—which locals call the "Red Road" because of its red lava paving—and drove about a mile and a half to Kapoho Kai Drive, the entrance to Kapoho Vactionland. Short coconut palms, *ohia* trees, and dense brush lined the drive. The Irelands' rental house was located less than a mile from the highway, on the second block. The two-story house, one-third of a mile from the ocean and a five-minute walk from tide pools, had a large, covered deck facing a grassy front yard lined with coconut palms and Norfolk pines. The Irelands would stay in the duplex's downstairs portion, a unit with three bedrooms and two bathrooms.

Kapoho Vacationland is one of many subdivisions in Puna that bear virtually no resemblance to subdivisions in most cities on the mainland. Their names—Fern Forest, Eden Roc Estates, Aloha Estates, Hawaiian Acres—conjure up images of exclusive, gated communities. In reality, they're substandard and sparsely populated, containing anywhere from 100 to 9,000 agriculturally zoned lots, many of which are vacant.

Structures in these subdivisions range from shacks to large architect-designed houses. Almost all of the roads are unpaved and privately maintained. In addition, most of the neighborhoods are without piped county water. Because the east side of the Big Island receives more than 100 inches of rain annually, rural residents can collect enough water in their catchment tanks to supply their households. As in Ida Smith's neighborhood, many lack commercial electricity and telephone service.

The County of Hawaii provides no rubbish pickup, so residents either must hire private garbage collectors or haul trash themselves to one of the county's "solid waste transfer stations," dumpsites scattered throughout the island. Sandy and Jim had a compost pile for their green waste but drove nine miles into Pahoa to dump their other trash.

Sandy and Jim were away skiing in Colorado. In their absence, Dana entertained her parents, taking them to the sites of recent lava flows, to a waterfall, and into Pahoa town, where they shopped and ate.

Pahoa is the unofficial capital of the Puna district, which is home to many hippies. Visitors to Pahoa often compare their experience to that of being in a time warp: The village looks like an Old West version of Haight-Ashbury, its main road dominated by tie-dyed clothing, long hair, and the sweet smell of marijuana. At the town's health food store, it was common to see hippies paying for their groceries with food stamps, jokingly called "Pahoa traveler's checks."

During one of these excursions, Dana noticed that her mother wasn't quite herself.

"Mama, you look so sad," Dana said. "What's wrong?"

"Something doesn't feel right," Louise said. "I'm sure I'll be better when Sandy is here and we're all together." Louise had been uneasy since learning that Sandy and Jim had left Dana alone to go skiing in Colorado. She had worried about Dana being on her own, so far away from her family. Although Louise knew Dana was safe now, she couldn't explain why she still felt apprehensive.

Although Jim and Sandy wouldn't return from their trip until a few days after Dana's twenty-third birthday on December 12, John and Louise threw Dana a small party that included her new friend, Mark Evans, from nearby Opihikao. Sandy had introduced Dana to Mark, a handsome 27-year-old carpenter with a passion for surfing, and the two hit it off. Dana's parents enjoyed his company at the birthday party. After the party, Louise asked to look at Dana's gifts again. Dana showed her the deck of tarot cards Sandy had given her before leaving for the mainland. Dana drew a card from the deck. It was the death card.

"I don't believe in those things," her mother said.

It rained for the next two weeks, so the Irelands passed the time doing Christmas shopping and playing gin rummy, Clue, Monopoly, and National Geographic Pursuit. They planned to drive to the Kona side of the island Christmas morning, a trip that would take about three hours. Kona is a popular tourist destination on the island's sunny western coast, and the Irelands planned to spend several days there. Since they would be away from home on Christmas Day, they decided to have their holiday dinner on Christmas Eve.

On the morning of the twenty-fourth, John and Jim used Sandy's car to go to a driving range, while Dana drove Louise and Sandy in the rental car to Kaiko'o Mall, a small enclosed shopping center in the heart of Hilo for some last-minute shopping. Louise bought Dana a mirror to hang in her bathroom at Sandy and Jim's place and rattan shelves for her bedroom.

The women ate lunch at Bear's Coffee Shop, a restaurant in downtown Hilo, before returning to Kapoho. On the drive home, Dana turned the discussion to the ageless question of what happens to people after they die.

"I think everyone ends up going to the same place whether they're good or evil," she said.

"Is it just one place?" Sandy asked.

"Well, I don't know, but I think at first they all just go to one place," Dana explained.

"Don't you think it's possible that when you die that there's so much opportunity or so many different places you can go?" Sandy asked. "I mean, it's such a huge universe."

"I don't know," Dana admitted.

"None of us knows," Sandy said.

"Well, Dana," said her mother, puzzled because Dana had never talked like this before, "I guess if anything happens to you, God will take care of whoever is left behind." Louise wondered if Dana had brought up the subject because of the Tarot cards.

As Dana drove home, she asked her mother if she

could invite Mark, who had no relatives on the Big Island, to join the family for Christmas Eve dinner. Louise readily consented. Mark's home had no telephone so Dana and Sandy decided to ride their bicycles to Opihikao to ask him personally.

It wasn't until they arrived at the vacation home that they remembered that Dana's bike had a flat tire. John offered Dana the rental car, but Dana said she preferred to borrow Sandy's mountain bike. The 15-mile round trip ride would be good exercise for the athletic Dana who had recently added surfing and scuba diving to her growing list of hobbies.

Dana and Sandy bicycled together almost every day, and Dana was familiar with the route to Mark's house. Although Sandy routinely rode her bike alone without incident, she had made it a point to discourage Dana from cycling by herself outside the immediate neighborhood. Sandy didn't think it was unsafe, but she felt responsible for Dana while she was in Hawaii, and exercised more caution with Dana than she did with herself. This Christmas Eve afternoon, however, Sandy's guard was down. Despite a nagging concern—which she wrote off as a big sister's overprotective instinct— she didn't to try to talk Dana out of riding to Mark's place alone.

She has regretted it ever since.

Chapter 4

Louise spent the rest of the afternoon cooking a traditional turkey dinner while John worked around the house and practiced his golf swing in the yard. Dana set off on Sandy's bike at around 3:00, slipping away without anyone in the family witnessing her departure. She was wearing denim shorts, a black halter top, and white tennis shoes—a sharp contrast to the warm, bulky outfits she typically wore on Christmas Eve in Virginia.

Dana first pedaled up Kapoho Kai Drive to Highway 137—Red Road—then headed south along the coastal highway toward Opihikao. Calling this main road a highway is misleading; for while it's officially a state highway, it's narrow and bumpy, at some spots consisting of a single lane.

Puna doesn't have the white sand beaches that attract droves of tourists to Hawaii, but instead features dramatic rock cliffs against which waves crash, creating a spray of white foam. The land off the Puna coast typically drops off precipitously to reveal a deep blue sea that is more suitable for fishing than for swimming. Only occasional sections allow swimming in relative safety from the sharp fingers of lava that reach into the ocean. Kapoho Vacationland, for instance, features tide-pools with an assortment of colorful fish. Dana, Sandy, and Jim had snorkeled there often.

Dana rode along the coast at a comfortable pace and absorbed the scenery. She was glad to be away from Springfield but missed her friends, especially her boyfriend, Jeff Stiles. Jeff was planning to visit Dana sometime after the first of the year, and she was trying to figure out how to break the news to him that she wanted to remain in Hawaii.

Perhaps not being able to talk to Jeff while in Hawaii was what drew her to Mark Evans, even though Dana's interest—unlike Mark's—was purely platonic. Before he met Dana, Mark was smitten with Sandy but knew she was off limits because of her relationship with Jim. Then, one day in November, he saw Dana sitting in her sister's car while Sandy was surfing at a spot called "Shacks." Dana was nearly fourteen years younger than Sandy, but the sisters looked strikingly similar. Mark approached the car.

"Hi," he said. "I'm Mark Evans. You must be Sandy's sister."

When Dana smiled, Mark felt that he had been given a second chance.

It wasn't long before he asked Dana out. Despite Dana's shyness, Sandy encouraged her to accept the invitation, and eventually she did. Dana and Mark went to a few movies together and later on a hike in

Waipio Valley, a lush area with breathtaking views of waterfalls and a pristine beach that was the setting for the final scene in the movie *Waterworld*. As was often the case with men who knew Dana, Mark hoped the relationship would blossom into something more than friendship. Unfortunately for him, Dana wasn't interested in Mark romantically; she thought of him more as a hiking companion. Yet Dana was a sensitive, compassionate person who felt bad knowing that Mark had no family in Hawaii with whom to spend Christmas. She was glad to be riding to his house so she could extend her family's hospitality.

A mile or so from Kapoho Vacationland, Dana rode past dense vegetation with intermittent breaks that revealed dramatic views of the sparkling blue ocean. At Isaac Hale Beach Park, in Pohoiki, the road turns away from the ocean, meeting it again about a mile later. Dana stopped there to watch the surf for a few minutes at Shacks before riding past a civil defense siren. The bright yellow horns, used to warn the public about tidal waves and other impending disasters, are mounted on poles throughout Hawaii's coastal areas.

The road just south of Pohoiki is only one lane wide, with ironwood trees on both sides. It rises and drops as it passes MacKenzie State Park, a beautiful picnic area on high cliffs overlooking the Pacific. The trade winds were blowing and the salt spray felt good against Dana's face.

She heard a car approaching and steered to the

right of the road to give it room to pass. Red Road had little traffic, yet there was enough that Dana didn't fear the isolation. If she got into trouble someone would soon come along to help.

Dana made a right turn off Red Road and arrived at Mark's two-story cedar house at about 3:30 P.M.

Mark and two of his friends heard the crunching of bicycle tires against the crushed lava rock driveway and glanced over the balcony to see Dana riding up to the house. She looked happy.

"Hi, Mark," Dana said. "I'm glad you're home. I came to invite you to have Christmas dinner tonight with my family. We're leaving for Kona tomorrow morning." She stood straddling the bike.

"That would be great," Mark replied. "I have to go shopping first, but I can meet you there later."

Dana visited for about a half hour, then told Mark she had to ride back so she could help her mother with dinner. Mark offered to put the bicycle in his truck and drive her there, but Dana declined. It was about 4:00 and would be light for a couple more hours. She couldn't resist the return bike ride along the coast on that balmy December afternoon.

As Dana rode away, Mark was thinking about how beautiful she looked. He admired her exposed legs, thinking what a shame it would be if she lost control of her bike and scarred them on the bumpy road.

Dana pedaled at a constant pace, glad that her mission had been successful. Mark would be a pleasant addition to the holiday gathering. Although he was no substitute for Jeff, he was a nice person and fun to be around.

At Pohoiki, Dana made a right turn into the parking lot of Isaac Hale Beach Park. She pulled over again to watch the surf, glancing at a group of teens and young men—some of whom she would meet later under much more sinister circumstances. Dana eased off the bike seat and stood straddling the bicycle while she focused her attention on the soothing rhythm of the waves.

A few minutes later Dana hopped back on the bike and headed toward Kapoho Vacationland. It wasn't long before three of the youths pulled out of the parking lot and headed in the same direction.

As Dana rode on this narrow road on an island in the middle of the Pacific Ocean, she felt lucky. It was a great place for bike riding. She rode with no purpose other than the enjoyment of her surroundings.

As soon as she turned onto the entrance to the Kapoho Vacationland subdivision, Dana heard another approaching car and again pulled over to the right. The car slowed to a snail's pace, and she heard loud music and male voices.

Dana quickly glanced around and assessed her situation. She was looking for an escape route, in case these guys proved to be more than just the typical jerks who liked to harass women out alone. Seeing nowhere to go, she pedaled harder. Her heart was pounding. Fortunately, she was now less than a mile away from her parents' rental home. She pedaled with renewed energy, taking comfort in the knowledge that the safety of her family was just moments away.

Chapter 5

At 5:00 P.M. on Christmas Eve, Sandy and Jim were at their home wrapping the last of their Christmas presents, while Louise was in the kitchen of the rental house basting the turkey. The ringing telephone interrupted Louise. She put down the turkey baster, wiped her hands on her apron, and picked up the phone.

"Hello?"

"Hi, Louise. This is Mark. May I speak to Dana?" He was calling from a pay phone near Sure Save Supermarket.

"Well, she's not back yet," Louise said. "What time did she leave your house?"

"About an hour ago. Maybe she stopped to watch the surf. She should be back soon," Mark said. "The reason I'm calling is that I was wondering if I could bring something tonight. Maybe some dessert or something?"

"Oh, no, you don't have to do that," Louise said. "We have everything we need."

"Well, how about some flowers?"

"That's really not necessary," Louise said. "But you can if you want."

"Great. I'll see you soon. Bye."

"Goodbye."

Louise relayed the conversation to John, who was a bit concerned that Dana hadn't gotten back yet. Expecting her to arrive at any moment, he went into the yard to hit a few golf balls and watch for her.

At about 5:15, Jim and Sandy were driving down Kapoho Kai Drive to the Irelands' rental house. They saw a crowd of people standing around a mangled black bicycle on the side of the road. Jim slammed on the brakes and jumped out of the car. He immediately recognized the bike as Sandy's. The pair rushed to the Irelands' rental home, where Sandy, shaken, asked, "Is Dana here?"

"Not yet," replied John, who was still outside practicing his golf swing. Louise, hearing the alarm in Sandy's voice, ran outside to find out what was wrong.

"Something terrible has happened," Sandy said, and described what she and Jim had just seen three-tenths of a mile down the road. John dropped his golf club. Louise forgot all about the dinner. As the family raced to the scene, Jim was in tears and Sandy was trembling.

The Irelands pulled up alongside the bent and twisted bicycle. Its seat was missing and one of its pedals was embedded in the cinder road. Next to the bike lay Dana's wristwatch with a ripped band, a foot-long hank of blond hair, and a white athletic shoe, still tied at the ankle. Anna Sherrell, one of the first people to stop, had moved the shoe, watch, and hair out of the road, hoping to preserve evidence of what she assumed was a hit-and-run accident.

What alarmed everyone were the tire tracks in the dirt. They showed that a vehicle had swerved— seemingly deliberately—right into the bike. At the point of impact, the bike tracks had made a gouge in the road. Then they just stopped. It was obvious from the tracks that the car had accelerated, turned around, and fled the scene. One of the bystanders, Paul Gomez,* took pictures of the tracks to preserve as evidence, in case other cars drove over them.

Dana was nowhere in sight. Thinking she might have been thrown into the nearby brush, the Irelands and several other people frantically combed the bushes looking for her. When they realized that Dana was not to be found, Anna's boyfriend drove her home and she called the Hawaii County Police Department.

Her phone call was logged in at 5:25 P.M. Anna described the accident scene, reporting the bicycle, shoe, hair, wristwatch, and tire tracks.

"Looks like their shoe was, like, clean on the other side of the road—up the road. Like it was a

---

*Not his real name

pretty hard impact," Anna told the dispatcher. "And it looks like they took off and spun out, man, and just kept going, according to the tracks. It doesn't look like anybody picked her up."

Less than one minute later a different dispatcher answered a call by John Ireland.

"I need to know if there's been an accident with a bicyclist in Vacationland has been reported," John said, obviously flustered.

"Vacationland?" the dispatcher asked, unfamiliar with Kapoho Vacationland. John explained that Vacationland was the main subdivision in Kapoho and told the dispatcher that the accident was on the road leading into the subdivision from Highway 137.

"Our daughter has had an accident in the road," John said. "The bike is totaled. There's pieces of her hair, a shoe, and no sign of her."

At 5:28 P.M., dispatcher Don Brescia put out a broadcast asking the patrol officer closest to Kapoho Vacationland to respond. Officer Bob Wagner, who was at the scene of another traffic accident on Kapoho Road, answered and was dispatched to the scene, arriving eight minutes later. After assessing the situation and setting up flares, Wagner asked the dispatcher to call Hilo Hospital to see if anyone matching Dana's description had been admitted. No one had, so Wagner called dispatch and asked for backup.

Within five minutes of Wagner's arrival, Sergeant

Gabriel Malani and Officer Harold Pinnow arrived. Sergeant Malani made a note that the scene
was already somewhat contaminated. He looked
for blood but found none. A thorough search of the
area turned up no additional evidence.

A neighbor drove Louise, Sandy, and Jim to Hilo
Hospital, the Ireland family assuming that Dana
would be taken to the hospital as soon as she was
found and wanting to be there when she arrived.

Five miles to the north in Waa Waa, Ida Smith
had already discovered Dana tossed in the bushes.
While the fire department was still trying to get help
to Dana, the police department had figured out that
she was the missing bicyclist and tried to get word
to her family. A police dispatcher called the wife of
the Irelands' neighbor to tell her what was happening so she could pass the information to John, who
had stayed behind in case Dana turned up in the
neighborhood. All the dispatcher could tell the
neighbor, however, was that Dana had been found,
that she was badly injured, and that she would be
transported to the hospital as soon as possible.

John drew on his inner strength as he had done
since childhood. He had survived orphanages,
World War II, and Korea, he told himself, and he
would survive the anxiety he felt tonight.

While John tried to reassure himself at the rental
house, Louise, Sandy, and Jim waited in frustration at the hospital. John had called them to say
Dana had been found but they could get no details
from anybody at the hospital. Shortly after 7:00

P.M. Jim approached a paramedic from a Hilo-based ambulance.

"Do you know when they're going to bring Dana Ireland here?" he asked. "She was in an accident in Kapoho. A bicycle accident."

The paramedic called fire dispatch. "The ambulance just left the scene and they're heading here now," he said. "It'll take a while for them to get here."

The ambulance arrived just before 8:00 P.M. As Dana was wheeled into the emergency room, Jim said, "Dana, we're with you." Louise called John and told him that their daughter seemed to be all right. John was relieved to hear the news. His relief, however, was short-lived. Two hours later, at about 10:00 P.M., Louise called again.

"John, it looks pretty serious. You should get to the hospital."

Neighbors drove John to Hilo. They all waited in the hospital's emergency room while a doctor operated on Dana. John and Louise sat helplessly, with the same apprehension they had felt three decades earlier when Sandy, then age seven, had had surgery for the tumor on her liver. That had ended well, they told themselves, and this would, too.

Shortly after midnight, the emergency room physician, Dr. Nigel Palmer, emerged and spoke privately to Sandy. After the discussion, Sandy slowly walked over to her parents and friends.

"Dana didn't make it," Sandy said in a barely audible voice. "She died in surgery."

Seconds later, Dr. Palmer approached John and Louise. He put his hand on Louise's shoulder. "Your daughter had a crushed pelvis," he said. "We tried to stop the bleeding but we ran out of time. If she'd gotten here earlier we might have been able to save her."

He didn't mention that she had been raped.

Chapter 6

When the sun rose above the ocean off the Big Island's eastern coast on December 25, 1991, it was a magical time for thousands of early risers eager to begin celebrating Christmas. But for police, it was the first day of a long, frustrating murder investigation. And for the Irelands it was the beginning of a gloomy future filled with questions for which no one had answers.

John, still numb from the shock of Dana's death, switched on the radio. What he heard stunned him even more. A newscaster reported that police believed Dana had been intentionally run over and abducted from the area. Why hadn't the police told him this? The Ireland family had left the hospital grief-stricken, but they had assumed Dana had died from an accident. It had never occurred to them that her death was deliberate. As the reporter read a phone number that people could call to report tips about the crime, John sat in disbelief. Dana had been murdered. Louise was inconsolable. "How could this happen to Dana—of all people?" she asked, dabbing her eyes with a soggy tissue. It was a question that would be repeated throughout the day as the Irelands called friends and relatives to tell them about Dana's death.

Heather Preast was celebrating Christmas with her parents when she got a call from Mike Dickerson telling her Dana was dead.

"That's the cruelest joke you could play on me," Heather said. "It can't be. You're a liar. I don't believe you. Don't tell me these things." She hung up.

Mike called back and told her it was true.

"I was devastated," she said, years later. "I broke down sobbing. I was in hysterics. I was in my parents' basement and I couldn't believe it. If there was anybody that really didn't deserve to die, it was Dana. She was such a good person. I couldn't name one thing that she had ever done wrong. Every day for two years I thought about her constantly. And now it's more like weekly and bi-weekly. It's just a pain real deep inside that'll never go away."

John Ireland's brother, Bob, flew to Hawaii immediately and agreed to identify Dana's body at the morgue.

News of the murder spread quickly throughout East Hawaii. Homicides are rare on the Big Island, especially random rape-murders. Ironically, a second Christmas Eve attack in Puna had been interrupted by a Good Samaritan the same night. A woman had met a man at a bar and left with him. The man had driven her to the parking lot of a shopping center in Keaau, about 15 miles from where Dana was found, and then begun to beat her with a crowbar. A passerby notified police, who stopped the beating and arrested the assailant. Even though that attack was vicious, it failed to evoke the same emotional response in the public as Dana's murder because many women jogged or rode bikes alone in broad daylight and recognized that what happened to Dana—her random abduction-rape-murder—could have happened to them.

On Christmas morning, Detective Steve Guillermo was still in bed when the phone rang at 7:30 A.M., jolting him awake.

"Hello?" Guillermo said.

"Rico, it's Cisco." It was Steve's boss, Lieutenant Francis Rodillas, using their nicknames for each other.

"Hey, what's up?" Guillermo wasn't quite awake yet.

"We had a homicide last night," said Rodillas. "You've gotta come out this morning."

"Yeah, right," Guillermo said. For an instant, Guillermo thought the lieutenant in charge of the Criminal Investigations Division was pulling one of his practical jokes. Often, during a routine phone call, the lieutenant would try to make one of his detectives believe a major crime had just been committed. But something in Rodillas's tone told Guillermo this was not a joke.

"No, really. We really had one last night," Rodillas said and filled Guillermo in on what he knew. "Meet me at the station around eight."

A half-hour later, Guillermo arrived at the Hilo police station, where Rodillas assigned him to lead the investigation. Little did he know the assignment would last into the following century.

At over 4,000 square miles, the Big Island is the largest of the Hawaiian Islands and is the biggest land area in the U.S. under the jurisdiction of a single law enforcement agency. Despite the large land mass—consisting of everything from deserts to jungles to snow-capped volcanoes—the Hawaii County Police Department in 1991 had an authorized strength of only 327 officers to police some 120,000 citizens. Resources were stretched thin.

The Big Island's population was as diverse as its geography. At the time of Dana Ireland's murder, 40 percent of the island's residents were Caucasians, locally called *haole*, the Hawaiian word for "foreigner." People of Japanese ancestry made up 22 percent of the population, followed by those of Hawaiian or part-Hawaiian ancestry at 19 percent, and Filipinos at 13 percent. The remaining six percent were African-Americans, Native Americans, and persons of unknown heritage. Perhaps because no one ethnic group holds the majority, the proverbial melting pot is more a reality in Hawaii than in most other parts of America. Members of various ethnic groups routinely intermarry, leading to individuals of mixed heritage, often referred to simply as "local."

Detective Steve Guillermo fit that category. His father was almost pure Filipino and his mother was mostly Hawaiian with a little Portuguese thrown in. The 33-year-old Guillermo, who could pass for Hispanic, had short black hair, dark eyes, and a neatly trimmed mustache. He was a just-the-facts-ma'am kind of cop with a mild temperament and an easygoing style. At five-foot-six, he looked more like a handsome schoolteacher or executive than an imposing police investigator, especially when he smiled.

Guillermo had been born in Kona, on the west side of the Big Island. Although his family lived in Honokaa, a sugar plantation town along the Hamakua Coast of the island's soggy east side, the Guillermos spent their summers in sunny Kona, and that's where they were when Steven Guillermo came into the world on July 31, 1958. His father worked for the telephone company while his mother stayed home and took care of their seven children. Steve was the middle child, with two older brothers, two younger brothers, and an older and younger sister.

When Steve was about 10, his family moved to Kona full-time. There he attended Konawaena Elementary and High School. At the high school, his basketball coach, Alfred Rabarra, was a Hawaii County Police Department patrol sergeant who coached in his off-duty hours. With Rabarra as his inspiration, Guillermo made it his goal to enter law enforcement.

After high school, Guillermo attended Hawaii Community College and then took a job driving a truck for a Kona hauling business. On weekends he played golf and fished on his father's boat. In 1978 Guillermo met his future wife, Trudy, at a high school graduation party for some of her friends. They would eventually marry in 1982.

Meanwhile, in 1980, Guillermo got a job with the Police Department. Two days before he was to begin recruit training, officers from the vice section asked him to work undercover. Guillermo accepted; at a local gym, he started playing basketball with members of a Filipino group from Wainaku, a neighborhood just outside Hilo.

The Wainaku gang, which was notorious for selling stolen guns, invited Guillermo to attend cockfights with them. In late 1980, vice officers armed with a search warrant raided a fight in Waimea. The man Guillermo was with was worried that his probation would be revoked, so he handed Guillermo his box, which contained an injured bird. Guillermo ended up getting arrested to protect his buddy, an act that elevated his status among the gang, giving him access to their activities. He was able to link a gun he bought from them to a sporting goods store burglary.

After 11 months, a man who had attended Guillermo's going-away party from the trucking job saw him at a cockfight, and recognized him as a young cop. Not long after that, a member of the Wainaku gang, Paterno Castillo, attended a housewarming party in Puna and saw a man there, Robert Della Sr., who resembled Guillermo. Thinking he was getting revenge on Guillermo, Castillo stabbed the man to death. Guillermo testified at Castillo's murder trial.

By then Guillermo had completed his recruit class. Working his way through the ranks, he eventually became a detective in Hilo's criminal investigations division. His biggest case to date had been a manslaughter investigation against Blaine Farris, charged with killing police Sergeant Ronald "Shige" Jitchaku during a late night brawl on Banyan Drive in Hilo on May 7, 1990. Emotionally, it was a tough case for Guillermo because Jitchaku had been one of the first officers he'd trained with in the field, and Guillermo thought he was a "real nice guy."

Now, Guillermo was one of nine detectives assigned to the criminal investigations division. Lieutenant Rodillas initially assigned detectives Jerry Coloma, Robert Kualii, and Edwin Tanaka to Guillermo's investigation team. Eventually, Guillermo would be the sole detective assigned to work the case full-time, with patrol officers helping with the legwork. No one envied him.

Chapter 7

The Puna District is almost 500 square miles—about the size of the island of Oahu or the state of Connecticut. Puna, which is made up of many small, tight-knit communities, isn't a mainstream tourist destination; it's more famous for its high-quality marijuana, called "Puna Butter." In the 1970s, marijuana patches were so widespread in Puna that hikers frequently encountered armed pot growers jealously guarding their crops. Marijuana patches were sometimes booby-trapped with fishing lines rigged with hooks dangling at eye level, rat traps that fired shotgun shells when activated, and punji sticks—sharpened bamboo sticks set in trails and designed to cut into the feet of trespassers. This kind of lawlessness prompted police officials to obtain federal grants for marijuana eradication missions by helicopter. Not long before John and Louise Ireland arrived in Hawaii, Dana and Sandy had heard a helicopter and looked outside to see it hovering over Sandy's property. A police officer was hanging from a rope looking into Sandy's garage. Sandy and Dana chuckled because Sandy was drying basil in the garage, and it seemed obvious that the culinary herb was what aroused the suspicions of the authorities. That kind of noisy intrusion offended many law-abiding citizens while it drove pot growers further underground, sometimes literally into subterranean lava tubes.

Many people moved to the area to get away from mainstream society and to surround themselves with nature. For that reason, a brutal crime in rural Hawaii was more shocking and horrifying than it would have been in a large mainland city. And police had more trouble getting help from citizens than they would have had elsewhere. Still, rumors flew, prompting countless tips to police.

The challenge facing the detectives was to determine which leads to pursue first. Detective Guillermo had to amass evidence for use at a trial. While most people were opening their Christmas presents, Guillermo and Rodillas headed for the collision scene and Kualii and Coloma went to the spot where Dana Ireland's body had been found.

The first piece of business at a crime scene is to interview eyewitnesses and to collect physical evidence. Unfortunately, police were aware of no one who had witnessed the vehicle-bicycle crash or the attack on Dana Ireland. What they did have was some physical evidence, which they set out to preserve. Because they didn't know which items would turn out to be important, they had to photograph everything, diagram precisely where each item was found, carefully pick it up without destroying any microscopic evidence that might be clinging to it, and place it in a zippered plastic bag or other suitable container. They would sign and date each package and then note the time each item was recovered. Residents in the area of the bike crash had blocked the road to safeguard the crime scene, and police were able to take more photographs to supplement the ones from the night before.

Luckily, the roads at both crime scenes were unpaved, so police were able to find tire indentations in the dirt at each location. They made plaster casts of the tracks and took pictures of several tire marks, including a single narrow gouge mark on Kapoho Kai Drive with larger double tire tracks leading to it. Detectives identified the gouge mark as the point at which the bicycle tire was driven into the road from the collision. Police call that the point of impact, or POI.

Now that it was light, police were able to spot a black bicycle seat in the thick grass growing off the side of the road near the tracks. They carefully slid the seat into a brown paper bag and later deposited it and Dana's crushed bicycle in a locked storage room at the Hilo police station. The bike was probably the most important piece of evidence from the Kapoho scene. Detectives hoped to find some of the automobile's paint on it so they could determine at least the vehicle's color, if not its make and year. Police also collected Dana's left shoe, her watch, and the clump of her blond hair.

At the Waa Waa scene, where the killers had

dumped Dana, police looked for more clues. A few yards from where sea turtles splash around looking for food, they found red panties, a badly damaged pair of Gap shorts, a child's left black McGregor jogging shoe with socks stuffed inside, a woman's right white Avia aerobic shoe, and a blue T-shirt with a print of a "woody" station wagon and the word "Jimmy'z" printed on it. Both the shoe and the T-shirt were spattered with blood. This early in the investigation, police had no way of knowing whether the T-shirt had been worn by the killer or simply discarded by a fisherman. They had to collect everything and analyze it. It was painstaking and time-consuming, but it was critical.

Careful gathering and control of evidence is also important for maintaining the chain of custody. Any item that might end up in court as evidence must be accounted for from the time of its seizure until it is presented at trial. When a cigarette butt is taken back to the police station in a plastic bag, for example, it is turned over to an evidence clerk, who signs for it, logs it in, and locks it up. When it's sent to the FBI for analysis, a similar procedure takes place. The purpose of this careful process is to prevent anyone from tampering with the evidence—or at least to make it easy to identify anyone who does.

Once police had gathered the potential evidence at the two crime scenes in the Dana Ireland case, Guillermo had the more gruesome duty of attending the autopsy. Because the body had multiple injuries, he knew it was important to determine which one had caused the woman's death so prosecutors could pinpoint who had inflicted that injury and charge the right person with the crime. At this point he didn't know if Dana Ireland had died from the car crash or from the blow to her head.

Dana's family wouldn't have recognized the corpse on the autopsy table. Not only had she been badly injured and pumped full of intravenous fluids, but she also showed evidence of the surgical efforts to save her. Part of her head had been shaved, she had many sutures on her head and body, and a large surgical incision extended from her abdomen to her pelvic area. The pathologist, Dr. Charles Reinhold, found numerous injuries to Dana's head but no evidence of a fractured skull or brain damage. Her left collarbone was broken; the right side of her neck and her right shoulder were severely scraped and bloody.

Dana's chest and back were covered with abrasions, cuts, and bruises. The doctor noted a bite mark on her left breast and discovered semen in her vagina. The semen remaining was minimal, as most of it had been lost in the emergency room during the unsuccessful effort to save Dana's life. Dr. Reinhold saved a sample of semen between two slides.

During the autopsy, the pathologist also found signs of extensive hemorrhaging, particularly in Dana's heart, lungs, stomach, and bladder. Her pelvic bone was fractured in two places. Her arms and legs were severely scraped and cut but weren't broken. Dr. Reinhold summed up Dana's appearance by saying she had "numerous external traumatic injuries to all major portions of the body." Her insides were just as bad. Reinhold concluded that Dana Ireland had died of a massive internal loss of blood.

Guillermo now knew she'd suffered traumatic injury, most likely from being hit by a vehicle, and that she'd been raped. But he still had no idea who was responsible. After attending the autopsy and collecting the physical evidence, he assigned Detective Kualii to interview the last person known to have seen the victim alive, Dana's friend Mark Evans. Mark had been headed to the Irelands' house for Christmas dinner when he'd come upon the "accident" scene. When Officer Wagner and Sergeant Malani stopped him there, he told them the bike belonged to his girlfriend. The police told Mark that Dana was at the hospital and then questioned him briefly. Mark told police Dana had left his house at about 4:10 that afternoon. The officers had duly recorded the information in their reports, along with the observation that Mark turned back without completing his trip to the Ireland house.

Days after the murder, John Ireland and his family began their own investigation. Sandy, a longtime resident of the area, was friendly with many Kapoho residents; she went door-to-door asking if anybody had seen anything that might be helpful to police in their search for the killers. She forwarded all tips to the police.

Sandy's neighborhood tour made it clear just how much Kapoho had changed over the years. Established residents told stories about "bad types" who had moved in or now hung around the area, and Sandy noticed previously well-kept homes that had fallen into disrepair—including one her parents had rented several years earlier. Sandy attributed some of the deterioration to hard drug use by people who were attracted to the area by its low rents. Nevertheless, she still felt safe in Kapoho. And the response of the Puna community to Dana's death was heartening.

Neighbors visited the Irelands carrying food and flowers, held community meetings about Dana's attack, and someone set up a reward fund. Some families donated as much as $1,000 to the fund, and smaller contributions came from families who could ill afford to give anything. The Ireland family itself contributed $10,000. When the Irelands left for Dana's funeral in Virginia, many friends saw them off at the airport, carrying leis and more money for the reward fund. Leis and tropical flowers began arriving in Virginia almost as soon as the Irelands got there. The gifts continued to arrive for days afterward.

The family held two services for Dana in Virginia and one in Hawaii. The first took place on January 2, in the same chapel where John and Louise Ireland had married almost 40 years earlier, at the Fort Belvoir Army post not far from their home in Springfield, Virginia. The chapel was filled with family and friends, and decorated with the flowers sent from Hawaii. Heather Preast, who'd heard about Sandy Ireland for years, had never met her. She gasped when she saw Sandy from behind at the chapel. For an instant, she thought it was Dana.

Lowell Kilday, the longtime neighbor of the Irelands, gave the eulogy. "Dana Ireland was for many years like another member of my own family," Kilday said. He knew Dana well enough to be sure she wouldn't want to see people grieving. "Dana was life, and Dana was light, and she was love, and she was caring, and she could not bear to see others suffer, no matter what the cause."

The retired ambassador explained how, as a child, Dana came to be known as "Magoo" and how she could stand up to the Kilday boys when they tried to intimidate her. On Dana's first day of kindergarten, Kilday recounted, Dana told the registrar at Keene Mill Elementary School that her name was Dana Kilday and that she was the younger sister of the six Kilday children. He reminded the mourners of Dana's love for animals and told them about the time she released her pet hamster because she couldn't stand to see any animal caged.

Kilday talked about Dana's athletic prowess and her scholarship. He went on to describe her devotion to her sister. "Sandy was at once her model, her mentor, her frequent companion, and her treasured friend," and the last months of Dana's life spent with Sandy and Jim were "some of the happiest she had known." Kilday concluded by praising John and Louise for the way they had raised Dana. "The deep love Dana drew from her parents was the basis of her inner security and her confidence in herself and in her ability to deal with the outside world."

The second memorial took place two days later at Louise's family plot in Davis Cemetery, in Shipman, Virginia, a little more than 100 miles southwest of Springfield. Some of Dana's ashes were laid to rest next to her maternal grandparents, amid the many flowers sent from Hawaii.

A final distinctly Hawaiian memorial was held on the spring equinox in Kapoho. Friends caught and prepared fish and made *haku* leis from foliage gathered in the nearby *ohia* forests. A Hawaiian minister presided over the ceremony; a devotee of Krishna Consciousness added an Eastern influence. Sandy gave the eulogy. "Spring," she said, "signified renewal and new beginnings, and it seemed an appropriate time to share with our community the essence of Dana." After the ceremony, Sandy, the minister, and a friend paddled out toward the open sea while those on shore threw hundreds of flowers and leis into the water. When the canoe reached an appropriate spot, Sandy scattered the remainder of Dana's ashes into the ocean her sister had loved. "Giving what little was left of my sister to the sea was a reality almost too painful to endure," Sandy later said. "Yet somehow the act itself proved transforming, and I felt release and emotional relief."

One of the early leads police pursued involved two people who had seen something peculiar at around the same time Dana had been run down on her bicycle. Eric Carlsmith and his girlfriend, Corina Kahookaulana, had been parking their Jeep in front of their driveway on Ililani Road near the intersection of Kapoho Kai Drive, where Dana's bike was found. They noticed a dark green Datsun pickup truck with gray primer stopped at the intersection.

"Hey, look. He's putting a little kid into the back of the truck," Eric said. He couldn't see the kid's face but assumed it was a child because a boy about 10 years old stood outside the truck. Eric noticed that the foot of the person being put into the truck didn't have a shoe. The man at the truck began to throw bushes from the side of the road into the back of the pickup. Eric didn't suspect foul play but thought the man might be stealing something.

The man glanced up and noticed Eric and Corina watching. He stared at them for what felt like two minutes, then bent down and grabbed an armload of bushes from the tire well on the left side of the truck. He said something to the boy, who walked to the cab and climbed into the passenger seat. The man then got into the truck and slowly drove down Kapoho Kai Drive in the direction of Red Road. He was about five feet nine inches and 220–230 pounds with a dark complexion and wavy, short black hair. By Eric's account, the man had big shoulders and a "fat gut." He wasn't wearing a shirt.

A short time later, Eric and Corina passed the spot where they had seen the man throwing bushes into his truck and noticed the crushed black bicycle and a white athletic shoe, as well as the set of skidmarks and tire tracks that indicated someone had made a U-turn. They stopped briefly to get a closer look before continuing. Later, after hearing Eric's story, police showed him a photo lineup, and Eric identified the man he saw as Ralph Rodrigues.*

That was just one of many tips that streamed into the police department. For example, within a few days of Dana Ireland's murder, police conducted a polygraph test on a person some surfers thought might be involved in her death. The man passed the test, though. Most tips, like that one, led nowhere, but some tantalized police.

One concerned a station wagon—rented by someone who lived near Waa Waa—that supposedly was returned with blood in it. As it turned out, the rental company had retrieved the vehicle the day before Dana's abduction and it contained no blood. Another informant told police that a resident of the area, Jim Orlando* might have been involved in Dana's death. During an interview with

_____
*Not his real name

police, Orlando admitted that he had yelled at a girl matching Dana Ireland's description on December 24, but said he never saw her again and had stayed at the beach area until his girlfriend picked him up after 5:00 P.M. Police found contradictions in Orlando's story; his girlfriend said she got off work at 7:00 P.M. and didn't remember picking him up. More important, police discovered that Orlando had been arrested three years earlier for sexual assault. He remained a suspect for years.

Many of the tips were second- or thirdhand, the kind that someone heard from a friend, who had heard it from someone else who "knew" what happened. Indeed many rumors swarmed around Puna after the murder. Quite a few were of the everybody-knows-who-did-it-but-is-afraid-to-tell variety, but some were much more specific. One of those came at the end of January from a former Florida boyfriend of Sandy's, George Mansfield,* who told police that he had received specific information from a person whom he would not name. Mansfield's informant told him that three brothers were involved in the crime, that their last name possibly started with an "L," and that the oldest of the brothers lived in Hawaiian Beaches, very close to Waa Waa, where Dana was dumped. One of the brothers was named Ralph. The detectives concluded that the information referred to the Rod-

---

*Not his real name

rigues brothers, Ralph, Andy,* and Jack.* Police therefore obtained an arrest warrant and picked up Ralph Rodrigues.

Rodrigues told detectives he had spent the entire day of December 24 with his wife at her home, some 15 miles from the crime scenes. He also said he knew who committed the crime and named a person living in the Ainaloa subdivision, a man police had not previously interviewed. That tip turned out to be another dead end.

Soon after that, police showed Eric Carlsmith a second photo lineup and this time he identified a different person, Herb Johnson.* Rodrigues and Johnson looked similar, so police thought it was reasonable that Eric could have made an honest mistake in his first identification. Police obtained a body warrant for Johnson. The county physician, Dr. Ben Hur, took blood and saliva samples and combed Johnson's pubic hair, then plucked pubic hairs and hairs from his head, beard, mustache, stomach, underarms, arms, and legs.

Police also got search warrants for Johnson's Datsun pickup truck and his sister's house. Detective Guillermo learned during a December 31 interview of Johnson that Johnson's son had lost one side of a pair of black high-cut basketball shoes. That attracted Guillermo's attention because of the child's black shoe found at the Waa Waa scene. He

_____

*Not his real name

asked Johnson to submit to a polygraph test. At first, Johnson consented, but a few days later his wife called the detective to inform him that Johnson wouldn't be taking the test. She insisted, however, that Johnson was with her at his sister's house from 2:00 P.M. on December 24 until 6:00 P.M. Christmas Day. So while police had enough suspicion to obtain a search warrant, they didn't have enough probable cause to arrest Johnson. However, he remained a suspect.

John and Louise Ireland called Guillermo constantly for updates. Louise, especially, was angry. She had learned that Johnson was under suspicion and couldn't understand why he wasn't in jail. "When are you going to pick him up?" she would ask during her daily calls.

Guillermo explained what would happen if police charged someone with Dana's murder before they had enough evidence for a conviction. A jury would find the defendant not guilty, and he could never be charged with the crime again because of the constitutional guarantee against double jeopardy. Guillermo understood the Irelands' frustration, but he had an investigation to conduct. "I'm not going to call you back every five minutes to tell you what I was doing for the last four minutes," he said. Fortunately for Guillermo, Lieutenant Rodillas was a supportive boss who fielded many of the calls from the Irelands and the public. That gave Guillermo more time to chase leads.

As it turned out, Johnson's pickup truck didn't match the description given by Eric Carlsmith. More importantly, he had a solid alibi for the time of the murder. Since Carlsmith's description of the truck was consistent with the tire tracks found at both scenes, police focused their attention on small pickup trucks, stopping people throughout Puna and questioning them. Nearly everyone who drove such a truck cooperated. Many gave tips about drivers of similar vehicles. Police interviewed scores of people, some of whom submitted to polygraph examinations. Many provided descriptions of suspicious characters and vehicles in the Kapoho and Waa Waa areas on Christmas Eve.

One atypical lead came from a Puna woman named Jean Fredrickson. She said she'd seen a tan van parked at the intersection of Ililani Road and Kapoho Kai Drive at about 4:40 P.M. on the day of Dana Ireland's abduction. Sandy Ireland had seen this same van cruising through the subdivision a few days earlier, with three men who she believed were acting suspiciously. Police eventually traced this van to 47-year-old Violet Harrison* and interviewed her and her 21-year-old son, Ray,** who had a police record for burglary and theft. Both mother and son denied being in the van anywhere near Kapoho Kai Drive on the day in question. The two volunteered to take lie detector tests. The poly-

---

*Not her real name **Not his real name

graph examiner concluded that both displayed deception in their responses.

John Ireland also got a tip about Harrison. He called Detective Guillermo, saying he had information from a confidential source that Ray Harrison had committed the crime. He asked if police had taken any teeth impressions from Harrison, raising the question because he was aware that Dana had been bitten on the left breast during the attack. Guillermo would neither confirm nor deny that dental impressions had been obtained from Harrison. Guillermo asked how John had gotten the information about Harrison but John refused to reveal his source.

All the same, Ray Harrison became a suspect.

Chapter 8

By mid-February 1992, police were focusing most of their attention in three directions: Ray Harrison, Herb Johnson, and Ralph and Jack Rodrigues. Police obtained a body warrant and took a blood sample from Harrison on February 12. When Detective Guillermo interviewed him, Harrison denied any involvement in the murder. His mother gave police permission to search her van; they found blood on both rear doors, on the right rear inner panel, and on pieces of plywood covering the van's floor. When police told Violet Harrison blood had been found in her van, she said she'd cut her finger and flatly refused to answer any more questions. Ray's 12-year-old brother, Perry,* told police that Roy did have the van on Christmas Eve, and said he remembered hearing his older brother talk about the murder shortly after it happened. Guillermo obtained additional statements incriminating Ray Harrison, but nobody could place him

---

*Not his real name

at or near the crime scene. Police sent samples of the bloodstained items to the FBI for analysis.

In early March 1992, Guillermo received an anonymous tip that 18-year-old Frank Pauline Jr. and someone named Gregory either were involved in the murder or had information about it. Guillermo interviewed Pauline on March 17. While Pauline admitted that he had a cousin named Gregory, with whom he often hung out, he denied any involvement in the Ireland case. He did tell police, however, that a week earlier he'd overheard an argument between two young men. Pauline said a man he didn't know told an acquaintance named Ian Schweitzer, "You think you bad 'cause you wen' run that girl down and fuck her."

He was speaking a dialect known in Hawaii as "pidgin." Most longtime residents of the state can switch back and forth between standard English and pidgin—as a way to establish their local roots. Yet, many working class citizens speak only pidgin, which has its own grammar and pronunciation. For instance, putting the word *wen'* in front of a present tense verb changes it to past tense. So, "you wen' run that girl down" translates to, "you ran that girl down."

Guillermo intended to follow up on the tip, but he continued to focus on Harrison, Johnson, and the Rodrigues brothers.

One of Guillermo's informants told him he had seen Andy and Ralph Rodrigues take their Datsun

pickup truck out for a test drive at about 4:30 P.M.
on December 24. The informant said when the
brothers returned two hours later, they looked nervous. Andy was no longer wearing his shirt and
jeans. The tipster said the brothers spent that night
stripping the truck of its engine and transmission.
They then dumped the rest of the truck. He also
told Guillermo that he'd seen Andy Rodrigues
wearing a T-shirt like the one shown on television
from the Waa Waa scene, where Ida Smith had
found Dana Ireland. Finally, the informant told
Guillermo that several weeks after the killing,
Ralph Rodrigues was bragging that he was getting
away with murder and there was nothing anybody
could do about it.

A few days later, the informant told Detective
Guillermo that he had made up the story about the
Rodrigues brothers' involvement in the crime because he was having a dispute with Ralph Rodrigues over the sale of marijuana. Guillermo didn't
know what to believe. He continued to seek more
information on all his prime suspects and hunt for
the vehicle that had struck Dana Ireland.

One suspected truck was the 1976 Toyota
pickup originally owned by Andy Rodrigues. Another was a 1974 Datsun pickup that had been
identified as being at the scene of the bicycle collision on Kapoho Kai Drive. Police never found the
Toyota, but they tracked down the Datsun and,
with the permission of its new owner, took hair,
fiber, and gravel as evidence. The owner of the

pickup at the time of the crime, Larry Nakamatsu,* was a felon. Although that information seemed promising in the beginning, Nakamatsu's girlfriend told police that she'd been with Nakamatsu the entire day of Dana Ireland's abduction and that they'd never left the house.

In the meantime, police became interested in another man. In December 1991, Roland Derienzo* had been the boyfriend of one of the first witnesses at the scene of the mangled bike. Police had interviewed Derienzo several times, not because he was a suspect but because he had been with his girlfriend that night and they thought he might have seen something that would help identify Dana Ireland's killers. Over the months since the murder, Derienzo's name came up from time to time in tips to police. Since the focus was on a small pickup truck, and because Derienzo's girlfriend had been with him most of December 24, police had never considered him a suspect.

That changed early in 1992, when someone called Crime Stoppers and said Derienzo had twice admitted to accidentally hitting Dana Ireland, pulling her into a van, raping her, and then dumping her while she was still alive. The caller said he didn't think the case should be classified as a murder. Shortly after that phone call, Detective Guillermo learned that Derienzo, who was on parole for a sexual assault conviction, was in the Hilo police station being pro-

---

*Not his real name

cessed for violating parole. Guillermo took advantage of the opportunity and had a chat with the man. Derienzo was very cooperative—almost too cooperative, Guillermo thought. But after Derienzo offered to give DNA samples, police cleared him as a suspect.

Literally hundreds of other people came under suspicion during the course of the investigation. One by one, detectives investigated all of them.

The Ireland family wasn't about to sit idle while the police probed the case. Eventually they hired a private investigator; they felt the police weren't capable of handling the job. While the private investigator followed up leads on the Big Island, John Ireland tried to make sure police were properly analyzing all of the evidence they had obtained.

As he often did, John called Detective Guillermo. "Have you tested the DNA?" he asked.

"Tests are still being conducted," Guillermo said.

John took a deep breath. "We're frustrated as hell with the length of time it's taking to analyze the evidence," he said, "but we know this is common in criminal investigations like this."

John was learning more than he ever wanted to know about homicide investigations through his affiliations with an assortment of organizations that provide information to crime victims, including the National Center for Victims of Crime and the Fairfax County Victims Support Unit. The more he learned, the more active he became in fighting for victims' rights. He became an advocate in the campaign for a Crime Victims' Rights Amendment to the U.S. Constitution and lobbied lawmakers for support. Because he was the father of a murdered woman, the elected officials made time for him. "Every chance I get, I go over to Capitol Hill," John said.

The Irelands were appalled when they learned that whoever was arrested for killing their daughter would never stand trial for first-degree murder, a crime with a mandatory sentence of life in prison with no chance of parole. In Hawaii someone could only be charged with first-degree murder if he killed more than one person, killed for hire, killed somebody while incarcerated, or killed a police officer, judge, prosecutor, or court witness. Hawaii had no death penalty; the stiffest crime for second-degree murder was life in prison with the possibility of parole. "I consider the sexual assault and murder of my daughter no less a crime than those murders considered first degree under Hawaii's criminal code," John said. He was equally shocked to learn that Hawaii was the only state in the Union without a law permitting crime victims to make victim impact statements to the judge at sentencing.

John lobbied the Hawaii state legislature to pass new laws. On a trip to Hawaii, he and Louise met with State Senator Andy Levin, who represented the Puna District, and convinced him to introduce one bill allowing victim impact statements and another making a rape/murder a first-degree offense.

Although the impact statement bill passed easily, the second bill was unacceptable to legislators in its original form. The legislation that eventually passed kept rape/murder a second-degree crime but allowed for enhanced sentencing of life in prison without parole for murders that were particularly heinous, atrocious, or cruel. Unfortunately, it wasn't retroactive, so it wouldn't apply to Dana Ireland's killers.

In Washington, John met with Hawaii Senator Daniel Akaka and tried to persuade him to authorize the use of military ambulances to transport injured patients from remote areas to hospitals. He didn't want any other victim to suffer what Dana had gone through while waiting for emergency care. While that effort was unsuccessful, Senator Akaka did play a key role in the installation of emergency telephones in rural parts of the Big Island.

Even while pushing for new legislation, John continued independently investigating Dana's murder. He learned that the unnamed lab used by the police department wasn't using the PCR (polymerase chain reaction) method of analyzing DNA, but instead RFLP (restriction fragment length polymorphism) analysis, which at that time was deemed more accurate and conclusive, but not suitable for the kind of degraded samples present in this case. It wasn't until the beginning of June that Lieutenant Rodillas informed John that the FBI had conducted the lab tests, but that they had come back inconclusive.

John immediately called Deputy Prosecutor Brenda Carreira, who told him she had reviewed the police evidence even though the case had not been officially sent to the prosecutor's office yet, and that it was unlikely she could win a conviction based on the evidence accumulated to date. "I don't know why it's taking so goddamn long to get that to a grand jury," John replied.

In August 1992, a woman named Elaine Buenaventura* told a Puna patrol officer she had some information that might be useful. Guillermo interviewed her and learned that her daughter's ex-boyfriend, Wayne Gonsalves, had told her daughter that it was just a matter of time before the police arrested him for a murder he didn't commit. She also said Wayne's brother, Frank Pauline Jr., had hinted that he and Wayne might have been involved in the slaying, or at least might know who had been. Although she said Pauline's story changed somewhat each time he told it, Elaine was convinced Pauline knew something about the murder. Over the months following the crime, police received several other anonymous tips naming Frank Pauline and Wayne Gonsalves.

On August 12, Guillermo interviewed Wayne Gonsalves. Gonsalves said he had been in the Pohoiki and Kapoho areas on Christmas Eve, riding with friends in a 1980 or 1981 Nissan king cab pickup truck. But he denied any involvement in the

_____
*Not her real name

crime, and said he had heard that a man named Ian
Schweitzer was involved. Shortly after Christmas,
Gonsalves himself had seen Schweitzer driving his
1957 Volkswagen Bug. The Bug had damage to the
hood, which was repaired very soon after. Gonsalves volunteered to take a polygraph test, during
which he said he wasn't present when Dana Ireland was run over and he didn't have knowledge of
the incident. The polygraph results indicated no
deception.

Almost a year after the murder, a Puna patrol
officer, Richard Marzo, arrested two juveniles for
several burglaries and thefts. During Marzo's interrogation, he learned that some time after the murder the boys had been riding with Frank Pauline Jr.
Pauline told them he was responsible for the Dana
Ireland murder and pointed out the Waa Waa trail
where she had been dumped. Marzo passed this information to detectives in the Criminal Investigations Division, adding that he and other Puna
officers had heard other rumors about Pauline's involvement.

In late February 1993, Marzo arrested Pauline
for burglary. During his interrogation Marzo mentioned the Dana Ireland case. Pauline denied any
knowledge of it, but acknowledged that people
were blaming him for it.

Marzo questioned another individual rumored
to be a confidant of Pauline, but he denied that
Pauline had told him anything about the murder.

He did say, however, that he had heard that Pauline was responsible for raping somebody else.

That was probably true. Pauline was a suspect in a rape, and police had obtained blood and hair samples from him and submitted them to the FBI for comparison with evidence from the victim. Marzo requested that the samples from Pauline be preserved and compared to evidence from Dana Ireland. Marzo's report was filed without further action being taken for several years.

Chapter 9

On September 10, 1992, Big Island residents heard this announcement, broadcast at regular intervals over all radio stations: "This is a civil defense message. The Pacific Hurricane Center has identified a hurricane named Iniki in Hawaiian waters. The hurricane is located approximately 400 miles south of the Big Island and is moving slowly north northwest."

If the hurricane kept its course, it would slam into the island's south coast by the next morning. Detective Steve Guillermo was pulled off the Dana Ireland case and ordered to help shut down county beaches as a precaution. While he was doing so, someone summoned him back to the office. A two-month-old baby was dead of head and leg fractures. The boy's 15-year-old mother said he had fallen off the bed, but her story didn't ring true. The teenager was arrested, and it was Guillermo's job to investigate. So, while many island residents were taping windows, stocking up on supplies, and hunkering down with loved ones, Guillermo had to call his wife and tell her she was on her own; he and two other detectives would be spending the night at the police station investigating a homicide. Steve and Trudy Guillermo wanted to start a family, but his work schedule wasn't making it easy.

Sometime overnight, the hurricane changed its course, missing Hilo altogether but whipping up waves in West Hawaii as it brushed past the Big Island, destroying four homes and 11 boats. The next day the brunt of the storm squarely hit Kauai, devastating the entire island.

Sandy Ireland and her husband, Jim, had moved to Kauai that May because the Big Island held too many painful memories. On September 11, 1992, Hurricane Iniki provided a distraction—albeit not the kind Sandy and Jim were seeking. Maximum sustained winds of 130 miles per hour and gusts up to 160 miles per hour thrashed the island, tearing roofs off houses, plucking trees out of the ground, and toppling power lines. When it was over, more than 10,000 buildings were damaged or destroyed, five people were dead, 100 were injured, and Kauai's trademark lush green cliffs were barren.

The hurricane knocked Sandy and Jim's rental house off its foundation. The restaurant where Jim worked was completely destroyed, and Sandy had been jobless before the storm hit, so they suddenly found themselves homeless and unemployed. It didn't faze them much, though. After losing Dana, the material inconvenience seemed trivial.

By Christmas Eve 1992, Kauai was on the road

to a slow recovery. Sandy and Jim were starting a new life on Oahu's north shore, famous for its high winter surf. On the Big Island, a year had passed since Dana Ireland's attack, and still no one was under arrest. That night the Puna community held a "Take Back the Night" march and vigil in remembrance of Dana Ireland. John and Louise Ireland flew in from Springfield to participate and Jim and Sandy joined them from Oahu. It touched the Ireland family to see some 150 people—including two elected officials—taking time out from their Christmas Eve festivities to mark the first anniversary of Dana's brutal slaying. For 10 months now, John had led a letter-to-the-editor campaign by Dana's family and friends. Despite the geographical distance separating Springfield from Puna, he'd been determined not to let Big Island residents forget his daughter's murder. The vigil proved they hadn't.

John and Louise returned to Springfield, where Dana's friends frequently dropped by to offer comfort. The Irelands didn't celebrate Christmas anymore. When Jennifer Shepherd visited, she noticed a marked change in John and Louise. John looked as if he'd aged far more than a year. Louise never laughed anymore and the twinkle was gone from her eyes. She was obsessed with her daughter's death, dragging out photos and news clippings about Dana for Jennifer to see.

"Talking to victims, I tell you, it's sad," Louise said. "I don't know whether it helps me or it doesn't. John does things that help him, but I kind of think about it all the time." She told Jennifer that her doctor had prescribed pills to make her feel better. "Nothing like that's going to help me," she said. "It never will. I'll just have to live day by day, that's all. We'll never get over it. The families I've talked to never get over it."

Jennifer sat teary-eyed and shared in Louise's grief. She knew there wasn't much she could say. John could see how painful the visits were for Dana's friends. He understood when they began to drop by less frequently and cards came in the mail instead. "They seem to be almost as devastated as we are," John said.

John buried his emotions in his work for victims' rights and in tracking down tips about Dana's case. He listened carefully to every lead, meticulously writing them down in a running log he kept on his desk. He got one in May 1993 from a Hilo resident who told him she'd had a conversation with another woman "who claims she knows a woman who knows a woman who is either the wife or girlfriend of the person who murdered Dana." The caller told John that the murderer was a relative of a police officer and that police were covering up the information. John dutifully passed this tip, as he had the others, to police, prosecutors, and his private investigator. Like those before it, this tip led nowhere.

But John didn't give up. He continued to use his Springfield home office as a command center. He was in frequent contact with police and prosecutors in Hilo, as well as with his Hawaii attorney, his private investigator, the state attorney general, and the mayor of Hawaii County. He was particularly concerned about the failure of the DNA testing and made repeated calls to both Cellmark Laboratories, a leading forensic facility, and the FBI forensics laboratory to find out if additional—and more reliable—testing was possible. He found out that PCR testing was possible on the semen samples and that the Hawaii County Police Department was considering having such a test conducted. John then called the FBI lab and learned that a PCR test had been conducted on the sample in early 1993 but the results were inconclusive because the semen specimen was too small.

It would have been easy for John to be overwhelmed by frustration and rage at the way police conducted their investigation. But he tried to stay focused on solving the case. He alternately pressured the authorities and did his own research on forensics. His log indicated each call made and whether it was returned. John asked probing questions, and when he wasn't satisfied with the answers, he pushed harder.

For example, he was unconvinced when police and prosecutors told him teeth marks on Dana's body couldn't be matched to a suspect. He began calling forensic odontologists, dentists who help investigate crimes. John then called Detective Guillermo and the prosecutor's office to ask if they would hire one of the odontologists on his list to examine the bitemark. Guillermo called back about a week later and said police would approach one.

On September 9, 1993, John and Louise Ireland participated in a telephone conference that also included Hawaii County prosecutors, Sandy Ireland, her husband, and Ireland attorney Sherry Broder. The conference left the Irelands dissatisfied. They didn't get responses to their questions about the possibility of using another investigating agency or an independent prosecutor, but prosecutor Jay Kimura said police were now looking at two groups of suspects.

Shortly after the conference John called Detective Guillermo and asked him about the suspects. Guillermo told John police weren't looking at two groups and didn't know why Prosecutor Kimura had said such a thing. He also said police had obtained some new evidence without specifying what it was.

Unhappy with the investigation's progress, John and Louise flew to Oahu in November to meet with the state attorney general, Robert Marks. The attorney general's office is located in downtown Honolulu in part of the state government complex that includes the capitol, Iolani Palace, and the governor's mansion, Washington Place. While the area was picturesque, John and Louise weren't there to sightsee. They were interested only in bringing Dana's killers to justice.

John asked if the attorney general's office could

appoint an independent prosecutor to review the evidence, citing, among other things, the apparent difference of opinion between the Hawaii County Police Department and the Hawaii County Prosecutor's Office. He inquired as to whether there was sufficient evidence for a conviction and requested the hiring of another forensic odontologist to ensure that the bitemark could be used as evidence. Then John expressed his displeasure with how the case had been handled from the very beginning, citing the failure of the police to protect the scene of the crash, to immediately take the autopsy semen as evidence, and to follow up on tips passed to them by him and others. He got no response.

While in Honolulu, John and Louise also met with the governor's chief of staff, Joshua Agsalud, and asked for support from the governor's office, telling Agsalud the police had badly botched the investigation. Agsalud was sympathetic, but that wasn't enough for John. "I want results," he said, "not sympathy."

The Irelands met again with state senator Andy Levin. Although John was grateful for the meeting, he came away from it feeling that Senator Levin was defending the police. He was particularly upset when Levin asked if the Irelands would fund a medical helicopter for the Big Island if they won their civil suit against the county. The Irelands were suing over the delay in getting an ambulance to Dana. John flatly refused, saying the county or state should have funded such a helicopter long ago.

Soon after the Irelands returned to Virginia, Attorney General Marks sent John a letter saying his office would be reviewing the evidence in the Ireland case, a decision agreed to by Hawaii County's police chief, Victor Vierra.

By the end of 1993, two years had passed since the murder and police still hadn't made an arrest. The police department had released virtually no information to the public, save an occasional quote to the news media that the investigation was "ongoing" and a comment a year earlier that they were testing the blood of "some suspects."

Criticism of the department escalated. The community and the Ireland family pushed police to solve the case. A self-proclaimed watchdog group, Citizens for Justice, made the Ireland case one of its priorities. The small but vocal group had banded together after a police sergeant fatally beat his wife and then faked a traffic accident. The group's role in that case as well as in the Ireland case was to keep pressure on police and prosecutors through public rallies, letters to editors, and testimony at Police Commission and County Council meetings. The group was responsible for bumper stickers reading INDICT DANA IRELAND'S KILLERS that appeared on cars all over the Big Island. It also pushed for an outside agency to review the police department's investigation.

In January 1994, John and Louise again flew to the Big Island to seek answers. One of their first meetings was with the Hawaii County Police Commission, a meeting that included Chief Vierra. John repeated his concerns over the many mistakes he said the police had made in their investigation. The commission directed Chief Vierra to return to its next meeting with a list of procedural changes that he would implement to make sure such failures didn't happen again.

John also met with Mayapple McCullough and Del Pranke, two of the major figures in Citizens for Justice. John said he wanted them to get involved in the case but told them not to interfere with the attorney general's investigation. During the same visit, John also met with the Puna representative on the county council, Helene Hale, telling her he was fed up with police incompetence. He said he wanted to meet with the entire county council.

Both John Ireland and Citizens for Justice constantly got tips about the crime. Some were specific, including names of suspects, while others were vague and not particularly helpful. Sherry Broder, John's attorney, called in late February of 1994 to tell John that police had never interviewed Hazel Allan, the passerby who had first reported the crime to the police. When John called Detective Guillermo about why police hadn't talked to the woman, Guillermo told him they had. A few days later Hazel called John directly and repeated her charge.

John was becoming a frequent speaker about crime before groups as varied as high schools and the National Police Academy. In a forum about rape, he spoke about the effects of the crime on the victim's family.

"The horror of my daughter's rape and murder is on my mind constantly," he said, "and I keep asking, 'Why Dana?' Her sister has suffered financial loss because of Dana's terrible death, and my wife and I have spent a considerable amount on private investigators and travel to Hawaii to keep the police focused on the investigation. Dana's mother is having a difficult time coping, and psychiatric counseling has not been helpful."

When John spoke to the International Association of Chiefs of Police, he gave them tips on how to deal with relatives of murder victims:

"As soon as possible, tell the family that the death is considered a homicide," he said. "Don't let the family learn of murder from the media, as in our case.

"Don't withhold information from the victims. Everyone but my wife and I was told Dana was raped.

"Keep the victims up to date on the progress of the investigation and give them all the information you consider will not jeopardize the case. The victims will not leak information.

"Don't lie to the victims. They will only lose faith in the police and go to other sources for information.

"Don't consider victims uninformed of investigative procedures and forensics. There are too many sources for this information and the many experts are only too willing to supply it to victims.

"Don't be disturbed by frequent calls from victims. They are going through a traumatic period of life and talking to police is good therapy.

"And, finally, if there is a victims' support service in your locale, direct the victim to them. The Fairfax County Victims Support Unit has been of considerable help in our ability to cope with the tragic loss of our daughter."

On March 1, 1994, John and Louise again flew to Hawaii and met with the lead police investigators, presenting them with 15 specific questions for which they wanted answers. Some of the questions dealt with evidence, like the teeth marks and DNA analysis, while others were about particular suspects. During the meeting, John asked whether police had talked to Hazel Allan since his call to Guillermo a week earlier. They told him that they hadn't, but said they'd interviewed her soon after Dana's murder. The next day police finally interviewed Hazel.

The following day John and Louise met with prosecutors, again with a list of specific questions. Before long John gave up asking the questions because the prosecutors' responses were vague at best. This time the prosecutors' investigator, Billy Perreira, told John he thought two groups were involved in the murder. He added that Dana might not have been raped, suggesting that she might have had consensual sex with Mark Evans when she went to his house to invite him to dinner. John and Louise were skeptical about the two-group theory and offended by the remarks about voluntary sex. John said he realized that defense attorneys might try to use the consensual sex theory to help their clients, but said that he knew that Dana wasn't promiscuous and that Mark was just a friend. The Irelands left the meeting frustrated and angry.

While John's relationship with the prosecution deteriorated, his relationship with the police improved despite the confusion about Hazel Allan's interview. Detective Guillermo seemed confident that police would solve the murder. He confirmed that Ray Harrison was the prime suspect and said the man's bite was "consistent" with the teeth marks left on Dana.

Nevertheless, John wasn't going to take anyone's word on anything. He continued to pursue his own investigation. Shortly after talking to Guillermo, he called Dr. Norman Sperber, a well-known forensic odontologist in Southern California, who had analyzed the bitemarks on Dana for the police department. Dr. Sperber told him that one of the bitemark samples taken from suspects could not be ruled out, but that the match wasn't strong. Dr. Sperber was basing his conclusions on photographs of the bitemark on Dana Ireland and bite samples from the suspects, but told John in a letter that he might be able to make a more definitive analysis if he had the actual tissue instead of photographs. John im-

mediately called police and asked them why they
hadn't sent the tissue. The response: Dr. Sperber
had never asked for it.

John was infuriated but relentless. He badgered
the police and the prosecutors to send the tissue
sample to Dr. Sperber, and when he couldn't get answers from them he checked with Dr. Reinhold, the
autopsy doctor, who still had custody of the tissue.
"No," Reinhold said, "the police haven't picked up
the tissue yet." John got more and more frustrated.

Likewise, police and prosecutors were getting
frustrated with John. They were sympathetic and
understanding toward the father of a murdered
daughter, but they didn't like John pursuing the
killers on his own, and they were concerned that
his leaks to the press could jeopardize their investigation and the eventual prosecution.

On May 23, 1994, Guillermo was working at his
desk when a secretary gave him the message that
would blow the case wide open. "There's a guy on
the line," she said. "Wants to talk to you about the
Dana Ireland case."

Guillermo picked up the phone. "CID, Detective
Guillermo."

"I don't want you to know who I am, but I have
information about the Dana Ireland murder," a
male voice said. "Three guys were there. One's a
guy named Frank Pauline Jr., and the others are
two brothers, Ian and Shawn Schweitzer."

"What else do you know?" Guillermo asked.

"Nothing. But Frank's brother can tell you more. He wants to talk to you. Name's John Gonsalves."

Guillermo knew of Gonsalves's reputation for dealing drugs. He was a bit cynical about why Gonsalves would want to come forward. "I'll be here till 4:30," he said, giving the caller the number of his direct phone line. "Have the guy call me."

Chapter 10

At 4:45 P.M. on Monday, May 23, 1994, Steve Guillermo's phone rang.

"CID, Detective Guillermo."

"Oh, hi. This is John."

"John who?"

"John Gonsalves." Gonsalves explained that his brother was Frank Pauline Jr. Gonsalves told Guillermo about a telephone conversation a week earlier during which Pauline had told him he had been with two brothers, Ian and Shawn Schweitzer, 20 and 16 years old at the time, and had witnessed the ramming, kidnap, and rape of Dana Ireland. Gonsalves told Guillermo that Pauline and the Schweitzer brothers had been in a pickup truck belonging to Ian Schweitzer's girlfriend at the time.

"You tell Frank to call me. I'm here," said Guillermo, who was very familiar with Frank Pauline and his criminal history.

In police jargon, Pauline was a 21-year-old "local male" and a habitual criminal. A year earlier, after Pauline had been arrested for robbing a jewelry store, a judge had ordered him to stay home pending the outcome of a trial and had put Pauline under electronic monitoring to make sure he did. Guillermo had had to go to court to report to the judge that Pauline hadn't responded to 15 of 40 telephone checks and that he had been spotted miles from his home. About a month after Dana Ireland's murder, Pauline had been involved in a hit-and-run accident while speeding on his motorcycle. The accident injured an 11-year-old boy. Although Pauline could have been sentenced to 10 years in prison, he only served 10 days in jail in a plea bargain that reduced the crime from a felony to a misdemeanor.

While he was on probation in that case, Pauline was accused of first-degree burglary. That case, too, had ended in a plea bargain. Pauline was in prison now, serving a 10-year conviction for the 1993 rape of a woman who had been riding in his car. When the car ran out of gas, Pauline, who was high on alcohol and cocaine, demanded oral sex from the woman while her three children slept in the back seat. After the woman refused, Pauline forced her out of the car and raped her. In that case, Pauline had pleaded no contest to sexual assault, his attorney saying he had been too impaired by the drugs and booze to remember what had happened. At his sentencing hearing, a judge ordered Pauline into custody immediately and told him to wait for a sheriff with an unarmed law clerk who doubled as a bailiff. Instead of waiting for the sheriff, Pauline just walked out of the courtroom. He fled to the island of Oahu, where he spent the weekend until police caught up with him.

Pauline's first brush with the law was at age 10, when he was a suspect in a burglary with two other youths. His juvenile criminal career progressed from thefts and burglaries to marijuana offenses, assault, and robbery. One time, Pauline "ratted out" his mother and two of his brothers, telling police they were processing marijuana plants in their home. Police soon arrived at the house, arrested the mother and brothers, and seized the marijuana. It seemed that Pauline was mad at his mother and this was his way of getting back at her.

Guillermo, who'd questioned Frank Pauline more than two years previously about the Dana Ireland case based on an early tip, had no trouble believing that Pauline was capable of participating in her attack. Guillermo didn't buy for a second Pauline's claim that he was just a witness to the crime. Guillermo knew Pauline as a chronic liar and realized he wasn't one to just stand by quietly and watch. In the jewelry store robbery, Pauline had claimed his cousin was the one at the scene, telling police that the cousin had a tattoo identical to his own.

Frank Pauline Jr. was the sixth of seven children. The elder kids had a different father, and their last name was Gonsalves. Although they were technically half-brothers and sisters, the family never made that distinction.

Frank's mother, Pat Pauline, was the dominant

figure in the family. After her first husband died in a motorcycle accident, she married Frank Pauline Sr. To differentiate between father and son, the family called Frank Jr. "Frankie Boy," or "Boy," a common nickname in Hawaii for a junior.

Frank was born on the Big Island and raised in the Hawaiian Beaches subdivision of Puna, home to many working class families and people on welfare. He attended Pahoa elementary and high school but dropped out in eleventh grade. Frank was a tough kid, who constantly sought attention from his family. His older brother, John, didn't have a job, but he drove expensive cars and motorcycles and carried large quantities of cash, which Frank sometimes helped him count. Frank himself began smoking crack cocaine at age 15, when the price of pot went up, probably as a result of the Police Department's marijuana eradication program. Cocaine became his obsession.

Frank's mother was leader of Da Us Guys Band, for which Frankie Boy played congas. She didn't want his older brothers to give him drugs, but sometimes they would leave it in strategic spots and look the other way. If not, Frank would steal drugs, steal money to buy drugs, or take the drugs by force.

Guillermo wanted to talk to Pauline, but it was his policy not to initiate calls to informants, so he kept working on the case while waiting to hear from the criminal. Pauline called twice during the next 10 days, but Guillermo was away from the office both times. Unwilling to delay the discussion any longer, Guillermo flew to Oahu on June 1 to interview Pauline at the state attorney general's office.

At more than 200 pounds, Pauline was either husky or overweight, depending on who was describing him. He had fluffy black hair, a mustache, and a goatee. His full, well-defined lips could alternate between pouting and grinning in the blink of an eye.

That day, Pauline wasn't very cooperative. He was relaxed and made eye contact with Guillermo, but he said he had been caught by surprise when the prison guards drove him from Halawa Prison to the attorney general's office. He said he wanted more time to think about what he'd witnessed, and didn't want Guillermo to read him his rights. When Guillermo persisted, Pauline told him Ian and Shawn Schweitzer had driven to his house on Christmas Eve and asked if he wanted to party with them. Pauline said that was unusual because he wasn't a close friend of the Schweitzer brothers. He said he had hesitated until they had shown him some cocaine. Pauline told Guillermo that he had trouble remembering the details because he'd been high on cocaine. He said he vaguely remembered something about Ian hitting Dana Ireland with a tire iron. He also remembered that the Schweitzer brothers had thrown away the clothes they'd been wearing, although he couldn't say where.

Guillermo, who had a low-key interrogation style, just nodded and let Pauline talk. He knew Frank well enough to realize that he would change his story. Later the detective would confront him with the inconsistencies. Pauline ended the interview by telling Guillermo he would write the detective a letter with details of the crime.

The letter never arrived.

Two weeks later, Guillermo got a phone call from a woman named Charla Figueroa. "This is Frank's girlfriend," she said.

"Okay," said Guillermo.

"He wants to talk to you but he doesn't know if he can trust you."

"You know what?" Guillermo said. "Until he tells me something, he probably has every reason not to trust me. I'm here. You tell me when he wants to call. I'll be here."

At 7:22 that evening, Guillermo got a collect call from an inmate friend of Pauline's, Norm Simpson.* Simpson, in prison for murder, asked Guillermo what the detective could do for Pauline. "He wants to come forward, but he wants a guarantee about some things," Simpson said.

"I don't even know what he has to say," Guillermo said. "I can't guarantee him anything." Guillermo reminded Simpson that it was Pauline who had called wanting to discuss the case. "If Frank decides not to talk, we're still going to have

---

*Not his real name

to go talk to the Schweitzers," he said, explaining that he was giving Frank an opportunity to talk first but that he couldn't wait forever.

Pauline called two days later while Guillermo was out, leaving a message that he was ready to talk.

After Guillermo drove back to the Police Department in his white Ford Bronco, he decided he would pay Pauline another visit the following day. While he was preparing for the interview, one of the other detectives got a phone call. "Turn on the TV," he said. "The police are chasing O.J. Simpson." The detectives stopped what they were doing and watched the infamous slow-speed chase along with much of America as the retired football star tried to flee in a white Bronco from what was being billed on the mainland as the Crime of the Century.

"Cisco, that could be you on there," Lieutenant Rodillas told Guillermo. Everybody laughed. It was just what Guillermo needed to help him relax before his meeting with Pauline.

The next morning, Detective Guillermo and his captain, Raymond Simao, flew to Honolulu to conduct the interview, again in the Attorney General's office. Again, Pauline was calm, and he looked the detectives in the eye. Immediately, he offered to take a polygraph exam, which Guillermo took as a good sign. After confirming that Pauline understood his rights, Guillermo asked him what had happened. Pauline leaned forward in his seat.

"Okay, one day my two friends came to pick me

up," Pauline said. "Ian and Shawn Schweitzer. They wen' ask me if I wanted to go party and I told them, yeah. So we headed towards the beach."

Pauline said that the Schweitzer brothers had picked him up at his mother's house on Aku Street in Hawaiian Beaches around lunchtime in Ian's purple Volkswagen. They headed "towards the end of Hawaiian Beaches," turning right onto Beach Road. Ian was driving, Shawn was in the front passenger seat, and Pauline was seated behind Ian.

"Okay, we made several stops to smoke cocaine. And after, well we kept continuing on little ways. We came out by an intersection going towards Kapoho and that's where we saw a girl standing up.

"As we were going past, my friend Ian looked towards the side and he said, 'Ho, look at that girl.' Then we continued to go forward down the road."

Guillermo asked if that was toward Pohoiki.

"Yes. Then we reached by these mailboxes area that we turned around," Pauline said. "That place is better known as Red Road where they call it. And we headed back towards the girl."

Guillermo wanted to know if Ian told him why he did that.

Ian didn't say at that point, but later he said he wanted to talk to the girl. "I guess to make a date or something," Pauline said. "Then we headed back and he was going faster and I was telling him for slow down. About forty to forty-five miles per hour because I looked at the speedometer. And then he just kept on going towards the girl. The next thing I knew, I felt like going over a speed bump real fast. How many times we went over? About I would say roughly two times. Going forward and reversing."

Guillermo was used to brutality and murder, but this was still shocking. He asked Pauline whether he'd seen the girl before they hit her. Pauline said they saw her walk across the road with a bike. He couldn't remember her hair color or what she was wearing. Guillermo asked Pauline what happened after they ran over her.

"He ran out. Him and his brother. And I was in the back trying for look. I didn't see what they really did but I know the body was in the front part of the car, in the trunk part of the Bug." Pauline said he didn't get out of the car. They drove back toward Hawaiian Beaches. "Then we made several stops and one of the stops was by some place by junk cars. Where there's cars. Lots of cars. Then we walked out of the car."

Guillermo wanted to know if Ian had asked Pauline to help him. "Yes. He asked me for come outside and help him carry the body out, so I did. We walked," Pauline said. He said he saw damage to the car's trunk.

"Okay," Guillermo said. "Then what happened?"

"Then we carried the body out. We laid 'em down and she was still alive. She nevah say nothing. Nevah really act up like she had been hurt.

Then Ian Schweitzer wen' end up having sex with her. It lasted for a short while. Maybe like a couple of seconds. Four-five seconds. Anyway, then he wanted me for go on top of her."

"To have sex with her?" Guillermo asked.

"Yes, and I wen' refuse. Told him I nevah like. And at the same time when he was having sex I was just kinda enjoying watching. I guess was 'cause of the drugs."

When Guillermo asked about Dana Ireland's injuries, Pauline said he saw blood coming out of her eyes, mouth, and nose. Ian told him they had to "knock her off," Pauline said. "He said if someone was to find her and she was to make it—live—she would tell on us and we all would get busted. So he told me for look for something. So when I wen' go back I found a L-shaped bar, tire iron.

"I walked toward the girl, and he told me for hit 'em. So I wen' swing all the way back and I wen' hit her on the head. Somewhere on the head. I'm not sure where," Pauline said, demonstrating the action by swinging an imaginary tire iron in his hands. To Guillermo the hand movement added authenticity to the story.

"Then I dropped the bar and I went towards the Bug on the driver side. I remained outside it," Pauline said. "I was feeling sick and I told Ian that I cannot do this so he wen' head back to her and I guess he wen' do um."

"Did he have the tire bar when he went back to-

wards her?" Guillermo asked. Pauline didn't answer, so Guillermo went back to Pauline's use of the
tire iron.

"Okay," Guillermo said. "When you hit her on
the head did you notice which area it was? Did you
notice if she was bleeding from that area or if there
was a wound where you hit her?"

"No, I cannot remember," Pauline said. "But I
know that the hit that I gave her was real hard. And
after that, after, I was leaning on the Bug and went
back in the Bug. And then later on, after, Ian and
the brother Shawn came back in. They closed the
front part of the trunk and then came in the car.
Then we left."

"When you hit her with the tire iron what was
your intention?" Guillermo asked.

"To make sure I killed her," Pauline said.

"To make sure she died?"

"Yes." Pauline said he couldn't remember
whether she was still alive at that point.

"So after Ian and Shawn came back in the car,
what happened next?" the detective asked.

"We headed back toward Hawaiian Beaches,"
Pauline said. "Through the back roads. Then we
made several stops to smoke cocaine again. And as
we stopped, Ian Schweitzer kept going back towards the front of the Bug to make sure that the
body was dead. Just to check on the body."

Now Guillermo was confused. "And this was after you guys left the area where he had sex with
her?" he asked.

"Yes," Pauline said. He explained that he didn't know if Dana's body was actually in the trunk, because he was in the backseat. He hadn't seen Ian unload the body anywhere else, and when they got back to the Schweitzers' house, he said, he saw that the trunk was empty when Ian opened it to wash off the blood. Ian then went into the house to wash off, telling his brother to put his clothes in the rubbish after showering.

Guillermo wanted to know what happened to the rubbish bag.

"Ian tied a knot in it and threw it on the right side of the house through a bush. And he left it there. Then, after all that was done we headed back towards my house on Aku Street."

At the Christmas party there, several people asked about the damage to the car, to which Ian replied "I just banged the trunk. Don't worry about it."

"Who asked about the damage?" Guillermo asked.

"My brother Wayne Gonsalves," Pauline said. "That's about it."

Guillermo asked a few more questions about the car, and Pauline told him that he had seen it painted yellow about two months after the incident. And he noticed that the front of the car had been lowered.

The only conversation Pauline had with Ian after the crime was Ian's warning him not to talk or he would "get me," Pauline said. "In what way I don't know."

Guillermo asked why Pauline was a little fuzzy on some details.

"Drugs. Cocaine to be precise," he said, explaining that he'd been smoking a lot of the drug prior to the crime. He said he was addicted.

With that, the interview ended, and Guillermo felt a sense of accomplishment. He believed the investigation was finally going somewhere. He thought Pauline's statement had too many details to be fabricated; he was particularly heartened by Pauline's description of the Volkswagen and its damage because the detectives had checked out many pickup trucks, but none of their bumper heights had lined up with the mangled bicycle. The Volkswagen's bumper height would match.

Immediately after the interview, Guillermo, Captain Simao, and Frank Pauline were on their way to the Big Island so Pauline could help police reconstruct the crime. The reconstruction started shortly after 4:00 P.M. at the Pauline home. From there they traveled down Kahakai Boulevard toward the ocean and then turned right on Red Road, heading toward Pohoiki. Pauline showed them where he and the Schweitzer brothers had supposedly stopped to smoke crack. To Guillermo, Pauline seemed to derive joy from talking about the drugs. Pauline directed the police to the place where he had first seen Dana Ireland, although he had a hard time finding the spot. He then took the detectives to a set of mailboxes fronting Kapoho Kai Drive on

Beach Road. "That's where we hit her," he said, without remorse. The mailboxes are one-third of a mile from where the bike was found, but they'd been shown in television newscasts reporting the Ireland murder.

Pauline then directed the detectives back toward Hawaiian Beaches, again pointing out spots where they'd smoked crack and finally to the general vicinity where they'd beaten Dana and dumped her. From there he led them to the Schweitzer home, where Guillermo and Simao saw a yellow Volkswagen that was missing its front fenders. Pauline told police this was the car he'd ridden in on Christmas Eve 1991, but said it had a new paint job.

The next day Pauline signed a formal statement and took a polygraph test. The examiner asked four relevant questions.

"Did you touch that girl other than what you told us?"

"Did you physically attempt to have sex with that girl?"

"Did you deliberately lie about touching the girl?"

"Are you making up this story?"

Pauline answered "no" to each question. The polygraph examiner concluded that the suspect was lying in response to questions one and three. When told that his answers showed deception, Pauline explained by saying he had helped Ian pull Dana's shorts down before Ian raped her.

Based on the information supplied by Pauline, Detective Guillermo obtained a search warrant for the Schweitzer property.

The Schweitzers were originally from the island of Oahu. Although, like the Paulines, they now lived in Hawaiian Beaches, theirs was a very different family. Both parents had legitimate jobs. Jerry Schweitzer worked for his contractor brother as a laborer and did some part-time jobs as a backyard auto mechanic. His wife, Linda, was a former bank teller who later went to work under a federal grant as a victim/witness counselor at the Hawaii County Prosecutor's Office. Her temporary job ended shortly after Dana Ireland's death, but long before the Schweitzer brothers were named as suspects. She also sold Hawaiian crafts that she wove out of palm fronds. The Schweitzer parents kept to themselves and weren't known as troublemakers. However, they were fiercely loyal to their sons.

Like Frank Pauline, the Schweitzer brothers had attended Pahoa High School. Shawn had played football and sung in the choir. Ian liked to work on cars. When the boys were younger, Shawn had helped Ian with his paper route, delivering the *Hawaii Tribune-Herald* by bicycle. One of their supervisors considered them "good kids," but another called them "bad-mouth kids" and said they were always bickering.

Their most serious brush with the law had been Ian's drunken driving arrest. Police had encountered Ian another time while he was working at a nursing home as a nurse's assistant. They responded to a call for help after Ian, who considered himself a ladies' man, got into a dispute with another male over a woman.

On June 26, Detective Guillermo drove to the Schweitzer home and handed the search warrant to Jerry Schweitzer. Mr. Schweitzer told Guillermo police couldn't take the Volkswagen, but Guillermo explained that it was listed on the warrant. The detectives took photographs of the property and of the evidence seized.

The owner of the lot next door gave them permission to search his property for the trash bag. Before long, Guillermo found a dark-colored plastic bag in the overgrown lot. He called to Detective Ed Tanaka, who took pictures of it before anyone touched it. Guillermo tried to dig around the bag so as not to disturb its contents, but it was old and it ripped along the edge, revealing what appeared to be clothing.

Hoping this was the break he needed, Guillermo looked inside. He saw a pair of shorts and a red shirt. Nearby, he found a gray tank top. Guillermo and Tanaka placed the plastic bag and the clothing into brown paper evidence bags, which they later took back to the police station for detailed inspection.

During their search, police noticed a young "local male" watching from the Schweitzer property. Detective Guillermo walked over to him, and the man identified himself as 18-year-old Shawn Schweitzer. Guillermo asked Shawn if he would accompany the detective to the Hilo Police Station for an interview. Before he could reply, Jerry Schweitzer stepped in.

"I'll take him there myself," he said. "Do I need an attorney?"

"That's your decision," Guillermo said. "Meet us at the Hilo station in one hour, that'll make it two-thirty." Meanwhile, police had the Volkswagen towed to the Police Department's evidence cage where it and a number of the seized parts would undergo a comprehensive inspection.

The interview with Shawn Schweitzer started at about 4:30 P.M., after police read Shawn his rights in the presence of Jerry Schweitzer and his oldest son, Kenny. Guillermo explained that he was investigating the Dana Ireland murder and that Frank Pauline had implicated Ian and Shawn Schweitzer. Lieutenant Francis Rodillas conducted the actual interview.

Jerry Schweitzer said his sons didn't hang out with Frank Pauline because of bad blood between the families. Shawn told Lieutenant Rodillas that he'd read about the murder in the newspapers and that he knew Frank Pauline. But he said he'd been home all day and night on December 24, 1991 and had nothing to do with the crime. He also told Rodillas that he'd heard about a month earlier that Wayne Gonsalves had said that Shawn and Ian were involved in the murder. He suggested a possible motive for both Pauline and Gonsalves to incriminate Ian and himself: The Schweitzer family had reported the activities of Frank's relatives to the police many times. Marco Salvador Jr.*—Frank's cousin—lived across the street from the Schweitzers, who had reported his alleged drug dealing, driving habits, and loud stereo.

Shawn asked if the police had found any of his shirts in their search of the adjacent lot, saying that he had thrown two of them there a year earlier. He also admitted having a black "Jimmy'z" T-shirt some years before, adding that Wayne Gonsalves had the same shirt in blue. Although initially denying any drug use, Shawn eventually told Rodillas he smoked marijuana and, on occasion, crack cocaine, but denied being a "druggie."

Shawn told Rodillas that his brother, Ian, had acquired the Volkswagen by trading it with Marco Salvador for another Volkswagen. He also said Ian had painted the purple car yellow and had accidentally damaged it after changing the color. According to Shawn, both front fenders and the front bumper had been damaged when Ian accidentally ran into his girlfriend's truck. He said he didn't know what had happened to the fenders. Shawn told Rodillas that his father had sent Ian to Kauai about a year earlier to get him away from the girlfriend, but that she'd followed him there, become pregnant, and moved back to Puna.

Rodillas thought Shawn's body language and

---

*Not his real name

other clues showed possible involvement. Shawn said he would take a lie detector test. "But not today," he added. That concluded the interview.

Three days later Lieutenant Rodillas interviewed Albert Ian Schweitzer on the island of Kauai. Ian understood what the interview was about because his mother had called him shortly after police searched the Schweitzer property. Ian told Lieutenant Rodillas that he was eager to give a statement to clear things up. Ian was somewhat more vague than his brother about his whereabouts and activities on December 24, 1991, initially saying he hadn't driven his Volkswagen that day. Later he remembered that he might have used the car that Christmas Eve to get to his uncle's house. He remembered helping his mother cook, but wasn't sure of the time.

Ian denied drug use other than marijuana and said he had painted the Volkswagen yellow because purple wasn't his color. He refused to take a polygraph test. When asked again if he knew anything about the crime, he told Rodillas to talk to Eric Carlsmith, who, he said, had witnessed the crime.

Lieutenant Rodillas ordered Ian Schweitzer to give a dental impression pursuant to a search warrant. Rodillas thought it strange that Ian never asked why police needed the impression. Police hadn't mentioned any toothmarks to Ian, but Dana Ireland had suffered bites, and Pauline's brother, John Gonsalves, had said that Ian had tried to bite her nipples off.

John Gonsalves wasn't the only member of the family to implicate Pauline and the Schweitzer brothers in the crime. Pauline's cousin, Marco Salvador Jr., told detectives that he'd heard from Frank's brother, Wayne Gonsalves, that Frank and the Schweitzer brothers had hit a girl on a bike and that Ian Schweitzer had later painted his car yellow. Detective Guillermo's interview of Wayne turned up essentially the same information.

Detectives interviewed many friends and acquaintances of Pauline's and the Schweitzer brothers'. It seemed clear that police finally had the men responsible for the attack on Dana Ireland. What they now had to do was compile enough evidence to get a conviction. Police had no eyewitnesses to the crime other than the suspects. All they had were the suspects' statements and rumors about the three men's involvement. That wasn't much upon which to build a solid case. And while few had trouble believing that Frank Pauline was capable of such a crime, the same couldn't be said about the Schweitzer brothers, whose only previous contact with the police involved traffic offenses and the incident at the nursing home.

Guillermo interviewed Pauline again on July 5, 1994. As soon as the interview began, Pauline said he remembered something that might help police recover evidence. He said Shawn Schweitzer was worried about fingerprints and had taken the tire iron out of the Volkswagen, put it in a plastic bag, and tossed it toward the back of a wooden shack on the Schweitzer property. Pauline said he'd been to the house several times before to lift weights with Shawn and friends.

Guillermo returned to the subject of the abduction. "How was everybody acting?" he asked.

"Shawn was freaking out. I was freaking out. Ian was cool—like he had done it before," Pauline said.

Guillermo asked Pauline whether he could remember anything else the men did to Dana Ireland or anything else that had happened when he and the Schweitzer brothers were with her. All Pauline could remember, he said, was that the Volkswagen had hit something when Ian reversed it by a nursery on Red Road and that the car had been trashed by repeatedly bottoming out.

Guillermo shifted the subject to Dana Ireland, asking Pauline if he could remember anything about her. Pauline said he remembered that she was white—which "was mandatory." Guillermo didn't ask Pauline what he meant, but found it odd that he would use the word "mandatory." Pauline also remembered that the woman was wearing tennis shoes, but he wasn't able to describe them. He said he couldn't remember just how the men put Dana Ireland into the trunk of the Volkswagen, but noted that when Ian opened the trunk on the trail off Beach Road, he saw that her legs were hanging out of the trunk toward the front and that her upper body was in back of the trunk closest to the windshield. Dana's position in the car would later become a big issue in the trial.

Guillermo asked Pauline if he had bitten the woman. Pauline said no, and said that he hadn't seen Ian or Shawn bite her, either. He agreed to provide a sample of his bite to prove it. The next day, Guillermo telephoned the forensic odontologist working on the case, Norman Sperber, and told him he would send Pauline's bite exemplar for comparison with photographs of the bitemark on Dana Ireland. He sent it on July 11, 1994.

Detective Guillermo gained enough information from Pauline's third interview to obtain another search warrant for the Schweitzer property, a warrant that was executed on July 6. The short search turned up a soiled black carpet belonging to a Volkswagen trunk.

The only major piece of physical evidence police had so far was the Volkswagen they had seized from the Schweitzer property in late June. Guillermo set out to trace its history. By interviewing several individuals who had owned or worked on the car, he found out that Pauline's cousin, Marco Salvador Jr., had once owned it but had sold it to someone who had traded it with Ian Schweitzer for a newer model. Everyone he interviewed agreed that the Volkswagen had been in excellent condition, with a first-rate purple paint job. After Dana Ireland's death, the car was painted yellow and looked shoddy.

On July 6, 1994, Detectives Paul Ferreira, Guillermo, and Norman Keamo, as well as their boss, Captain Raymond Simao, examined the

Volkswagen with Moses Suzuki,* the person who had sold it to Marco Salvador Jr. Suzuki identified the car as one he'd owned, pointing out some repairs he'd made. He also showed the detectives more recent damage to the car, including two cracks on the front part of the body and a damaged bumper bracket. The detectives took photographs to use as evidence.

In July and August, Detective Guillermo got disappointing news from Dr. Sperber. Neither Pauline's nor Ian Schweitzer's bitemarks matched the bite found on Dana's left breast. Hoping their third suspect would produce a match, police got a search warrant for a bitemark exemplar from Shawn Schweitzer. That, too, came back negative. This didn't prove that Pauline and the Schweitzer brothers weren't involved in Dana Ireland's attack, but it did indicate that they hadn't bitten her. It also meant that Guillermo would have to find other physical evidence to tie the suspects to the crime. Pauline's confessions alone weren't enough. Guillermo knew that history is replete with innocent people making false confessions. He needed corroborating evidence. And he needed to find out who bit Dana Ireland during the assault. Was there a fourth person involved in this crime?

On August 9, 1994, Guillermo called John Ireland and told him police had new evidence in the

---

*Not his real name

case. He said that Ray Harrison was no longer a suspect, that there were new suspects, and that police had obtained a warrant to search one of their properties for evidence. He didn't want to tell John too much because police still needed to gather more evidence before the case could go to a grand jury.

John was grateful for the information but said he wanted to make sure this "new information" wasn't just a ploy to get him to back off on the civil lawsuit the family had filed against the County of Hawaii for its failure to reach Dana in time to save her life. "I won't believe otherwise until a grand jury hands down an indictment," he said. By now, the burden of making the case to present to a grand jury lay almost solely on Guillermo.

The detective was working full-time on the investigation. His only workday respite was basketball at lunchtime with some police officers and prosecutors, a routine that cleared his head and kept him looking fit. Eating snacks on the fly, he interviewed acquaintances of Pauline and the Schweitzer brothers, people who knew the history of the Volkswagen, and others who might have information on the crime.

Guillermo hoped there was some physical evidence that would connect the Volkswagen to Dana's bicycle. He knew paint transfer would be the most likely link, so he had a Hawaii County Police Department evidence technician take paint scrapings from the bicycle seat and the trunk of the Volkswagen and sent them to the Honolulu Police Department's crime lab for analysis.

Even though the police were now focusing on Frank Pauline and Ian and Shawn Schweitzer, they couldn't ignore the possibility that others were involved in the crime or even that one or more of the prime suspects weren't really involved. It was important for Lieutenant Guillermo to continue gathering evidence associated with the crime itself, rather than just evidence relating to the three suspects.

Chapter 11

On August 11, 1994, Hawaii residents woke up to newspapers that said police had talked to a new witness in the Dana Ireland case who had been in the car with two others when she was hit. Several days later, Chief Vierra gave an interview to television station KGMB, saying the witness had come forward several weeks earlier and provided police with important new evidence. This witness had also passed a lie detector test, Vierra said.

John Ireland was skeptical. Chief Vierra had just announced his retirement and John suspected he was speaking to the news media because he wanted his career to end on a high note.

Little by little, information on the new witness leaked out. First, it was revealed that he was a prison inmate, and later, on August 14, Pauline's name became public. The Schweitzer brothers' names wouldn't be released for more than a year.

In December 1994, Hawaii residents finally learned details about the case. The *Hawaii Tribune-Herald* published an interview with Frank Pauline in its December 11 edition, a story prosecutors had notified the Irelands about in advance. Pauline spoke by phone to news editor Hunter Bishop from jail. Bishop wrote that Pauline had said that he was only along for the ride and was sickened by what happened to Dana Ireland. Pauline told Bishop that the two guys he was with threatened his life. He said he had vomited after seeing them hit, grab, rape, and beat the woman. He was speaking publicly, he told Bishop, because his brother, John Gonsalves, had urged him to tell his story, fearing that the two brothers who had actually committed the crime would pin it on Frank. According to Pauline, months earlier Gonsalves had consulted a psychic who had convinced him of Pauline's innocence.

Four days later, the *Tribune-Herald* reported that John Gonsalves had agreed to a plea bargain in a 1992 case in which he had been charged with conspiracy to distribute six pounds of cocaine. Also indicted were his mother, Pat, and his cousin, Marco Salvador Jr. The case had ended in a hung jury, and the state had agreed to the plea bargain to avoid a second trial. Circuit Judge Riki May Amano sealed the details of the agreement, but sentenced Gonsalves to five years' probation and 90 days in jail for the crime—which could have resulted in a sentence of 10 years in prison. It was widely assumed that Gonsalves got his break for calling police about his brother's involvement in the Dana Ireland murder case.

Once the public learned that Frank Pauline and

the Schweitzer brothers were the prime suspects, people who had not previously spoken to police came forward to offer information. One of them was 22-year-old Leroy Kanakanui, who would die in a car accident less than two years later. Kanakanui, like many who offered incriminating evidence against one or more of the suspects, was not acting from purely altruistic motives. He volunteered information under an agreement between his attorney and the prosecutor's office that if his evidence proved useful in the Ireland case, he would get some leniency in his own. Kanakanui was originally charged in February 1991 with first-degree burglary and possession of burglary tools, but ended up pleading guilty to second-degree attempted burglary, thereby reducing his maximum sentence from ten to five years.

In an October 1994 interview at the Hilo jail, Kanakanui told Guillermo that almost a year after Dana Ireland's murder he had been smoking crack cocaine with Frank Pauline when Pauline told him that he had killed someone with a tire wrench and that her pelvis and hip area "felt like Jell-O." A month after that, according to Kanakanui, they were again smoking crack when Pauline told him that the person he had hit with the tire wrench was Dana Ireland. According to Kanakanui, Pauline went on to say that he and Shawn Schweitzer had carried Dana into Ian's purple Volkswagen, that "we" bit her on the breast, and that "they" raped her. Finally, Kanakanui told Guillermo that he had told all of this to his girlfriend while he was in jail, ordering her to write down the names Frank Pauline Jr., Ian Schweitzer, and Shawn Schweitzer. His girlfriend did so, but subsequently lost the paper.

John Ireland continued to talk to anyone he felt could put pressure on the authorities to indict Pauline and the Schweitzer brothers. In December 1994, he talked to Hawaii Representative Patsy Mink's office manager in Washington and was told that the Congresswoman would be briefed on the matter. The next month Mink wrote to the chairman of the Hawaii County Council, asking that the council meet in a private session with prosecutors to seek answers to questions that John had posed: Did Pauline take a polygraph test? Had police questioned the Schweitzer brothers? Had the case been forwarded to a grand jury, and if not, why? The county council chairman politely refused to convene the meeting, saying any leak of information could jeopardize the police investigation.

In December 1994, three years after the murder, an article appeared in the *Hawaii Tribune-Herald* about the postponement of veteran police officer Richard Marzo's planned retirement. Marzo hoped the recently appointed police chief would follow up on the stalled Dana Ireland case. He told the *Tribune-Herald* he had given a report to detectives in December 1992 detailing information he'd heard about Frank Pauline while arresting some juveniles. Marzo said the detectives had ignored his report.

A police spokesman denied the allegation, but less

than a month later a detective interviewed one of the juveniles. The boy denied telling Marzo that Pauline showed him where Dana Ireland was dumped, but did say he'd overheard Pauline at a party telling someone about hitting a girl riding a bicycle on Red Road. He also identified photos of Ian and Shawn Schweitzer as possible acquaintances of Pauline's.

Tips continued to reach police, some naming different suspects, others confirming information already obtained. It was a time-consuming process for Guillermo to check them all out, but by doing so, the detective was gradually building a case against Pauline and the Schweitzer brothers. Some of the most important evidence came from Pauline's own relatives.

On January 4, 1995, Detective Guillermo again interviewed John Gonsalves, who had called him the previous year to tell him that his brother, Frank Pauline, was involved. John told Guillermo he didn't connect his brother to the Ireland slaying until several months before his first call to police—and only then because a psychic told him that one of the men responsible for Dana Ireland's murder was a close friend or relative of John's. Gonsalves asked his mother if she knew anything about the murder, and she said she suspected that Frank either had knowledge of the crime or was present. It wasn't long after that conversation that Gonsalves confronted Frank, who admitted his involvement. Gonsalves said he had no independent information about the case.

Steve Guillermo and Detective Paul Ferreira conducted the next interview on the island of Maui. It was a follow-up to a telephone call two weeks earlier from Margaret Stone, who had been staying in Hawaiian Beaches with her sons William and Andre Chung, on Christmas Eve 1991. Stone told Detective Ferreira that Frank Pauline went to their house that night and pulled down his pants to show them blood on his pubic hair and then talked about running over and raping a girl. Stone knew Pauline's reputation as a liar, however, so she paid little attention to his account. The next day he came to the house again and this time showed them a bat that he said he had used on the girl. Stone still didn't believe him, so she never said anything about it until she heard that Frank Pauline was a suspect in Dana Ireland's murder.

Police interviewed 21-year-old William Chung next. He told the detectives that Frank Pauline came to his house on Christmas Day 1991 with his twin sons and at some point started telling Chung and his brother about what had happened the day before. According to Chung, Pauline said he hit "one *haole* girl" on the head with a cut-off baseball bat as they cruised past where she was standing with a bicycle. They then got out of the car, yelled at her to get up, and then drove off, leaving her there. Chung told the detectives that he thought Pauline might have known the victim, as he said, "Yeah, that bitch not going bother me anymore." According to Chung, Pauline told him, "We wen' rape and beat up the *haole* girl." Chung explained that Pauline showed him the bat allegedly used to hit Dana. He described it in detail and said that Pauline threw it in the brush near his house. He said Pauline didn't name the other people in the car.

Police then interviewed William's 22-year-old brother, Andre, who denied hearing Pauline say anything incriminating about the murder, but said he remembered Frank Pauline's coming to his house in the late afternoon of December 24, 1991, asking to borrow his pickup truck. He said his mother refused to let Pauline borrow the truck. Andre Chung remembered that Pauline was in the company of others, but said he didn't know who they were. He did remember that Pauline was wearing a woody design T-shirt. Chung gave police permission to search his truck.

These were just more bits of information to add to the rapidly growing file on Pauline and the Schweitzer brothers. Nevertheless, police continually checked other leads, administered polygraph tests to eliminate other potential suspects, processed tips on pickup trucks, and sought additional citizens who might know something about the crime. Long before anything about Pauline appeared in the newspapers, many people had heard that he was involved in Dana Ireland's attack. But in those accounts the Schweitzer brothers weren't always named as his accomplices.

Police ventured outside Hawaii to interview people. In one case, detectives traveled to Arizona to interview a former Hawaii resident in prison for murder. The man, a friend of Frank Pauline's, denied knowing anything about Dana Ireland's murder. When Detective Ferreira showed him a photo of the woman and asked him if he recognized her, he said that he thought he had seen her in the Puna area. Ferreira thought the inmate appeared disturbed. The felon did consent to a bite impression and polygraph test. A comparison of his bite impression with the wound on Dana's breast proved negative, but the polygraph examination showed deception in questions about the crime. Police had no evidence that the man was present at the time of the murder so they dropped him as a suspect.

Back in Hawaii, Detective Guillermo was unable to find any more eyewitnesses to Dana Ireland's slaying. Virtually all the evidence police turned up was either circumstantial or hearsay, and Guillermo knew prosecutors would want physical evidence. To that end he had no good news yet.

In early 1995, Detective Guillermo started receiving collect telephone calls from Frank Pauline. Much as he wanted to talk to the man, he had to refuse the calls. Pauline's attorney had instructed the Hilo detectives not to talk to him because he was exercising his constitutional right to remain silent. These calls continued over the next few months, but police refused them.

Police weren't the only ones getting phone calls from Pauline. One night John and Louise Ireland were asleep when their phone rang at about midnight.

"Hello?" Louise said. John picked up an extension in the spare bedroom.

"Collect call from Frank Pauline Jr. Will you accept the call?"

"Uh, yeah," John said. He was groggy and not thinking clearly.

"I don't know what to say," Pauline said. "It looks like you people are upset. I know who really killed your daughter."

"This conversation is ended, you son of a bitch," John said. "I hope you rot in jail." He slammed down the phone. John and Louise were furious, but Pauline's call showed that their campaign for justice wasn't going unnoticed.

In mid-April, Guillermo received a call from Pauline's public defender on Maui, where Pauline was then incarcerated. She told Guillermo Pauline was declining assistance from her office and wanted to talk.

Not long after, Pauline's brother, John Gonsalves, called to say that Pauline really wanted to talk to Guillermo and that he would be calling soon. On April 20, 1995, Pauline did call and told Guillermo he would give him the identity of the person responsible for the murder of Dana Ireland. Pauline said the last person present at the murder was another brother, Wayne Gonsalves. He said Wayne was the person who raped Dana Ireland. Police returned Pauline to Hilo for a formal interview.

This time Pauline told this story: He and Wayne were at home on December 24, 1991, when the Schweitzer brothers came by in Ian's purple Volkswagen. All four of them headed down Kahakai Boulevard toward Beach Road. Ian was driving and Wayne was in the front passenger's seat. Shawn Schweitzer was seated behind Wayne, and Pauline was behind Ian. They pulled over to smoke some crack cocaine at the end of the pavement on Beach Road. While stopped, Wayne Gonsalves and Ian Schweitzer switched seats. From there Wayne drove to Kapoho, where they saw Dana Ireland standing by the road. Wayne drove the Volkswagen alongside her and started asking her questions, which she ignored. Wayne drove toward Pohoiki and then turned the car around and headed back toward Dana. Making no attempt to slow down or avoid her, he ran into her. Pauline wasn't sure whether the car actually ran over her or just hit her and threw her aside. Wayne and Ian then got out, picked her up, and positioned her between the front and rear seats. This contradicted his earlier version that placed Dana Ireland in the trunk. She was bleeding, Pauline said, and both Wayne and Ian got blood on their clothes. Wayne then drove back toward Hawaiian Beaches on Beach Road. Before they got to Kahakai Boulevard, Wayne pulled over to the right side of the road and stopped. He and Ian Schweitzer carried the bleeding woman in front of the car. Wayne then got on top of her. Pauline assumed he was raping her.

Pauline told the detectives that when he asked what Wayne was doing, his brother told him to shut up. Pauline said he suggested getting an ambulance. According to Pauline, Wayne said, "Fuck you. You like me to go to jail?" Pauline then ran down Beach Road toward Hawaiian Beaches. About a half hour later, when Wayne and the Schweitzer brothers picked him up, Dana Ireland was no longer in the car. They drove to the Schweitzer home, where they washed the car and Ian changed clothes. Pauline said he saw Ian throw some clothing into the bushes next to the house. They then drove to Pauline's house, where Wayne changed clothes and put his bloody clothing into a plastic bag, which he tossed into the bushes. When Guillermo asked Pauline if he had told anybody else about the incident, he said he had mentioned it to a friend, but didn't name the people in the car. He said he had also told his parents but didn't relate that Wayne was involved. Pauline told Guillermo he'd lied earlier when he said that he hit Dana Ireland with a tire iron. Pauline said a psychic had persuaded him to confess the whole story.

Guillermo didn't know if Pauline was once again ratting out a family member or was simply making up a story. In either case, on April 22, 1995, the detectives took him on another crime reconstruction. This one closely followed what Pauline had said during the most recent interview. In neither this reconstruction nor the previous one did Pauline identify the correct location of Dana Ireland's collision nor the exact place where she was found nearly dead. Nevertheless, Guillermo thought the new scenario might be worth pursuing.

He got permission from the owner of the former Pauline property to conduct another search. Three days later Guillermo scoured the home and area immediately surrounding it. He found a tire iron under some carpet and a piece of metal that looked like a Volkswagen part. Since the find seemed to corroborate Pauline's story, Guillermo interviewed Wayne Gonsalves at his home in Kurtistown, a small Puna community about halfway from Hilo to Volcano Village.

Wayne said he'd had very little contact with the Schweitzer brothers, but said Frank and Ian Schweitzer cruised and smoked cocaine together. Wayne said his only relationship to Ian was working on Volkswagens together. He told Detective Guillermo that he had helped repair damage to the trunk and one of the front fenders of Ian's purple Volkswagen shortly after Christmas 1991. He also said he was present when Ian painted the car yellow.

Guillermo obtained a warrant to take teeth impressions, blood, and a saliva sample from Wayne Gonsalves. When the teeth impressions were taken, it was noted that Wayne was missing an upper front tooth. Rumors were circulating that Wayne was knocking out his teeth so they wouldn't in-

criminate him. When Guillermo questioned him
about it, Wayne explained that he lost the tooth in
a fight with "some Samoans." He denied any involvement in the murder of Dana Ireland.

Later the same day, the detectives and Dean Yamamoto, an evidence specialist for the Honolulu
Police Department, recovered some wood and a
four-foot-by-four-foot piece of blue carpet from the
former Pauline home. Both were stained with
blood. Yamamoto took those objects and the rusted
tire iron recovered earlier back to the Honolulu Police Department crime lab for analysis. Less than a
week later the evidence technician told Guillermo
that in the carpet he found pinkish rope, which contained a few pieces of light hair. He found a similar
strand of hair—with root attached—on the tire
iron. Guillermo hoped he finally had the physical
evidence police so badly needed.

Police didn't tell John Ireland about the latest de-
velopments. It was standard police policy to withhold certain evidence—even from relatives—that
only the perpetrators would know. John was getting much of his information from Hawaii news reporters, who called him for comments any time
something new developed.

First Deputy Prosecutor Charlene Iboshi, who
was now in charge of the case, was keeping John as
informed as possible but John was still dissatisfied.
In early January he and Louise met with Iboshi and
her boss, Jay Kimura, along with Mayor Steven Ya-
mashiro, recently appointed Police Chief Wayne

Carvalho, and an attorney from the county corporation counsel's office. John wanted to know when police would fulfill the promises about solving the case and getting an indictment. Again, the county officials asked for his patience.

On several occasions in late 1994 and early 1995, Iboshi told the Irelands that the evidence was still insufficient to establish probable cause. She said she might have to make a deal with Pauline in order to get a guilty plea. Pauline's attorney had approached Iboshi with such a proposition, but she'd turned it down. She told John she didn't want to make concessions and would do so only if prosecutors reached an impasse. John Ireland didn't want that to happen.

In early February the Irelands met with Governor Ben Cayetano, asking him to get Attorney General Marjorie Bronster involved in the case. The Irelands continued to pass on tips and rumors to Detective Guillermo, still not convinced that the police finally had the right suspects. But John felt more confident that the new police chief and the new lead prosecutor would eventually solve the case. John's main contact at the police department now was Lieutenant Morty Carter, who had taken over as head of the criminal investigation division. With the change came more frequent calls from the police, which made John feel that he was getting more information.

Despite the improved communication, John continued to complain about the slow wheels of justice. He knew that police had to analyze evidence, interview people, and follow leads but they'd been doing that for more than four years and had assured him a year earlier that indictments were imminent. While John sat at home frustrated, police were busy consulting expert witnesses about the hair found on the rope and carpet and about the type of vehicle that might have made the tire tracks and caused the damage to the bicycle.

Guillermo continued to work overtime on the case. He needed corroborating information on much of what Frank Pauline had told him. Pauline's story changed with each telling and he was a known liar and blowhard. Prosecutors kept reminding the detective that the case couldn't be built on a confession alone, that Guillermo needed to get other evidence. In mid-1995 police interviewed Pauline's cousin, Alfred Piltz,* who was in the Hilo jail on a burglary charge. Piltz was willing to give teeth impressions and to take a polygraph test, but he denied a claim by Frank Pauline that the two discussed the Ireland case. He told police that while Frank wasn't friends with the Schweitzer brothers, Frank's brother, Wayne, was. Piltz's polygraph exam was inconclusive. He was sniffling and coughing and changing his breathing during the test so the examiner was unable to determine whether his answers were deceptive.

Guillermo also interviewed Frank's mother, Pat.

---

*Not his real name

She told the detective her son was calling and writing frequently, complaining about being assaulted in prison by guards and other inmates. Guillermo replied that he would check into it and then questioned her about the night of Dana Ireland's murder. Pat said Frank hadn't left the house until 8:00 or 8:30 P.M. She told Guillermo about an argument between Frank and his girlfriend over her engagement ring. The ring was missing and his fiancée suspected him of selling it to buy cocaine. Pat also remembered Wayne's leaving with Ian Schweitzer in Ian's Volkswagen around 4:00 P.M. but didn't remember his returning home. She told Guillermo she had confronted Wayne about any possible involvement in the Ireland murder and that Wayne had said he would surely remember if he was there, but remembered nothing. Pat Pauline told Guillermo, however, that she thought Wayne was lying and that he would never admit his involvement to her or to the police.

Why were both Frank and his mother saying Wayne was involved?

Chapter 12

When Ken Baker pulled into the Hilo police station's parking lot on June 21, 1995, a light rain began to fall. Steam rose from the still-hot pavement, creating a yard-high layer of mist. Beyond it, a 180-degree double rainbow arched above the jungle that grew across the street from the police station.

Baker was the director of the accident investigation division of Northwestern University's Traffic Institute, internationally recognized for its expertise on all aspects of vehicular safety. He was in Hilo because Detective Guillermo wanted his opinion on how Ian Schweitzer's Volkswagen struck Dana Ireland's bicycle, whether Dana was on the bike at the time, and what her injuries could say about the events of December 24, 1991.

Once inside the building, Baker forgot the island's tropical beauty and went right to work. After looking at the police reports and crime scene photos he told Detective Guillermo that some of Dana Ireland's injuries were consistent with her having been hit from behind. He examined the bicycle and the Volkswagen and told Guillermo that he would send him a list of forensic pathologists who specialized in traffic collision cases.

Baker was just one of several experts and agencies Big Island police consulted for analysis of the physical evidence. The Honolulu Police Department crime lab reported that it found no paint transfer from the Volkswagen to the bicycle, or vice versa. Technicians detected none of Dana Ireland's hair on the rope or carpet found in Ian Schweitzer's Volkswagen or on the tire iron found across the street from Pauline's house. Even the bitemark comparisons initially showed no match. Detective Guillermo sidestepped each disappointment and kept digging for evidence.

DNA—deoxyribonucleic acid—is found in the nucleus of every cell in a person's body and is unique to each human being. Therefore, scientists can test any human cells found at a crime scene for their DNA signature, or unique structure, and then match them against samples taken from suspects and victims.

In the early 1990s, DNA techniques weren't very sophisticated, especially when the samples were small or degraded. For that reason the FBI was unable to obtain a DNA profile from the vaginal swabs or slide smear taken at the hospital from Dana Ireland's body, even though the items contained minute amounts of semen.

However, FBI technicians were able to find DNA samples from blood on a gauze pad used when treating the dying woman at the crime scene as well as from one of her shoes, one of her socks, her panties, and the discarded "woody" T-shirt.

The FBI also profiled the blood samples from Herb Johnson and Ray Harrison. Those didn't match anything found at the crime scenes or during the autopsy, so both men were eliminated as suspects.

In the five years since the murder, forensic science hadn't stood still. When Detective Guillermo learned about advanced DNA techniques now available to the FBI, he called and asked which procedures they'd used in the Ireland case and whether they'd consumed the entire semen sample in the 1993 test. Guillermo followed up with an inquiry about whether the FBI could use mitochondrial DNA (mtDNA) analysis on the Ireland case evidence previously tested using older techniques. MtDNA, which doesn't come from the nucleus, contains far more copies of DNA than nuclear DNA. Using the polymerase chain reaction (PCR) technique, which makes multiple copies of a small amount of DNA, scientists can extract a large amount of information from a small or degraded sample.

The objective at this point was to find DNA traces from Frank Pauline and the Schweitzer brothers at the crime scenes or on evidence from Dana Ireland's corpse.

On October 2, 1995, Guillermo was in the office with the TV on again for the verdict that acquitted

O.J. Simpson. Although the not-guilty verdict astonished a lot of people who'd followed the case,
Guillermo wasn't surprised by it. He thought the
Los Angeles Police Department had jumped the
gun by filing charges right away without taking
time to build a strong case. "If we'd gone to the
grand jury as soon as Pauline first talked," he said
to his fellow detectives, "we might be in the same
situation today as the LAPD."

Guillermo devoted the rest of 1995 to follow-up
investigation, including Pauline's claim that his
brother, Wayne, had been involved in the crime.
Guillermo checked with Wayne's dentist and learned
that the man's tooth had been knocked out in the
1980s. In addition, the Pauline family produced a
time-dated home video of the Christmas Eve party
showing Wayne at the Pauline home at the time of
Dana Ireland's attack. Guillermo verified the time
and date on the video by interviewing other people
from the party. Wayne was eliminated as a suspect.

While police did confirm Wayne's alibi for that
night, they never found anyone who could provide
an alibi for Frank Pauline.

At last, in early January 1996, police sent the
case against Pauline and the Schweitzer brothers to
the prosecutor's office. The next month the county
agreed to pay the Irelands $452,500 to settle their
lawsuit over the delay in getting help to Dana.

* * *

At the time of Dana Ireland's murder, then-
Prosecuting Attorney Jon Ono had assigned the

case to one of his 12 deputies, Brenda Carreira, who handled violent felony cases. She worked with police on the case until September 1994, when Ono's successor, Jay Kimura, reassigned the case to Charlene Iboshi. He later named Lincoln Ashida as Iboshi's second chair.

Both members of the team grew up on the Big Island and both were of Japanese descent. Iboshi, 44, was the county prosecutor's second in command. Although most of her duties now were administrative, her boss knew her history as a thorough litigator and trusted her to oversee this critical case. Iboshi had brown eyes and wore her dark brown, chin-length hair parted on the left. She was cordial but abrupt and came across as somewhat self-conscious. The 34-year-old Lincoln Ashida, who loved speaking to the media, would be the spokesman for this duo. He was five-foot-five and trim, with dark brown hair, a youthful face, and a charming smile. Known among his colleagues as a clotheshorse, he was always impeccably dressed in one of a closetful of tailored suits. Although he had never worked with Iboshi on a case before, he respected her and they got along well. Ashida specialized in sex crimes and had previous experience prosecuting Frank Pauline. He was also the lawyer who had prosecuted the man who stabbed the Steve Guillermo lookalike, and he was part of the group that played basketball with Detective Guillermo at lunch time. He would be a good second chair for Iboshi.

The prosecutors were not only facing public pressure to indict and try the defendants; they were also facing a legal deadline. While murder has no statute of limitations, the law requires that prosecution for kidnapping and rape begin within six years of the crime. The defendant has the right to a trial within six months of indictment, a period that can be extended only by consent of the defense. The prosecutors in the Ireland case, then, had to obtain a grand jury indictment against the defendants no later than December 24, 1997. And they had to be ready to go to trial by June 24, 1998.

The grand jury met for its first session on April 29, 1996. A follow-up session was scheduled for May 30. Witnesses were subpoenaed for that date, but the grand jurors themselves didn't get the word. The judiciary blamed the grand jury foreperson for not notifying the others, but whatever the reason, the foulup didn't sit well with the media, the public, or John Ireland, who compared Hawaii's justice system to Murphy's Law. "Doesn't anyone over there give a damn?" John asked more than once.

Ultimately, the grand jury would meet nine times. The Irelands knew about the sessions in advance and after each one prosecutors told them the essence of what had happened. Even so, John was frustrated at the slow pace of the case. He repeatedly called police and prosecutors and he and Louise flew to the Big Island several times to speak with them in person. On October 17, 1996, the Irelands' attorney, Sherry Broder, joined the family at one meeting. Lead prosecutor Charlene Iboshi did most of the talking, discussing new evidence being analyzed and previewing the upcoming grand jury sessions. She also told the Irelands that Frank Pauline would soon be indicted for another unrelated sexual assault. But no indictments for Dana's murder would come before Christmas.

Louise Ireland reminded Charlene that prosecutors had told them she would decide on indictments by September 1995, more than a year earlier. "We've had it up to our ears with promises of indictments. All we get are delays," Louise said. "I wonder if you'll ever be able to indict those animals."

Prosecutors were struggling with a weak case. They still had no eyewitnesses, little physical evidence, and only the confession of a habitual liar, so as grand jury sessions took place the investigation continued. Charlene Iboshi, known for her attention to detail, wanted all other suspects eliminated before she sought indictments against Pauline and the Schweitzer brothers.

In late February 1997, a low-pressure system brought unusually cold and stormy weather to the Big Island. The high temperature in Hilo dipped to 74—the lowest high in recorded history. A foot of snow fell on Mauna Kea, closing the road leading to the 13,796-foot summit. Winds swept through town at 60 miles per hour, gusting to 80 miles per hour and knocking down trees, blowing roofs off buildings, ultimately damaging 300 houses. Thunderstorms and flying branches temporarily knocked out power to thousands of residents across the island. Civil Defense chief Harry Kim said it was the strongest wind since 1986.

It was against that backdrop that Charlene Iboshi called the Irelands and told them she had enough evidence to indict Frank Pauline and Shawn Schweitzer, but not enough to indict Ian Schweitzer. She didn't mention that investigators had found a witness, Shayne Kobayashi, who was willing to testify about statements Shawn had made admitting involvement in Dana Ireland's attack. They still hadn't found anyone—except Frank Pauline—to incriminate Ian. Iboshi told John and Louise she might be able to get indictments in April or May but she wouldn't commit to a specific date. She still had problems with the case, she said, and needed the additional time to obtain and analyze evidence.

John Ireland set a deadline—May 31, 1997. Of course, he had no way to enforce the arbitrary deadline, but he felt that he had to force some action in the case. That date came and went with nothing but rain. Hilo Airport's rainfall tally for the week leading up to the deadline was nine and a half inches, and forecasters said additional rain was on the way. They were right. More than 22 inches fell in June.

On July 29, with the Hilo courthouse full of cameras and reporters, the grand jury handed down an indictment against Frank Pauline on charges of kidnapping, first-degree sexual assault, and second-degree murder.

"It's about time," John said. "One down, two to go."

John was realistic about the case, correctly predicting that the defense would seek delays that could stretch it out for at least another year.

Frank Pauline Jr. appeared before Circuit Judge Riki May Amano for arraignment on the morning of July 31, 1997. Outside, a steady rain beat down on Hilo. Inside, Pauline's court-appointed attorney, Brian De Lima, entered a not-guilty plea on his behalf. Pauline's mother, Pat, was there to show her support. During the hearing, Judge Amano issued a gag order prohibiting lawyers and law enforcement officials from discussing the case with anyone, including the media. She then set the trial date for January 19, 1998.

Meanwhile, the case against the Schweitzer brothers was on hold pending a decision by Family Court on whether to try Shawn—who had been 16 at the time of Dana Ireland's murder—as an adult. Since prosecutors charged the brothers together, the case against Ian Schweitzer couldn't go forward until the jurisdictional question was settled. The answer came on August 25, 1997, when Family Court Judge Ben Gaddis ruled in favor of the prosecution and at the same time issued a gag order similar to the one in Circuit Court.

Finally, on October 9, 1997, a grand jury returned a true bill of indictment, charging Ian and Shawn Schweitzer with second-degree murder, kidnapping, and first-degree sexual assault. It was John and Louise Ireland's forty-fourth wedding anniversary, and they considered the indictments their anniversary gift.

Five days later Ian and Shawn Schweitzer appeared before Judge Amano for arraignment with their attorneys, James Biven and Ira Leitel. Both defendants pleaded not guilty to all charges. Judge Amano set a trial date of April 6, 1998—nearly six months away—and issued another gag order.

In mid-October the Schweitzer brothers' parents, using their home as collateral, secured their sons' release on $70,000 bail each. The court set the standard conditions of bail, including a curfew, no use of alcohol or drugs, and no contact with witnesses. Frank Pauline remained in prison.

In the American legal system, trials are the exception rather than the rule. Most criminal cases—around 90 percent—never make it to a jury. They end with plea bargains in which prosecutors offer a reduced charge in return for a guilty or a no-contest plea. Defendants go to trial only as a last resort, or in cases where only a trial will satisfy the community. The murder of Dana Ireland fell into the latter category.

Unlike in television and motion picture dramas, there are few shocking revelations during a trial. Attorneys can't spring a surprise witness on opposing counsel and they can't introduce evidence not already disclosed to the other side and approved by the judge. Trials aren't games; they follow strict rules of procedure, including pretrial motions.

One of the most common motions seeks to dismiss charges against a defendant. Frank Pauline's attorney, Brian De Lima, made the first such motion in the Ireland case. He argued that no one had been able to link any forensic evidence to his client or to the Schweitzer brothers. He cited the prosecution's failure to match the bitemark found on Dana Ireland's breast to any of the defendants, and argued that a tire iron couldn't have caused her head injury. He also objected to an investigator's having testified before the grand jury about a witness he'd interviewed, making the testimony hearsay. Finally, De Lima told the judge that the prosecution had failed to list forensic experts on its list of witnesses, making it difficult for the defense to prepare for trial. Judge Amano ordered the prosecution to give De Lima all relevant documents, but declined to rule on the motion to dismiss the case or to suppress the investigator's testimony.

Perhaps the most important pretrial motion was Brian De Lima's request in mid-December that the judge exclude Frank Pauline's confession because the first time he talked to Detective Guillermo he hadn't signed a waiver of rights. Meanwhile, the prosecution asked that De Lima be removed from the case because he had previously represented four prospective prosecution witnesses in the case—including Jim Orlando, a former suspect.

January 1998 was Hilo's driest month in recorded history, with 0.14 inches of rain compared with the average 9.6 inches. The El Niño weather pattern, which warms the Pacific Ocean, disrupted the trade winds that usually carry rain clouds to East Hawaii. Lawns and fields of wild orchids turned brown, and small farmers who made their living growing crops like ginger and heliconia or papayas and bananas feared losing their livelihood. Homeowners who relied on rainfall to fill their catchment tanks flushed their toilets selectively. Some paid $100 a load for tanker trucks to haul water to their property. Many filled jugs with drinking water from county spigots on the side of the road. The drought created a fire hazard, prompting the mayor to order a state of emergency and ban outdoor burning. Because of the still air, Kilauea Volcano's gaseous emissions—called "vog"—hovered above Hilo and Puna, causing distress for people with breathing problems and producing an uncharacteristically hazy sky. Moist, tropical air was nowhere to be found.

People waiting to get into Judge Amano's courtroom on January 19 could see the volcanic peaks of both Mauna Kea and Mauna Loa looming above

Hilo, unobstructed by clouds even if somewhat faint behind the vog. Someone remarked that it wasn't unusual to see snowcaps on those peaks during January. That wouldn't happen this year.

When the hearing got under way, Judge Amano denied Brian De Lima's defense motions. Then she shocked court observers when she removed De Lima as Frank Pauline's attorney, agreeing with the prosecution that his having previously represented four prospective state witnesses constituted a conflict of interest. This was a serious blow to Pauline, as De Lima was one of the best criminal defense attorneys on the Big Island. As it turned out, none of those witnesses would actually be called to testify at the trial.

Outside the courtroom, Pauline's mother went ballistic. Pat Pauline said she'd trusted De Lima to defend her son so she'd kept quiet until now. "I know my son didn't kill Dana Ireland because he was out buying cocaine," she told reporters. Sometime after Ireland's attack, Frank had met a friend to smoke crack, she said. According to Pat, the friend told Frank that he and two other men had attacked Dana Ireland. Pat complained to the reporters that police didn't believe her son when he told them about the conversation with his friend and that they didn't believe her when she gave them Frank's alibi for the time of the murder.

The next attorney to go was Ira Leitel, Shawn Schweitzer's lawyer. Judge Amano removed him from the case after ruling that the prosecution could call Marco Salvador Sr.* as a witness. Because Leitel had represented Salvador on three unrelated drug cases, it would be a conflict of interest for Leitel to cross-examine him. Leitel told the press he thought the prosecution listed Salvador as a witness for the express purpose of having him dropped as Shawn Schweitzer's attorney and as a ploy to delay the trial; prosecutors would have a strategic advantage if they tried Pauline's case first. Leitel might have been right; Gonsalves never testified in the trials, either.

In a separate ruling, the judge ordered that Shawn and Ian Schweitzer be tried separately because Shawn's case couldn't proceed until his new attorney had time to read all of the documents in the case. Two weeks later Judge Amano granted Biven's motion for a delay in Ian Schweitzer's trial so he could send sperm and hair samples to independent labs. Biven didn't want to rely on the FBI for the analysis.

Meanwhile, Judge Amano appointed Clifford Hunt, a Honolulu attorney, to represent Frank Pauline. Now all three defendants had counsel, but it would take some time for the newly appointed attorneys to read through the huge stack of police reports in preparation for trial.

In early May the prosecution went to court again,

*Not his real name

asking Judge Amano to issue an arrest warrant for Ian Schweitzer, who had violated conditions of his bail by testing positive for marijuana and by threatening a prosecution witness. Prosecutors made a similar request for Shawn Schweitzer, who had committed the same sins as well as causing a disturbance while drinking alcohol. At the conclusion of the hearing, the state got its wish. The Schweitzer brothers "blew it," Amano said, by not following her orders. They would stay in jail pending trial.

At the end of May 1998, Cliff Hunt asked Judge Amano for a delay in Frank Pauline's trial, which was supposed to begin July 27. He cited a heavy workload and inadequate time to prepare. The judge granted him a delay until May 3, 1999. If the schedule didn't change again, the Schweitzer brothers' trials would come before Frank Pauline's.

Louise Ireland was livid at the latest postponement. "I don't know how much longer I can take this," said the 74-year-old woman. "I'll be dead before the trial is over." Her husband was equally perturbed but said he understood the need for a delay.

In early August, Shawn's new attorney, Keith Shigetomi, asked the judge for a change of venue—to move the trial to another island—arguing that his client couldn't possibly get a fair trial on the Big Island because of all the publicity. The judge denied Shigetomi's motion, heading off another potential delay.

Barely a month later—less than a month before

the trial was supposed to begin—the Schweitzer brothers appeared in court again for what most assumed would be a routine hearing. Astute observers immediately sensed something in the air, however, when they noted that Shawn's former attorney, Ira Leitel, was seated in the gallery. When the hearing started Charlene Iboshi dropped a bombshell by asking the judge to dismiss charges against the brothers because of "unforeseen circumstances." Judge Amano dismissed the charges "without prejudice," meaning the state could file them again later. The judge released the defendants from jail but told them and their attorneys that they were still under a gag order.

Reporters looked at each other, stunned. Iboshi wouldn't explain this turn of events to them, but they pored through court documents and found that a DNA signature from semen on the hospital sheet upon which Dana Ireland had lain didn't match that of either Frank Pauline or the Schweitzer brothers. John Ireland confirmed that the dismissal was related to DNA evidence and said he'd known about it for a week. "I guess I've learned to roll with the punches," he said, "but Louise—this just about devastated her. The best way I can describe it is it's like seeing the light at the end of the tunnel, and all of a sudden that tunnel collapses."

The sheet was among a number of items that had been sent to the FBI laboratory in January 1992, less than a month after Dana Ireland's murder. The police department had asked the lab to check it for hairs, fibers, semen, and blood. At the end of April the FBI had sent police a report indicating that they had detected nothing on the sheet. They did find DNA on vaginal swabs, but it was too degraded to produce a profile.

Public reaction was predictable. Would this case ever end? Was there a fourth perpetrator? Were these suspects even involved? The community was outraged. They had very little information about the case and what they had made the authorities look incompetent. A former Hawaii County prosecutor wrote a letter to the *Hawaii Tribune-Herald*, criticizing Judge Amano's gag order and the prosecution's handling of the case.

Some people talked about taking matters into their own hands. In late November posters appeared in Pahoa, near the Schweitzer home, with photographs of Ian and Shawn Schweitzer and the words WANTED DEAD—IAN & SHAWN SCHWEITZER.

Chapter 13

In April 1999, the prosecution's lead investigator, Billy Perreira, got a phone call from the mother of a Hawaii prisoner who had been transferred to a penitentiary in Minnesota. The inmate, Mike Ortiz, had been at the Big Island jail for theft while the Schweitzer brothers were there. Perreira vaguely remembered hearing that Ortiz had called a year earlier, claiming to have information about the Ireland case, but to his knowledge Ortiz had been transferred to the mainland prison before anyone followed up on it.

On May 5, Perreira flew to Honolulu, where he interviewed Ortiz by videoconference. Ortiz's only request was that he not be transferred back to a Hawaii prison. Apparently, Minnesota's Prairie Correctional Facility in Appleton was more pleasant than the ones in the Aloha State. Ortiz's biggest fear was that his name would appear in the newspaper. Perreira reassured him that even if prosecutors had to file documents in court, they would use only Ortiz's initials. The newspapers wouldn't know the inmate's name. Ortiz agreed to talk.

Perreira turned on his tape recorder. While Ortiz was telling his story, the tape jammed. Perreira scrambled to start a backup machine, which he had brought just for such a malfunction, and then got Ortiz to repeat the statement.

Mission accomplished, Perreira returned to Hilo with his tape. When he got there, it occurred to him that it was critical to get a videotape of Ortiz so the defense attorneys could evaluate his demeanor.

On May 13, Perreira made the long trip to Minnesota. He left on a red-eye and arrived in Sioux Falls, South Dakota, the following afternoon. Perreira placed a phone call to the prison's security agent and explained that it was important that the other inmates didn't see him when he arrived. Two-thirds of the prisoners were from Hawaii and would recognize him as a "local boy." They would know something was up. Perreira rented a car and drove three hours through back woods country that conjured up images of the movie *Deliverance*.

When Perreira got to the prison, he met with the warden, who stashed him in a room in the medical unit while someone went to get Ortiz. In a few minutes a guard opened the door and in walked Ortiz. He recognized Perreira immediately.

"What's up?" Ortiz asked.

"I'm here 'cause I want to get you on video," Perreira said. Ortiz backed away.

Perreira spent six hours trying to persuade Ortiz to go on tape. During the negotiations Ortiz didn't ask for any concessions from prosecutors. His only concern was for his safety. In prison, no one likes a "rat." Finally, he agreed.

Originally, Perreira's plan had been to elicit the same statement that he'd already recorded on the audiotape. But during his six hours in the medical unit, it occurred to him that Ortiz could change some or all of his statement. That would give the defense something to pick apart at trial. So Perreira just had Ortiz state his name and explain that he'd been incarcerated with Ian Schweitzer, that the information on the audiotape was true and accurate, and that he hadn't made any agreements with the state in exchange for the statement. That done, Perreira made the exhausting trip back to Hilo.

On Sunday, May 16, 1999, the *Tribune-Herald* ran a front-page story saying a grand jury would re-indict the Schweitzer brothers that Wednesday. All day Wednesday, TV news crews and local newspaper reporters waited outside the grand jury room, videotaping witnesses, including Perreira, as they entered the secret proceedings.

Inside, Perreira testified about what Ortiz had told him two weeks previously. That kind of hearsay testimony wouldn't be admissible in a trial, but it was allowed during grand jury hearings, where prosecutors need only prove they have probable cause to take someone to trial.

Another witness, Shayne Kobayashi, testified that Shawn Schweitzer had told him he was involved in the Ireland case. And finally, Steve Guillermo testified about information he had received from another jailhouse snitch, Brien Sullivan, who had shared a cell with Shawn Schweitzer at Hawaii Community Correctional Center for three and a half months.

After the prosecution concluded its presentation, the grand jury issued a true bill, re-indicting the Schweitzer brothers. John Ireland was glad about the indictment but didn't expect the case to end soon. "I'm just drained, and I know this is going to drag on for a long time," John told a reporter. Louise added: "I have no life, because wherever I go or whatever I do, I don't enjoy it."

Chapter 14

A new Frank Pauline sat in Circuit Judge Riki May Amano's courtroom on April 13, 1999. Clean-shaven, wearing a dress shirt and tie, and sporting a short, stylish haircut, the 26-year-old man in glasses had lost weight and looked more like a Harvard Law School student than one of the Big Island's most notorious criminals. He sat with his attorney, Cliff Hunt.

Although Hunt had been born and raised in Hawaii, he would have to work hard to win over these jurors. Not only was he a *haole*, but he also lived on the island of Oahu, making him an outsider on two counts. Hunt, 44, had brown hair and a pale complexion, partly the result of spending months indoors preparing for this case. Unlike the state's attorneys, who had the resources of the Police Department and the Prosecutor's Office behind them, Hunt had only the assistance of a private investigator, Dan Boe, and a legal assistant, Maria Dumlao. Dumlao, who sat at the defense table, was a petite and attractive young local woman perhaps chosen to show that Pauline couldn't possibly be a rapist if she were willing to work on his case.

Discreetly seated behind Pauline in plainclothes were two prison guards wearing simple waist pouches containing their guns and handcuffs. It would be too prejudicial for the jury to see Pauline in restraints and prison garb or to catch sight of uniformed guards carrying firearms. At another rectangular table to the right of the defense team sat Charlene Iboshi and her co-counsel, Lincoln Ashida. The empty jury box was to their right.

About 90 prospective jurors filed into the courtroom for the first round of preliminary screening. Among them was Mayapple McCollough of Citizens for Justice fame, wearing a large pair of dark glasses. As she took a seat on one of the wooden benches, two reporters sitting in the front row looked at each other and raised their eyebrows. *Was McCollough part of this jury pool?*

When all the prospective jurors were seated, Judge Amano's law clerk counted them. She glanced at a clipboard, frowned, and counted again. She looked puzzled. "Is there anyone here—besides the media—who's not a juror?" No one answered. The law clerk counted again, went to the bench, conferred with another clerk, and then walked back into the courtroom gallery. "I'm counting an extra person," she announced. "Is there anyone in the courtroom who isn't a juror?" After several seconds of silence, McCullough sighed and then slowly raised her hand.

"I'll have to ask you to leave the courtroom for a few minutes until the other spectators come in," the law clerk said. McCullough slinked out, looking as if she'd blown an undercover operation. When she returned to the courtroom to watch the proceedings, she sat in the back row not far from Pauline's family. During jury selection, Pauline occasionally turned toward the back of the courtroom and made hand gestures and facial expressions to his mother. At one point he placed his fingertips to his lips, indicating his desire for some non-institutional food. Astonishingly, no one objected when one of his relatives returned shortly before the lunch break with a container of fast food from a nearby restaurant. This practice would continue well into the trial until TV reporters questioned authorities about it.

In the meantime, Judge Amano's law clerk/bailiff, Michelle Agsalda, introduced herself to the pool of jurors, asked them to remove any hats, sunglasses, or gum, and then took her position at the bench and banged her gavel. "All rise."

A door behind the bench opened, and Circuit Judge Riki May Amano walked in and hefted her short, stocky frame up onto the seat behind the bench. A sturdy pair of glasses rested on her nose; her hair was parted slightly to the right of middle in a simple, efficient cut that showed her ears. Although the judge was only 46, what had been salt-and-pepper hair when she was first appointed to the bench in 1992 was losing its pepper and would be mostly salt by the time the Ireland cases reached their conclusion.

Judge Amano was a workaholic, legendary for holding meetings with lawyers on weekends, holidays, and late into the night. The mother of adult twins, she had married her childhood sweetheart while they were both still in high school. Unlike some teenage mothers, however, Amano had never used motherhood as an excuse for curtailing her education. When the twins were children, Amano and her husband took the girls with them to college and, later, law school. Before she was appointed to the bench Amano had worked with her attorney husband in private practice, representing auto insurance companies.

Judge Amano introduced herself to the packed room of prospective jurors, most of whom appeared to wish they were somewhere else. Then her clerk announced how many jurors had been summoned and how many had already been excused. Amano ordered bench warrants for those with unexcused absences and set bail at $100. The jury pool snapped to attention. After a beat, the judge added that she would "stay" the order—pending further investigation.

"Aren't you glad you showed up?" Amano asked. Nervous laughter trickled through the gallery. When it subsided, the judge introduced the attorneys and read the grand jury indictment, which specified the charges against Pauline. "The indictment is not evidence," Amano explained.

The judge began the tedious process of screening the jury pool for anyone who might be ineligible to serve because of felony convictions, physical or mental conditions, severe conflicts of interest, or extreme personal hardship. Judge Amano then explained that the remaining prospective jurors were to fill out a questionnaire; they would later get appointments for individual questioning about their exposure to pretrial publicity. She wanted to be sure they could disregard news accounts of the case and base all conclusions solely on the evidence presented in court.

When the first group of prospective jurors left, the judge repeated the process with additional panels. The courtroom wasn't large enough to hold all the people necessary to ensure a final count of twelve jurors and four alternates who hadn't already formed an opinion in this highly publicized case.

By the end of the day, some 300 people had appointments for individual questioning. Those who survived would be instructed to return on May 24 for final jury selection.

On the afternoon of April 14, a 5.5 magnitude earthquake jolted the south side of the Big Island. The quake, which was also felt in Kona, rocked three buildings off their foundations, ruptured gas and water lines, and knocked out electricity for an hour to the 1,500 residents of Pahala. Fortunately, the quake didn't generate a tsunami, but 50 people had to be evacuated from Ka'u hospital.

Frank Pauline was in court on May 24, but his lawyer, Cliff Hunt, was nowhere in sight. Attorney Tom Bush made a special appearance on Pauline's behalf. He handed Judge Amano a large envelope which the judge said contained correspondence addressed "To whom it may concern." The judge called the attorneys and Pauline to the bench, where they held a lengthy whispered conference. Following the conference Amano said that she would postpone the remainder of jury selection until July 19 with the trial to follow immediately. She didn't elaborate.

The prosecution team didn't know the contents of Hunt's letter but knew it documented his request to delay the trial for personal reasons. In court, Charlene Iboshi objected for the record. "The state appreciates Mr. Hunt's personal situation," she said, but she stressed that the Ireland family and the community deserved to have the case proceed.

Despite Iboshi's posturing for the Irelands and the people of the Big Island, Lincoln Ashida welcomed the delay. It would give the state additional time to prepare. More important, it would postpone the inevitable failure he expected at the conclusion of this weak case. He was glad he wasn't the lead attorney. In the legal community, you're only as good as your last trial. He didn't want to be remembered as the prosecutor who let Dana Ireland's killers get away with murder.

John Ireland wanted to know the grounds for Hunt's delay. "If he's got a legitimate reason like surgery or something with his family, I go along with it. But I don't buy the secrecy," John told the *Hawaii Tribune-Herald*. "I feel that the public and we as victims have the right to know the reason." It was never revealed.

The 119 prospective jurors who survived individual questioning returned to court on Monday, July 19, 1999, for final jury selection. This process is called *voir dire*, a French term that means "to look, to speak." In many jurisdictions, a judge will dismiss any prospective juror who has heard any details of a case or knows any of the attorneys or potential witnesses. On the Big Island, such a practice would make it impossible to find a jury. Jurors often know one or more of the witnesses at least casually. The challenge for the judge is to find jurors who can put aside any biases and evaluate the acquaintances' testimony the same way they would any other witness. Jurors can be dismissed "for cause" if it appears they can't be fair. Lawyers also can exercise "peremptory" challenges, for which they don't have to show cause or explain their rationale. In the Pauline trial, the prosecution and the defense were each allowed 12 peremptory challenges. As the selection process progressed, Pauline's attorney, Cliff Hunt, appeared to target females for dismissal, especially those who were young or *haole*. The prosecutors would try to bump anyone who was critical of police or any young man who was likely to identify with Pauline.

Up until this point, Charlene Iboshi had been the only prosecutor to question the jurors. But in a strategy session during a court recess, Billy Perreira, the prosecutor's investigator, threw out a suggestion: "Why don't you let Lincoln do some jury selection this afternoon?"

Iboshi looked at Ashida. "You want to?"

"Sure," Ashida said. He knew that his role as second chair would probably require him to cross-examine some of the expert witnesses. When he did, the jurors would see his tough side. It was important to establish his warmth and sense of humor first and to drop little hints about his local roots. Besides, Ashida loved playing to an audience.

Attorneys like a jury with two or three leaders and the rest followers. They try to identify the most likely candidates during *voir dire*. In addition to screening jurors for potential bias, *voir dire* gives the attorneys an opportunity to educate the panel about the issues in the case and to screen out people who don't seem receptive. This would give Ashida a chance to see which jurors he wanted to bump from the case. His goal was to find the ones who could be fair. If they grew to like him in the process, that would be even better.

One of the jurors Ashida questioned was 53-year-old Lisa Kaneshiro. Although Ashida had no way of knowing that Kaneshiro would be the jury forewoman, he could tell immediately that she would be one of its leaders. She'd already served as a juror on five cases—including two murder cases—and she'd been the forewoman on one of them. Ashida began to charm her, and in the process the other prospective jurors who watched.

"I have a son, Scottie, who's three and a daughter, Katie, who's five," Ashida said. "We live in Hilo. I grew up in Papaikou, went to Hilo High School, but now we live in Hilo. One day I opened the cookie jar and found it empty. Then I saw Scottie with cookie crumbs on his face. Ms. Kaneshiro, do you think it would be reasonable to conclude that Scottie ate the cookies or would you need a witness who actually saw him eat the cookies?"

"I would conclude that Scottie ate the cookies."

"Well, how about this," Ashida said. "I asked him, 'Scottie, did you eat the cookies that were in the cookie jar?' He said, 'Yes, Daddy, I ate the cookies.' So I said, 'I'm glad you told the truth, son, but I'm going to have to punish you for eating the cookies.' Then Scottie said, 'No, Daddy, I didn't eat the cookies. Katie ate the cookies.' Ms. Kaneshiro, do you think people sometimes lie to get out of trouble?"

"Yes."

"Do you think it's more likely that someone would lie to get out of trouble or to get into trouble?"

"I think they would lie to get out of trouble."

This line of questioning was clearly designed to

instruct rather than to elicit information. Now the jury knew that Ashida was a father, his roots were in a rural area on the east side of the Big Island, and that someone's credibility would come under attack during the trial. Furthermore, Ashida had Kaneshiro on record under oath that she believed people lie to get out of trouble. He hoped she and the others would remember that as the trial progressed.

Defense attorney Cliff Hunt took a different approach. He asked another juror, "What if Scotty saw Katie take the cookie and lied to protect her?" He was laying the foundation for a defense argument that Pauline had made up his story in exchange for leniency for his brother's drug case.

By the end of the second day, Kaneshiro was one of the eight women and eight men sworn in as jurors. Despite Hunt's efforts, the panel included three *haole* women. Seated alongside the jurors were four alternates, two men and two women, who might have to fill in for any of the 12 jurors who couldn't see the trial through to the end.

Before Judge Amano sent the jurors home for the night, she gave them her standard instructions: "Don't discuss the case with anyone, not even each other. Don't let anyone discuss the case with you. Don't read any newspapers, watch any television news, or listen to any radio news. Don't conduct your own investigation. And keep an open mind."

About three miles from the courthouse, signs were posted at Honolii beach, closing it until further notice. While the lawyers were picking the jury, a shark had attacked a 43-year-old surfer. With the help of a friend, the man was able to paddle through the murky waters to shore. He was treated at the hospital for a puncture wound and released. The shark escaped unscathed.

Lincoln Ashida wondered if Frank Pauline would do the same.

Chapter 15

By 9:00 the next morning, the hallway outside the courtroom teemed with reporters and spectators waiting to get inside for the start of the 10:00 A.M. trial. TV reporters who had flown in from Honolulu used this time to interview spectators for the trial of what one newscaster described as one of the most disturbing murders in Hawaii's history. A woman wearing a bicycle helmet carried a sign proclaiming that women should have a right to ride their bikes without being raped and murdered. No one disagreed.

Judge Amano had consented to television coverage of the trial. Months earlier, Court TV had considered doing gavel-to-gavel coverage of the case, but the cable network abandoned that plan after learning that attorneys expected the trial to last six weeks. The judge allowed only one TV camera in the courtroom and restricted it to a platform at the right rear of the room. The platform, which had been built just for that purpose, was a first for Hilo. Videotape recording equipment that allowed stations to share the camera's feed was hidden be-

hind a portable wall in a corner of the hallway outside so jurors wouldn't know the magnitude of the
publicity or inadvertently see images on the moni-
tors when they passed through the halls during
court recesses.

Hilo didn't have a dedicated courthouse. The judiciary shared the building with other state agencies, creating a security nightmare. Citizens were
free to enter the building without the metal detec-
tion and X ray screening that have become com-
monplace in most courthouses across America.
Because of the building's poor design, witnesses,
lawyers, victims, and reporters shared the same
waiting area in the hallway. Jurors would have to
walk past them to take smoke breaks and to go out
for lunch.

Now, the jurors waited in a jury room sand-
wiched between two courtrooms. The door to
Judge Amano's courtroom was locked while the
judge heard unrelated Family Court matters inside.
A deputy sheriff wheeled a portable metal detector
into place in front of the courtroom. Even this
makeshift security checkpoint was a rarity in the
Hilo courts. The metal detector heightened the an-
ticipation as people began lining up; the trial had
all the excitement of opening night on Broadway.

Once inside, people quickly filled the wooden
benches in the gallery and strained to scrutinize the
players. Frank Pauline looked as much like a
lawyer as anyone in the room. He wore black
slacks, a long-sleeved white shirt with a button-

down collar, and a blue tie. Cliff Hunt sat to his right in a slightly rumpled dark blue suit. To their right, next to the jury box, was the prosecution team. Lincoln Ashida was wearing a dark blue Italian suit. His shoes appeared as if they'd been spit-polished and looked every bit as expensive as the suit. By contrast, his supervisor, Charlene Iboshi, wore a functional navy blue polyester skirt suit. On her feet were blue flat-heeled pumps designed for comfort rather than style. It was going to be a long trial and winning a fashion award was the least of her concerns.

Noticeably absent from the courtroom were members of the Ireland family. John, Louise, Sandy, and Jim were on the witness list, and the judge had imposed a rule banning any potential witnesses from sitting in the courtroom. The witness exclusionary rule was designed to keep witnesses from comparing testimony to get their stories straight. Typically, not all witnesses on such lists end up testifying. Sometimes lawyers put people on the list simply to keep them out of the courtroom—a trick used by both prosecutors and defense attorneys to keep certain people away from the scrutiny of the jury.

Ashida glanced down at his folding calendar. Attached to it was a yellow note with the single word "INTEGRITY" printed in bold capital letters in felt-tipped ink. It was Ashida's reminder to focus on the integrity of the case rather than on community pressure. He used the same message as the screensaver for the computer in his office. Ashida felt defensive because of the DNA. He knew he couldn't control the evidence in the case, but he could control the integrity he brought to the trial. Despite the tremendous pressure he felt knowing the prosecuting attorney's career was on the line, the note was Ashida's reminder not to treat this case any differently from all the others he'd prosecuted over the years. He took a deep breath.

With the Ireland family holed up in a rented oceanview condominium next door to the courthouse, Charlene Iboshi began presenting the state's case. In her opening statement, she told the jurors that Dana Ireland, a beautiful blond, was on a path to a wonderful life when Pauline and his friends took her on another path—"a brutal path to her death." Iboshi described Dana's bicycle ride from her parents' rental home in Kapoho to Mark Evans's house in Opihikao and her stop on the ride back to watch the surf at Shacks in Pohoiki.

Iboshi pointed at the young man in the white shirt and blue tie. "Witnesses will say that this defendant, Frank Pauline—also known as Frankie Boy—was with Albert Ian Schweitzer and Shawn Schweitzer in a Volkswagen," and followed the girl on the bicycle, Iboshi said. "They strike her—hit her—and her bike falls on the ground. The impact was such that Dana Ireland's shoe flew across to the other side of the street."

Then, instead of getting help for Dana, Iboshi said, Pauline and the Schweitzer brothers drove her to another location. "She was beaten, sexually penetrated, struck, disabled, and just thrown away in the bush and left to die," Iboshi said, with just the right amount of contempt in her voice. She then described how Dana Ireland had died at the hospital later that night.

Pauline's conscience began to bother him, Iboshi said, telling the jury about the defendant's statements to police and his reconstruction of the crime. She acknowledged Pauline's subsequent recantation but added, "His confession is backed up by the evidence," including a bitemark on Dana Ireland's breast which an expert witness would testify was consistent with Pauline's lower teeth. With that, Charlene Iboshi sat down.

Lincoln Ashida thought Iboshi's opening was "decent to good." But during a break, Brian De Lima, the attorney who'd originally been assigned to represent Pauline, took Ashida aside. De Lima was a defense attorney, but, above all, he was a connoisseur of the art of practicing law, no longer representing Frank Pauline but rather acting as an impartial observer. "She should have used the word *rape* every chance she got." Ashida was just glad he wasn't the one addressing the jury. The prosecutors were bound to lose, and the defeat would be magnified by the scrutiny of the news media.

After the break, it was Cliff Hunt's turn to open. He took the jury on what he called a "tour of the events." At the scene of the wrecked bike, he said, police took measurements and interviewed witnesses. All of the initial statements and evidence pointed to a pickup truck or a van. "There is no way that a Volkswagen could have been involved in the accident," he said, explaining that he had an expert to substantiate that. Hunt told the jury that a doctor at Hilo Hospital took vaginal swabbings and recovered Ireland's hospital sheet, which police later sent to the FBI for testing. He said a DNA expert would testify that the FBI "botched the job."

Meanwhile, said Hunt, Dana Ireland's father, John Ireland, "was becoming very impatient with the progress of the investigation." He put pressure on police. Then, at the end of 1993, Frank Pauline's half brother, cousin, and mother were arrested in "one of the biggest drug busts on this island," Hunt said.

While Pauline's brother, John Gonsalves, was awaiting trial, he persuaded his baby brother to call the police from prison and tell them about the Ireland murder. "Frank Pauline tells his brother he loves him so much and he would do anything to help him," Hunt said. As a result, Gonsalves was "richly rewarded for his participation"—given a deal for no jail time in exchange for his cooperation in the Ireland case. Hunt said Gonsalves wouldn't be the only questionable witness the prosecution would put on the stand. The jury would also hear from "guys locked up in jail."

Frank Pauline sat tall, his face revealing no emotion. Hunt then told the jury about the sperm found on Dana Ireland's hospital sheet and sent to an independent lab. "The sperm DNA did not match Frank Pauline Jr.'s known DNA—because he provided a sample. Did not match Shawn Schweitzer's DNA profile. Did not match Ian Schweitzer's DNA profile," Hunt said. "They were all excluded." Hair found at the scene and in the trunk of the Volkswagen was also compared to Pauline and the Schweitzer brothers, Hunt said. "No match. Excluded."

The next day the courtroom gallery was still more than half full, but not as packed as it had been the previous day. Apparently some of the spectators had discovered that trials can be tedious and that the wooden benches for the public don't budge when pressing against tailbones. Some speculated that the benches seemed designed to ensure the rotation of spectators.

The prosecution strategy was to start with "emotional" witnesses, the kind who offer little evidentiary value but elicit sympathy from jurors and draw them into the story. Portraying Dana Ireland as a human being and not just a police statistic would make it that much easier to evoke contempt for the person who had harmed her. The evidence linking Pauline to the crime could wait.

"Please call your witness," Judge Amano said.

"Sandy Ireland."

Sandy walked through the hushed courtroom to the witness stand, where she raised her right hand and swore to tell the truth. Sandy was slim, with shoulder-length blond hair, and looked younger than her 43 years. She was visibly shaken and barely audible as she described her dead sister in the present tense. "She's a very gentle and loving person. Very, very, very, very shy," Sandy said. She told the jury about Dana's visit to the Big Island and about her parents' arrival from Virginia for Christmas. Sandy's resemblance to Dana was uncanny, and Charlene played it up for the jury. She showed Sandy a portrait of Dana Ireland and held it up for the jury to see. "Is this what she would have looked like on December twenty-fourth, nineteen-ninety-one?" Charlene asked.

"Yes," Sandy said, her voice cracking,

Sandy's face revealed obvious pain as she recalled that her family hadn't seen Dana leave the house for her bike ride to Mark's place on Christmas Eve. "She sort of just slipped out—she slipped away," Sandy said. She then described how that evening she and Jim had come upon a group of people standing around the black mountain bike on Kapoho Kai Drive. "I saw the condition it was in. I was really frightened," Sandy said, fighting to keep her composure. "I saw the hair—a lock of her hair—on the road and her shoe and a watch—broken watch."

She told about the horror of driving to her parents' place looking for Dana, and discovering that her sister hadn't come home yet. "That's when I knew something really bad had happened," she said, closing her eyes as if to shut out the pain.

A juror wiped tears from her eyes.

Charlene asked Sandy if she had ever seen Dana alive again.

"No, I never saw her again alive or dead," Sandy said, "I never saw her again."

Mark Evans was next. During the years since Christmas 1991, he had grown a beard and mustache to complement his thick head of tousled brown hair. Mark testified that he and Dana had met at the beach about a month before her death, and said he'd received a note from Dana inviting him to Christmas dinner. He recounted how Dana had arrived at his house on the black bike the next day to extend the invitation in person while he and two friends were putting a roof on his lanai. She spent 20 to 30 minutes there, he said, and then declined his offer to drive her back in his truck.

"And as she rode away, what were you thinking?" Charlene asked.

"I was thinking to myself that she was a beautiful person and the road is so messed up and she was wearing shorts and it could be very easy to wipe out going down the road because it gets steep at the bottom," Mark said. "And as she rode away, it's funny, but I thought to myself, 'Oh, don't fall and scar up your beautiful legs.'"

Mark testified that he had tried to call Dana about an hour later but was told she hadn't returned home yet. He said he had called the Ireland home again after that and got no answer but drove there anyway. He told the jury about seeing a number of police cars as he neared Kapoho Kai Drive and thinking it must be a Christmas Eve DUI road-block. One of the officers stopped him and asked for his identification. Mark said he then noticed the smashed bicycle and recognized it as the one he had seen Dana riding earlier. "I told him that was my girlfriend's bike," he said.

Mark testified about going home, calling the hospital, and talking to Sandy, who told him he should go to the hospital. "I walked into the emergency room, and Sandy told me that somebody had hurt Dana," Mark said.

The next person to provide pieces of the puzzle, Anna Sherrell, walked to the witness stand with her head high and her shoulders thrust back. She testified that she and her boyfriend had been driving to Pahoa when they had stopped to look at a white tennis shoe on Kapoho Kai Drive. "It's a brand new tennis shoe. It's about my size. I wondered where the other one was," she said. After she stopped, Anna saw the wrecked bicycle. "It was almost un-recognizable as a bike when I first glanced at it," she said. "So I started looking for a body in the bushes." She never found the body, but she found the lock of hair and wristwatch and noticed tire tracks that she described as "acceleration marks" on the cinder road. It looked as if someone had made a U-turn in the road, she said. Trying to be helpful, she put the watch and lock of hair on the side of the road and searched through the bushes trying to find the bicyclist.

Under cross-examination, Pauline's attorney,

Cliff Hunt, quizzed Sherrell about her use of the phrase "acceleration marks." He wanted to know if prosecutors had coached her. Sherrell said that although she had met with Charlene Iboshi and the prosecutor's investigator, Billy Perreira, earlier in the week, she had told police about the "acceleration marks" from the beginning. Deputy Prosecutor Lincoln Ashida was scheduled to play a tape of Sherrell's call to police immediately after her testimony, and Hunt knew that. When the tape was played, Sherrell didn't use the phrase "acceleration marks." She said the tire tracks looked as if the driver had "spun out." This was a small point for the defense, which had already planted the seed that the prosecution was being overzealous in its desire to win this case.

At the end of the day, Judge Amano sent the jury home until Monday morning. It was Thursday, and the judge was reserving Fridays for other court matters. As the jurors went into the jury room, Frank Pauline was led out through a back door by a guard. Just before he got to the door, he turned to the back of the room and stuck his tongue out at a freelance TV cameraman.

The weekend was tough for Louise Ireland. The 75-year-old woman was going stir-crazy on the ninth floor of the high-rise condo next door to the state building. Although the unit had a breathtaking view of Mauna Kea and Hilo Bay, she didn't like being that high off the ground and it bothered her that her unit also overlooked the place where Frank Pauline spent his days. She alternated between frustration and relief over not being allowed in court. "I don't know if I could stand it," she said. But Louise would be in court soon enough—not as a spectator but as a witness.

"I can't wait to get a good look at that ol' Pauline," she said. "I wish they had the death penalty over here. It's terrible what that savage did to Dana. I swear, if I had the chance, I'd shoot him myself, and I'd go to bed smiling."

"Oh, Mom," Sandy Ireland said, laughing. "You wouldn't know what to do with a gun if you had one."

"I don't care," Louise said, undeterred. "I'd shoot all three of 'em, if I ever got the chance. I'm not afraid to go to jail. I'm old. It's no difference if I go to jail or into a nursing home."

The Irelands had several friends attending the trial and giving progress reports. Louise constantly asked them, "How do you think it's going? They will find him guilty, won't they?"

"I believe there's enough to hang those guys," John interjected too many times to count. "The prosecution has a pretty strong case."

"But what about the DNA?" Louise would ask. And then she'd answer her own question: "I don't believe in that DNA. I really don't. I just know ol' Pauline and those Schweitzers are the ones that did it."

* * *

Monday morning when the trial resumed, Charlene Iboshi called Louise Ireland as the state's first witness of the day. Dressed in white slacks and a white blouse covered by a royal blue sweater, Louise walked to the witness stand with poise. Once there, Dana's mother turned and glared at Pauline, then looked away. She did it again and again.

Under questioning by Iboshi, Louise described rushing to the site of the crushed bike on Christmas Eve. "After that I kind of went blank," she said. "I went into orbit. I just couldn't believe this had happened." She told about waiting for Dana in the emergency room. She had seen Dana being wheeled past. "I didn't expect her to die. I was sitting there waiting," Louise said. "We waited there, not knowing she'd been murdered and raped." She glared at Pauline again.

Iboshi showed Louise a photograph of Dana and her mother that had been taken shortly before Christmas 1991. "This is the last picture we have of her," Louise said. "And I cherish it. She was my baby." One of the jurors—a blond woman in her forties—slipped a tissue under her glasses to wipe tears from her eyes.

Louise didn't stay on the stand long. Wisely, Cliff Hunt didn't cross-examine her.

Afterward, Louise was exhilarated. She'd conquered her feeling of helplessness and taken action against the man accused of murdering Dana. What pleased her even more was that she'd looked him in the eye. "That was my highlight," she said, "looking at him and thinking, 'You ugly ol' bastard.'"

Back in the courtroom, another witness, 29-year-old Alex Frenchy, testified that he was an acquaintance of Frank Pauline's. He said he had been at the Shacks surfing spot in Pohoiki from about 8:00 A.M. on Christmas Eve 1991.

Sometime in the afternoon Pauline and the Schweitzer brothers had stopped by in Ian Schweitzer's Volkswagen. They had some beers, Frenchy said, and stayed about 45 minutes. During that time, a woman matching Dana Ireland's description rode toward Kapoho on a bicycle. A while later, Pauline and the Schweitzer brothers took off in the same direction. Frenchy said the Volkswagen was in excellent condition and had a custom purple paint job.

Several weeks later Frenchy saw the Volkswagen again. "It looked shitty," he said. The front end was damaged, the fenders were missing, and it had a poor-quality yellow paint job.

Under cross-examination by Cliff Hunt, Frenchy admitted he had started drinking early Christmas Eve day, with the intention of getting drunk. When asked whether he was drinking domestic or imported beer, he said he didn't know the difference. He also couldn't say whether Pauline and the Schweitzer brothers left before or after the bicyclist. "I don't remember," he said. "I was pretty drunk."

Sandy, 14, John, and Dana Ireland, 8 months, pose during a vacation in Bermuda.
Courtesy of Louise Ireland

Dana Ireland started playing soccer at age 11 and played through high school.
Courtesy of Louise Ireland

Dana Ireland, shown here at age 22 during one of her frequent hikes on Old Rag Mountain in Virginia's Shenandoah National Park, loved nature.
Courtesy of Louise Ireland

Dana Ireland, shortly after graduating from high school. Her sister described her as "very, very, very, very, shy."
Courtesy of Louise Ireland

Louise and John Ireland pose during one of their many visits to Hawaii seeking information about their daughter's murder.

Photo by Chris Loos

Veteran Hawaii County police detective Steve Guillermo worked on the Dana Ireland case for 9 years. His testimony was instrumental in obtaining convictions for Dana's killers.

Photo by William Ing

Circuit Judge Riki May Amano presided over the Dana Ireland trials. Her salt-and-pepper hair would be mostly salt by the time the case reached its conclusion.

Photo by William Ing

Prosecution investigator Brian Antida, left, and Ken Baker, accident investigation specialist, show the jury Dana Ireland's mangled bicycle as Judge Riki May Amano looks on.

Photo by William Ing

Convicted killer Frank Pauline, Jr., as he appeared prior to his trial.
Photo by William Ing

Ian Schweitzer's yellow Volkswagen still shows evidence of its former purple coat of paint.

Photo by William Ing

Sandy Ireland points to a map during testimony at Frank Pauline's trial.

Photo by William Ing

Victim witness counselor Dena Aindow, left, sits in court with Louise, John, Sandy, and Jim.

Photo by William Ing

Frank Pauline's attorney, Cliff Hunt, right, confers with Lincoln Ashida and Charlene Iboshi during a court recess.

Photo by William Ing

Frank Pauline, Jr., appears in court with a new image.
Photo by William Ing

On the witness stand, Louise Ireland identifies one of the last pictures ever taken of her daughter.

Photo by William Ing

Television crews follow Shawn Schweitzer away from the Hilo courthouse.

Photo by William Ing

Ian Schweitzer, right, stands with his attorney, James Biven, during his sentencing.

Photo by William Ing

Chapter 16

From the beginning of the trial, Deputy Prosecutor Lincoln Ashida had been virtually sitting on his hands while Charlene Iboshi questioned the witnesses. Iboshi had been a sharp trial attorney earlier in her career, and she was a master at putting together a case, but it was apparent that her years as an administrator in the prosecutor's office had rusted her courtroom skills. Iboshi would later say the Ireland case took on a life of its own and made her tongue-tied in situations that would usually seem routine. As she examined witnesses, Ashida—considered the best litigator in the prosecutor's office—was champing at the bit to get a crack at one. His attitude about the case was changing. Up until now, he'd thought of his role as Iboshi's writer and researcher, whose job it was to encourage her. "People know we have a shitty case. We're not expected to do miracles," said Lincoln, who was always eloquent in the courtroom but often profane when speaking in private. "If a fucking jury lets him walk, then it's on their head."

Now, the prosecution's investigator, Billy Perreira, encouraged Lincoln to take a more active role in the trial. "Brah, you gotta take over," Billy said, using pidgin for "brother."

"Brah, I cannot tell her that," Lincoln said. So Billy told her.

Lincoln got his chance to question his first witness when the prosecution called Dr. Kanthi Von Guenthner, a forensic pathologist with the Honolulu Medical Examiner's office who had performed close to 5,000 autopsies. She was a very effective witness as she spoke directly to the jury. Born in Sri Lanka, Dr. Von Guenthner was striking, with an olive complexion, large eyes, and shoulder-length black hair. Von Guenthner hadn't performed the autopsy on Dana Ireland but testified about the woman's injuries after examining autopsy notes, photos, X ray reports, and reports by experts. She waived her usual $225-an-hour fee for the "hours and hours" she spent working on the case, she said, as a "contribution to the community."

Von Guenthner said that some of Dana Ireland's injuries, including her head injury and scraped legs, were the result of being hit by a vehicle while riding her bicycle. But she said the bitemark on Ireland's left breast, fingernail marks on her right breast, and vaginal bruising were caused by an assault. Severe bruising to both sides of Dana Ireland's neck was "consistent with some kind of pressure being applied to the neck area." Other injuries, including a broken pelvis, a broken collarbone, and a gash to the head, could have been caused by either the collision or the assault. Bruised tissue between the outer surface of Ireland's scalp and her skull bone could have come from a "glancing blow" from the pointed end of a tire iron, Von Guenthner said, adding that it was "quite possible" that the woman's head was moving during the blow. It also was "highly possible," she said, that the victim's head was wrapped in a T-shirt when it was bashed.

During Cliff Hunt's cross-examination, Von Guenthner conceded that the T-shirt theory was speculation, but said she had reached that conclusion because police had found a bloody T-shirt at the scene and Ireland's head was the only part of her body that was bleeding profusely. Most of Ireland's other bleeding was internal, she said. A "direct full blow" couldn't have caused the head injury because that would have led to a crushed skull and severe bruising to the brain. But a sharp edge of the bicycle or vehicle also could have caused Ireland's head injury in the collision.

Hunt didn't buy the tire iron theory. He suggested that Von Guenthner only mentioned it after prosecutors told her about Frank Pauline's admission that he had hit Dana Ireland with the tire iron. He asked why she hadn't given that explanation of the head injury when she responded to questions from police in 1998.

"I was not aware that some tire irons have that sharp edge," she said, explaining that the blow would have had to come from the straight end of the tool.

Dr. Von Guenthner used a full-scale skeletal model of a pelvis to demonstrate the location of fractures to the right and left sides of Ireland's pubic bone. Because Dana Ireland's pubic bone, located in the front, was broken, but the back of the pelvis wasn't, Von Guenthner concluded that the injury was caused by "a considerable amount of force" from the front.

Under cross-examination, Cliff Hunt used the pelvic model to illustrate that Dana Ireland would have been leaning forward while riding the mountain bike. He repeatedly asked Von Guenthner if the pelvic injury could have resulted from the bike seat's ramming into Ireland's pelvis after the car hit the bike.

"Could the vaginal bruising be caused by the bike seat?" Cliff asked.

"Absolutely not," Von Guenthner said. "Not inside the vagina."

Throughout the testimony, Hunt kept insisting that Von Guenthner respond either "yes" or "no." At times the exchange became heated. But the doctor never wavered from her position.

The next day the jury got its first accounts from witnesses who'd seen Dana Ireland alive after the attack. Ida Smith described sitting in her kitchen preparing dinner for her husband at about 4:45 P.M. on December 24, 1991, and hearing what she thought were children playing. Ida's composure on the witness stand changed, and it was clear she was fighting back tears. This was going to be painful for her, even after eight years.

"I just heard, 'help me,' and I thought kids were having a game," Ida said. The sound persisted, so she went to investigate. "I just got nosy. I thought maybe the little kid got locked in the basement next door."

Ida said when she went out of her house she could tell the sound wasn't coming from the house next door. It was coming from the direction of the ocean and she wondered if a car had gotten stuck in a ditch or crashed. She testified about following the sound down her driveway to the road, shouting "I'm coming—where are you?" She described going to the narrow fishing trail leading from the road to the ocean. She saw nothing, she said, so she followed the sound down the trail.

"And that's when I found her," Ida said, breaking down and blowing her nose. "She was all bloody, and I didn't know what to do. She just looked pretty bad." The way Dana was positioned in the bushes made it appear "like somebody just picked her up and threw her down," Ida said. Her head faced the ocean, her denim shorts lay around her ankles, and her halter top was shoved up around her neck.

Several courtroom spectators sniffled.

"I kept asking her, 'Who did this to you?' and she didn't know," Ida said. "She thought I was a man and was incoherent." Ida described removing both the shorts wrapped around Dana's ankles and the remaining athletic shoe at Dana's mumbled request, praying with her, and running back to her own house to get a quilt. Shortly thereafter, she said, she stopped a passing motorist and asked her to call for help.

Charlene Iboshi approached the witness stand and showed Ida Smith a portrait of Dana Ireland, holding it so the jury could see it.

"Is this the woman you found discarded in the bushes?" Charlene asked.

"She didn't look like that when I found her," Ida said, wiping her nose with a tissue.

Defense attorney Cliff Hunt cross-examined Ida about the condition of the trail leading to where Dana was found. "A low vehicle, a vehicle that rides very low, would probably hit its oil pan on the road?" Hunt asked, implying that the Volkswagen couldn't have maneuvered onto the trail.

Ida responded that she had seen vehicles get stuck on that road. Hunt then hammered at Ida about inconsistencies between her testimony and what she'd told police eight years earlier. Ida testified that shortly after the incident she wrote everything down on her computer and gave it to police, but that police had evidently lost her account.

On redirect examination by Charlene Iboshi, Ida said that she was giving her best recollections and that she had been interviewed "constantly." She told Iboshi that she still cried often and continued to see Dana Ireland in her mind. "It was Christmas Eve," she sobbed. "It was supposed to be a joyous season."

Cliff Hunt's re-cross examination was scathing. He asked Ida if she knew what "browbeating" meant and whether police had done that to her? No, Ida said. Some of the spectators felt that Hunt was the one doing the browbeating. They thought it hurt his case.

Next, Peter Teijeiro testified that he was driving on the Old Government Beach Road in lower Puna on Christmas Eve 1991 with his girlfriend, Ronlen Kaalakea, her brother Chad, and a friend named Brian.

"Out of nowhere this *haole* lady came out of the bushes and flagged us down," Teijeiro said. Smith directed them to Ireland, who was in shock, Teijeiro said. "She looked like somebody had beat the crap out of her." Teijeiro said he tried to keep the injured woman calm while Brian and Ronlen went to call for help and Smith ran back to her house for more blankets to try to keep Ireland warm. "I held her hand and told her everything would be okay," he said, adding that Brian and Ronlen returned with a nurse friend who had tried to stop the blood oozing out of Ireland's head.

Under cross-examination, Cliff Hunt asked Teijeiro if the nurse used a piece of clothing to stop the bleeding. He hoped to offer an explanation for the blood-soaked shirt found at the Waa Waa scene matching the description of a shirt owned by Frank Pauline.

Teijeiro said he wasn't sure what the nurse had used to stop the bleeding. "I know she used something out of the first aid kit," Teijeiro said. "What it was, I'm not sure."

Another witness, Officer Harold Pinnow, testified that on Christmas Eve 1991, his sergeant sent him from the scene of the crushed bicycle in Kapoho to Waa Waa to investigate a rape report. He said when he arrived at 6:20 P.M. he found a woman surrounded by several people who told him her name was Dana. "Now I knew that this was the girl that we were looking for," Pinnow testified. "She looked like she had been seriously injured." He notified Sergeant Malani by radio and asked him to make sure the Fire Department was on its way. Pinnow testified that as he left Kapoho Kai Drive he asked the police dispatcher to send an ambulance to Waa Waa.

Under cross-examination by Cliff Hunt, Pinnow testified that Ida Smith told him that Dana said "a friend" or "a friend of a friend" attacked her.

Johnson Kahili, a paramedic with the Hawaii County Fire Department, testified about Dana Ireland's many visible injuries including a long gash to the right side of her head. "Her skull was visible through that large laceration," Kahili said, adding that Dana was pale and in shock. "She was conscious but she wasn't very coherent," Kahili said. "She was confused, combative."

Mary Sakahashi, a nursing supervisor at Hilo Hospital, told the court the patient was close to death when the doctor conducted a sex assault examination that consisted of vaginal swabbings and preparation of slides for review at the hospital's lab.

"She was pronounced dead shortly after the specimens were obtained," Sakahashi said. Warren Sako, who had been a medical technologist in 1991, testified that he had examined the slides and found sperm.

Now that the prosecutors had presented evidence that Dana Ireland was dead, it was time to start linking her death to Frank Pauline. They called William Chung III, a sous-chef at a steak house, who testified that in 1991 he lived in Hawaiian Beaches about two or three roads away from where Pauline lived.

Upon hearing this, Pauline leaned toward his attorney's legal assistant with a puzzled expression on his face. "Who is this?" he whispered. If Maria Dumlao answered, her response couldn't be heard from the front row of the gallery.

Chung testified that he and his brother were in their parents' garage with Pauline on Christmas Day when Pauline admitted to attacking Dana Ireland. According to Chung, Pauline said he and his friends were talking to "one *haole* girl" on Christmas Eve, telling her that they wanted to have sex with her. She refused and rode away on her bicycle. "They came up behind her with a bat and hit her on the head" and then "stomped on her" and "fucked her brains out," Chung said.

Under further questioning by Charlene Iboshi, Chung said that Pauline hadn't named the people with him during the attack. "I never knew who was with him," Chung said. "He just said he and his friends."

When Charlene asked Chung to identify Pauline in the courtroom, Chung pointed in the direction of the defendant. Defense attorney Cliff Hunt, however, wasn't sure that Chung actually pointed at Pauline.

"Please describe the man you saw," said Iboshi.

"Grayish hair, long-sleeved shirt," Chung said, describing the plainclothed prison guard sitting behind Pauline. The misidentification prompted a rare grin from Pauline, who had shown little emotion in front of the jury up to that point.

Fuck, Lincoln Ashida thought. Outwardly he tried to downplay the significance for Iboshi's benefit. "It's not that bad, Charlene," he said. "It just shows them how much Frankie's changed."

It turned out that Chung was nearsighted. The prosecutors considered recalling him to the stand to explain his vision problems but decided against it because they didn't want to make a big deal of it in front of the jury. Instead, they produced Chung's older brother, Andre, whose sole purpose was to identify Pauline. He did so without hesitation. Under cross-examination by Cliff Hunt, Andre Chung denied that prosecutors coached him about which person to finger as Pauline.

In between the testimony of the two brothers, former detective Edwin Tanaka, now a lieutenant, took the stand. Tanaka, a 23-year veteran of the police department, had been assigned to the Ireland case in the early 1990s. Now part of the records and identification section, Tanaka showed the jury Ireland's mangled bicycle, her wristwatch, the clump of her hair, and the tennis shoe police had recovered from Kapoho. He also displayed items found in Waa Waa near Dana's injured body, including her denim shorts, her black halter top, the other tennis shoe, and the bloody T-shirt found at the scene.

People in the courtroom began to fidget after almost a day of technical witnesses; at this point, prosecutors called Sandy Ireland's husband, Jim Ingham, to the stand. He was tall and slim, with brown hair and glasses, dressed in a suit and tie. Jim's gentle voice described how the couple noticed a smashed bicycle beside the road as they were driving to Christmas Eve dinner at Sandy's parents' place. They recognized the bike as the one Dana had been riding.

"I started calling out her name and looking in the bushes for her," Jim said. "It was obvious to me she'd been hit by a car."

Jim recounted how he and Sandy looked in vain for Dana at their parents' rental home and then returned to the site of the crushed bicycle, where other people and eventually a police officer were also searching for Dana. "While we were at the scene, the officer indicated that somebody had been found, and he thought it would be a good idea to go to the hospital," Jim said. At the hospital he stood outside checking each arriving ambulance until the ambulance carrying Dana finally reached the emergency room. She was in obvious pain and straining at the straps that bound her to the gurney, Ingham said, nearly losing his composure. Hunt's cross-examination was mercifully short.

At 7:00 the next morning, July 29, a full moon glistened above Mauna Kea and then slowly sank behind the mountain and disappeared. It was more dramatic and inspiring than a sunset on the Pacific. Anyone who was awake for this display pitied the people who slept late.

In court later that morning, the pathologist who had conducted Dana Ireland's autopsy took the stand. With deep-set eyes and a high forehead, Dr. Charles Reinhold's appearance complemented his gruesome occupation. "Dana Ireland died from massive blood loss due to multiple trauma injury throughout her body," Reinhold said. He testified that she lost so much blood from all her injuries that her blood no longer had the ability to clot. Lincoln Ashida asked him for a conclusion about what might have caused those injuries.

"The combination of injuries indicates to me

that this is not due to a single mechanism or a single episode such as falling onto the ground due to a motor vehicle accident," Reinhold said.

Hunt jumped to his feet. "Objection!"

"Approach," Judge Amano said, switching off the microphone in front of her in the signal for a bench conference—where lawyers can discuss legal points without the risk of influencing the jury. No one in the gallery could tell what the judge and lawyers were saying; all they could do was watch their body language. When it was the judge's turn to speak, Lincoln Ashida nodded and smiled. To the jury, it might have appeared that the judge was siding with the prosecution. That was what Ashida wanted them to think. No matter what a judge said during a bench conference, Ashida always nodded and smiled in deference to the judge. He was well aware that the courtroom held few diversions for a jury waiting for a bench conference to end. The paneled walls were blank, save for a clock above the exit door behind the gallery and American and Hawaiian state flags adorning the bench. Now, the jurors watched the whispering figures at the bench and glanced impatiently at the gallery.

When the lawyers returned to their places, Judge Amano ordered Reinhold's response stricken from the trial transcript and asked the jury to disregard it. Lincoln's grinning and nodding had been nothing more than bravado.

The testimony resumed with Dr. Reinhold saying

he had collected vaginal swabbings that confirmed the presence of sperm in Ireland's body. In an attempt to defuse inevitable testimony that the sperm found on Ireland didn't match samples submitted by Pauline or his two accomplices, Lincoln posed this question to Reinhold: "Is there any way for you to tell that the sperm that you saw were deposited as the result of a sexual assault?"

No, Reinhold said. The tests only confirmed the presence of sperm. This response left open the unspoken possibility that Dana Ireland had engaged in consensual sex with someone prior to the attack on her.

Under cross-examination by Cliff Hunt, Reinhold agreed that DNA testing can be used either to identify or exclude an individual as the source of sperm. Hunt was laying the groundwork for the defense's case.

Another witness, Steven Dearing, identified a Jimmy'Z T-shirt police found near where Ireland's battered body had originally lain shortly after the attack on Christmas Eve 1991. Dearing, a former neighbor of Andre and William Chung, testified that a month before Dana Ireland's death he saw Pauline wearing the shirt, which had a picture of a woody surfing station wagon on it.

"This was the shirt that he was wearing that day," Dearing said. Under extensive cross-examination, Cliff Hunt quizzed Dearing about the circumstances of the encounter with Pauline and his motive for testifying against him. Dearing said he went to his neighbor's garage after his son's go-cart was "hijacked." Frank Pauline was there and walked toward Dearing as if he wanted to fight. After a standoff, Pauline turned his back but didn't walk away. Dearing said the image of the woody on the back of Pauline's T-shirt was burned into his mind.

Dearing looked like a bouncer for a rough bar, with bulging biceps and tattooed forearms. He didn't appear to be the kind of person who would take kindly to being threatened.

Cliff Hunt questioned Dearing about an interview the man had given seven years later to the prosecution team's investigator, Billy Perreira.

"You're asked by Mr. Perreira if you can identify that shirt in this photograph and you say it looked different, correct?" Hunt asked.

"Uh . . ."

"Yes or no?"

"It looked different 'cause it was covered with blood," Dearing said.

"I thought it was burned in your mind."

"Well, before it wasn't covered with blood. When I saw the shirt I about puked because it was covered with blood."

Another witness, Lynn Matthews, owner of a custom auto painting shop in Hawaiian Beaches, identified photos of Ian Schweitzer's purple Volkswagen. Matthews said Schweitzer and "a Filipino kid" had come to his shop in September 1991 where "the kid" purchased a newly refurbished

1957 baby window Volkswagen—so named because it had a small oval rear window.

On that day, Matthews said, Ian Schweitzer arrived in a 1968 Volkswagen. After the purchase, Schweitzer and his friend dismantled the two cars and exchanged parts.

"They swapped interiors, the rims and tires, and then the cars," he said. By the time they were through, Schweitzer ended up with the purple Volkswagen.

Some time later, Matthews saw Schweitzer's Volkswagen again. "It was painted yellow," he said. "It wasn't a very good yellow paint job." This testimony bolstered Alex Frenchy's earlier account.

At the end of the day, after Judge Amano dismissed the jury for the weekend, Cliff Hunt demanded a mistrial because of Dr. Reinhold's opinion earlier about the cause of Dana Ireland's death. Hunt cited an order Amano had issued requiring all expert witnesses to provide written reports containing their opinions and conclusions. Reinhold's autopsy report contained no opinions or conclusions about the cause of Ireland's injuries, Hunt said.

Hunt told the judge he had specifically asked Lincoln Ashida if he expected to ask Reinhold for conclusions about the cause of Ireland's injuries, and Ashida had said no.

"This morning Mr. Ashida begins to elicit opinions from him as to what were the causes of the injuries," Hunt said, in his appeal for the mistrial.

Ashida argued that a mistrial wasn't necessary

because the judge corrected the problem when she struck Reinhold's response and told the jury to disregard it. "We believe that the court's prompt action cured any error," Ashida said.

Judge Amano agreed and denied Hunt's mistrial request. "I believe that the jury can reach a fair decision," she said. "There's no basis for a mistrial at this time."

Friday, July 31, was Detective Steve Guillermo's forty-first birthday. He and his wife went to Wailoa State Park, a recreational area on a pond, located right behind the courthouse. Despite the park's many picnic tables, the Guillermos weren't in the park for a birthday lunch; they were there to meet a three-year-old boy. Their efforts to conceive a child had failed, and they were working with Hawaii's Department of Human Services to adopt one.

The boy, Alika, arrived at the park with his foster parent, a single woman in her early sixties. He wanted to walk to the water's edge, so Guillermo went with him. Alika was quite a talker for a boy his age. While he chattered away, he began throwing rocks in the pond, trying to hit the mullet that were swimming there. One of the rocks splashed water on Guillermo, and Alika laughed with delight. Guillermo knew then and there that he would adopt the boy.

Back in court on Monday, the prosecution called convicted sex offender Shayne Kobayashi, the witness who had testified at the grand jury about Shawn Schweitzer's incriminating statements. The bearded and mustached 24-year-old Kobayashi said he went to Pohoiki on Christmas Eve 1991 to surf and then drank beer there with some friends. While he and his friends were drinking, Frank Pauline, Ian Schweitzer, and Shawn Schweitzer arrived in a vehicle together and joined the group.

"We was talking story and kicking back," Kobayashi said. Sometime in the afternoon Dana Ireland rode up on her bicycle "not more than 20 feet away" wearing shorts and a shirt. Under questioning by Lincoln Ashida, Kobayashi said he was certain Ireland noticed his group " 'cause she wen' look our way." She rode her bike into the parking area and stopped to look at the ocean, Kobayashi said.

"People in our group was talking, 'Oh, look at that nice lady over there,' " Kobayashi said. Courtroom observers doubted that the language was that mild. They also noted the contempt in Ashida's voice. Kobayashi testified that Ireland stayed about five minutes and then headed in the direction of Kapoho Vacationland.

Kobayashi said that after Dana left, he and the others made plans to drive in their separate cars to an area above Pahoa School to smoke pot and drink. Kobayashi and the others went south on Red Road, taking a 20-minute route to the area above the school. Pauline and the Schweitzers headed in the opposite direction, the same route Dana Ireland had taken earlier. The trio never did join the rest of the group above the school, Kobayashi said. A day or two later, Kobayashi recognized Dana Ireland in photographs. "I seen the reward posters, and I seen 'em on the news."

Kobayashi said that although he had told police in early 1992 that he didn't know anything about the Ireland case, he decided in 1997 to come forward with information about the case "for justice." By then Kobayashi was in prison serving a 10-year sentence for second-degree sexual assault. He had yet to attend classes for sex offender, drug, and anger management. "My deal was for get out of prison and for be placed on parole after I do my classes," Kobayashi said. In exchange, Kobayashi agreed to testify in the Pauline and Schweitzer trials. Kobayashi told this jury that he also provided other information to Big Island police but didn't elaborate on the nature of that information because it was inadmissible in Pauline's trial. Prosecutors were saving that for the Schweitzer trial.

Under cross-examination, Kobayashi testified that he was originally indicted for first-degree sexual assault on a 13-year-old girl. He said he was later indicted for jumping bail and faced up to five additional years in prison for that charge. He acknowledged that he shaved up to eight years off his sentence by coming forward but insisted that wasn't his sole motivation for testifying for the state. "I feel that's the right thing—and I wanted for get out of prison, too," he said.

Lieutenant Paul Ferreira, who had been a detective at the time of the crime, testified about chauffeuring two police detectives and Pauline when they went on the reconstruction tour on June 18, 1994. Ferreira said he picked the three up from the Hilo airport and drove them to the Puna district, where Pauline directed him first to the Hawaiian Beaches subdivision and then to Kapoho. "He was nervous, but he was normal," Ferreira said. "He was cooperative and talkative."

Pauline pointed out the mailboxes at the end of Kapoho Kai Drive—about a half-mile from where Dana Ireland's mangled bike was found. "He saw her on the bicycle and also he said that's where the accident occurred," Ferreira said.

During cross-examination, Ferreira maintained eye contact with the jury and barely glanced at Hunt. He said police didn't videotape, audiotape, or photograph any of the reconstruction tour. Ferreira also acknowledged that the areas where Dana Ireland and her bicycle were found had been marked with memorial markers and were common knowledge among area residents.

Another witness, Fred Perreira, testified that he had received a call in May 1994 from Pauline's brother, John Gonsalves, seeking advice. He had advised Gonsalves to tell Pauline to go to police with information about the Ireland case.

During cross-examination, defense attorney Cliff Hunt asked Perreira if he was a psychic.

"No, not a psychic," Perreira said. "Someone who gives advice. I have intuition."

"Were you known as someone who gives advice based on being able to be aware of things or perceive things that most normal people cannot perceive or become aware of?"

"No," Perreira said. "Your typical person has intuition."

Some of the spectators wondered if Perreira had "intuition" about the outcome of this case.

Chapter 17

Up until now, the picture of Frank Pauline that was developing through witness testimony contrasted starkly with the clean-cut choirboy image he projected in court. No matter how many times a judge tells jurors to base their deliberations solely on the evidence, individuals in the jury box can't help trying to assess whether a defendant looks guilty. The defendant sitting quietly between Cliff Hunt and his female assistant projected the impression of a respectable young man not likely to ravage a young woman for sport.

That façade was about to crack.

On Tuesday, August 3, prosecutor Lincoln Ashida began direct examination of Pauline's cousin, Marco Salvador Jr., who was serving time in an Oklahoma prison for a 1993 drug conviction on the Big Island. Handcuffs and shackles restrained Salvador, but courtroom observers still found him a frightening figure—especially when he smiled in their direction. Sporting a mustache and disheveled hair, this man in brown prison garb twitched and had a wild look in his eyes.

Salvador had lived across the street from the Schweitzer family in 1991. He testified that he used to own the Volkswagen that Ian Schweitzer obtained shortly before Dana Ireland's death. When Schweitzer took possession of the car, "it was in top shape," Salvador said. "Never had any dents or anything." Salvador said he had noticed that after December 24, 1991, the car underwent alterations and received a new paint job.

Salvador testified about a phone conversation on Christmas Eve between his cousin—Wayne Gonsalves—and Pauline. "I heard from my cousin himself the night of the incident," Salvador said, adding that he hadn't come forward with the information right away because "nobody ever did ask me any questions."

Prosecutor Lincoln Ashida established that Salvador received nothing from prosecutors in exchange for his testimony. Salvador said he came forward because he had a daughter himself. "If this was my daughter, I would take things in my own hands," Salvador said.

Pauline jumped out of his seat, clutching his right wrist with his left hand. "Then tell 'em who did 'em," he shouted. "Tell 'em the truth you fucking liar." In that short outburst, the jury got a glimpse of Pauline's quick temper and heard the heavy pidgin accent that belied the Harvard-student look his attorney had worked so hard to create.

After Pauline regained his composure, his attorney cross-examined Salvador extensively about his criminal record and his motivation for cooperating with police in 1994. "I don't expect nothing from the cops. Nothing at all," Salvador said. "I'm doing my time now. I don't expect nothing."

Salvador wasn't the only prison inmate to testify that day. Shannon Rodrigues, serving two life sentences for a double murder near Hilo Airport, testified that Pauline had admitted his involvement in the Ireland case to him when the two were incarcerated together at Maui Community Correctional Center. Pauline had told Rodrigues that Pauline had been cruising with his brothers on Christmas Eve 1991. "They seen this girl, they had sex with her, but he did not kill her," Rodrigues said.

Jeffrey Alfonso, John Gonsalves's brother-in-law, was serving time in a federal prison in Oregon for a drug conviction. He testified that in late 1993 he and Pauline were driving on a back road in Puna to go fishing. "I pointed out where I thought they found Dana Ireland's body, and he insisted that that wasn't, that it was farther down, toward Hawaiian Beaches."

After Pauline went to prison for the other rape conviction, he would call Alfonso once a week or so, Alfonso said. One day Pauline told Alfonso about the Dana Ireland attack. "He said he had nothing to do with the rape, but was at the scene, and he couldn't see her suffering so he grabbed a tire iron and did what he had to." Alfonso said Pauline told him about it because he needed to get it off his chest.

Alfonso maintained he didn't expect anything in exchange for his testimony. But during cross-examination Cliff Hunt read from a letter Alfonso sent to federal Judge Helen Gilmore saying that the U.S. Attorney prosecuting his case promised him a reduced sentence in return for his testimony in the Dana Ireland trial. Alfonso said he never did get his sentence reduced and would be released in three months, after serving his full sentence, with time off for good behavior and participation in a drug rehabilitation program. Hunt spent about half an hour reviewing Alfonso's extensive criminal record—primarily assault and drug cases. Alfonso's responses were cocky and sarcastic.

Time would tell whether the jury believed the prisoners or whether they would disregard them as opportunists who had fabricated stories—stories that didn't match.

That same day, Pauline's ex-girlfriend, 24-year-old Charla Figueroa, testified. Figueroa was an attractive woman, with waist-length straight black hair and styled bangs falling to the left. Her chocolate lipstick matched her perfectly manicured acrylic nails. Nervously wringing her hands and speaking in a soft voice, Figueroa testified that she'd been Pauline's girlfriend from late 1989 to early 1994 and had lived with Pauline at his family's home. She testified that Pauline was in and out of his mother's house during the 1991 Christmas Eve party. She said she couldn't remember when he was in and when he was out.

When asked about a T-shirt Pauline owned that matched the description of the blood-soaked one found near Dana Ireland, Figueroa said that she had seen Pauline wearing the shirt before Dana Ireland's slaying and that she had washed it. The next time she saw it was on a television newscast after Pauline made statements placing himself at the crime scene and implicating the Schweitzer brothers.

"I was in shock," Figueroa said, " 'cause that's the first time I found out that he was a suspect for this case." During her testimony, Figueroa avoided looking at Pauline until prosecutor Charlene Iboshi asked her to point him out.

"Can you identify Frank Pauline Jr.?" Iboshi asked.

"Yes."

"Can you tell the judge and jury what he's wearing?"

"I can't see what he's wearing," Figueroa replied.

"Do you recognize where he is sitting?" Iboshi asked.

Attorney Hunt urged Pauline to get up. "Stand up. Stand up," he said. Pauline rose and Figueroa identified him. After she did, she put both hands over her face and wiped her eyes.

"Is it hard for you to be here?" Iboshi asked.

"Yes, it is," she said.

Figueroa, who was in tears or close to them for the remainder of her testimony, said that after Pauline had gone public about his involvement in the case, he had told her that he had withheld the information from her because he didn't want her to know about it.

"Why did he tell you that?" Iboshi asked.

"He said he was protecting me and my kids." Figueroa and Pauline were the parents of twin boys.

Under cross-examination, Figueroa said the Pauline family's Christmas Eve party was a tradition. Frank Pauline was supposed to give her an engagement ring, she testified, but he couldn't find the box and everybody ended up looking for it. Frank got into an argument with his mother, Pat, who accused him of selling the ring to buy drugs.

"How did that make you feel?" Hunt asked.

"Hurt," she said.

"You weren't just hurt—you became very angry with Frank, didn't you, that day?"

"No I didn't."

"Didn't you tell Detective Guillermo that you were still very angry with him because you thought he might have traded it or sold it for drugs?" Hunt asked. Pauline's attorney was trying to establish a motive for Figueroa's testimony against the defendant.

"I wasn't very angry," Figueroa said. "I told him I was upset if he did trade it for drugs. But I also calmed Frank down and told him that I still loved him."

Figueroa testified that Pat Pauline had expected her to do a lot of work around the house while no family members lifted a finger. Figueroa had moved out of the house shortly after Pauline went to prison in 1994.

Figueroa described Pauline as possessive and macho. She said he got into many fights, bragged a lot, and lied about his exploits.

"He was kind of a mouth?" Hunt asked.

"Yes."

Figueroa said Pauline still called and wrote to her from prison. In one letter he had written that he'd implicated himself to help his brother, John Gonsalves.

Hunt asked if this had happened during the period shortly after the media became aware of Pauline's statements about being present during Ireland's attack.

"Yes," Figueroa replied.

"At one point the media started circling like vultures," Hunt said. Then, glancing at the reporters on the front-row bench, he apologized. "I'm sorry, I didn't mean that."

Figueroa's grandmother, Louise Furtado, testified next. She said that on Christmas Eve 1991 she had arrived at Pauline's house after dark, parking her car across the street. As she got out, she saw Pauline exit a white or cream-colored Volkswagen. "He started walking forward with his head down and his chest heavy," Furtado said. He wasn't wearing a shirt and he was crying.

Sometime in 1994, Furtado said, Figueroa and her children were living in Mountain View, a subdivision on the road to Hawaii Volcanoes National Park. Pauline called from prison, in tears, and spoke to Furtado. "He wanted me to tell her that he was involved with the Ireland case, that he had hit Ireland with a tire iron, and that he didn't know how to tell her." Pauline told her the Schweitzer brothers made him do it "so that he couldn't squeal on them," Furtado testified. "One hit her with a stone, the other punched and kicked her, and he hit her with a tire iron."

That night, in the Hilo Lagoon Center next door, John and Louise Ireland were among the thousands of people statewide who learned what happened in court by watching the news on television. John, especially, was frustrated at being excluded from the courtroom. At least Louise had been called as a witness and that gave her a sense of purpose. By now John was resigned to the fact that the prosecutors wouldn't call him to testify because they didn't want Hunt to cross-examine him about the pressure he'd put on authorities to solve the case.

This trip, like all the others, was costing the Irelands a lot of money. In addition to coach class airfare and the condo, they also had to spend $700 a month for a rental car. "I guess we've spent about one hundred thousand dollars coming back and forth," John said, "but that's what you have to do."

"It's terrible what happened to Dana," Louise said. "Those three guys just have to be put away for good."

"I used to be very liberal," John said. "But not anymore. I didn't believe in the death penalty, but in certain cases I think it's justified."

The next day the state called one of its star witnesses, John Gonsalves. Frank Pauline's 32-year-old brother testified that on Christmas Eve 1991 he had attended a large family gathering in the garage at his mother's house. Sometime in the early afternoon, he said, Pauline got into the argument with his girlfriend over the missing engagement ring. Following the dispute, Pauline went into the house and slammed the door. Gonsalves didn't see his brother again until early that evening when he went outside and saw the Schweitzer brothers and Pauline standing by the purple Volkswagen Bug.

"When I went outside I saw Shawn and Ian and they were all talking about they had hit a dog and they were laughing," Gonsalves said. The lower left side of the apron and part of the hood or fender of the Bug were "smashed like they did hit a dog or something," he said. "Frank looked like he was real angry and like he was doing drugs."

Prosecutor Iboshi asked Gonsalves whether anyone else was with Pauline and the Schweitzer brothers. "I really feel there was somebody else," Gonsalves said. "I cannot picture him no matter how hard I try." Iboshi didn't pursue the subject.

Gonsalves testified that more than three years later, in May 1994, Pauline had called him from Halawa prison. According to Gonsalves, Frank told his brother that he was having problems at the prison and had to "get the hell out of there."

"Frank, can I ask you something?" Gonsalves said. He mentioned Kapoho and Frank became silent for what felt like a long time.

"Who told you?" Pauline asked when he finally broke the silence. Gonsalves said nobody had told him anything. He just had a hunch. Frank then had confessed his involvement in the crime, Gonsalves testified. He claimed Pauline had told him that he and the Schweitzer brothers had seen Ireland at Pohoiki. "He told me that he and Ian and Shawn was driving and they saw this girl on a bike and they were giving her gestures, and when she refused Ian got all mad and he told Frank, 'Eff this,'" Gonsalves testified. "And he wen' bang the girl. He ran over her. He supposedly ran over her again, and then they grabbed her and took her."

According to Gonsalves, Pauline and the Schweitzer brothers put Ireland in the car and took her to a trail. "Ian was raping her, and Frank told me that he was kind of freaking out already, and Ian made Shawn have sex with her, and if not, he was going to hurt Shawn, too," Gonsalves testified. "Ian was biting her breast, and all kind of sick stuff," he said. "Ian was like possessed or something," and they were scared. "He told me that he was there, but he did not rape the girl."

Pauline grabbed a tire iron, Gonsalves said. "He said he was scared and he thought that was what he had to do." And then "he just wen' whack 'em over the head. She was begging them to stop, saying, 'Please, I'm not going to say nothing,' " Gonsalves said. Afterward, they left her in "side road bushes." When asked what kind of car the guys were in, Gonsalves answered that his brother first told him he was in Ian's girlfriend's pickup truck and later told him it was the Volkswagen Bug. The truck would be consistent with the police department's initial leads.

Gonsalves urged Pauline to go to police, telling him, "Even if you don't go, I gotta go," he testified. Eventually he convinced his brother to talk to the police.

After Gonsalves called the police, they asked Gonsalves to take "embarrassing" DNA tests to exclude him as a suspect, he said. "I told them I could not believe that they would ask me to do that, and I was very offended." He testified that he consulted an attorney, Joy Hutson. He then told the jury about his arrest for conspiracy to distribute cocaine and his plea bargain for a suspended jail term along with an opportunity to wipe his record clean. Gonsalves insisted, however, that he had never asked for anything in exchange for his testimony against Pauline. "I agreed to testify truthfully regardless of the agreement," Gonsalves said. "I would never sell my brother out, but the truth is the truth."

Charlene Iboshi asked Gonsalves to identify Pauline in the courtroom. While doing so, Gonsalves's voice broke. Afterward, Gonsalves put his head down on the witness stand and then came up crying with his face in his hands.

Cliff Hunt's cross-examination focused on Gonsalves's "sweetheart deal" with the government on the drug offense, which Hunt was trying to suggest was payment for turning in his brother. Gonsalves's responses were prompt and confident. He denied being a drug dealer. He testified that he had gone to police after Pauline confessed to him about his involvement in the attack on Ireland. "I did it because of the whole situation," Gonsalves said under follow-up questioning by Iboshi. "That's bad what had happened. Her family deserves to get justice and peace." Gonsalves testified that he thought Pauline "was going to come clean, too."

On re-cross examination, Hunt paced, his hands clasped behind his back. "This was your civic duty to tell the police what you knew, correct?"

"How would you feel if it was your daughter?" Gonsalves responded.

"I'm asking you the questions here," Hunt said.

"I did it because I'm human and I have a heart," Gonsalves replied.

Following Gonsalves's testimony, Judge Amano called a recess and left the courtroom. While the jurors were still in the jury box, Gonsalves stood up in the witness box and turned to his brother. "I love you no matter what," Gonsalves said, placing his right hand over his chest. "Search your heart."

Pauline smiled.

After the recess, with the jury still out, Hunt asked the judge to find out if any of the jurors had heard or seen Gonsalves's comment and gesture. One by one Amano brought them into the courtroom and asked, "Did you see or hear John Gonsalves do or say anything after the court recessed?"

It turned out none had.

Chapter 18

After John Gonsalves's testimony, Cliff Hunt asked for another mistrial, saying he hadn't received a three-page report from the prosecution's accident reconstruction expert, Kenneth Baker, until the previous day. "The state has had almost eight years and close to 7,000 pages of discovery to get its theories straight and line up its experts to prove its theories," Hunt wrote in his motion for a mistrial. "Yet when the defense seeks a report from its experts concerning those theories, the state moans and groans about the difficulty of producing a couple pages of documents containing those theories."

Hunt also complained that Baker's analysis of the defense expert's computer simulation of the bicycle accident was done on invalid computer software and asked that Baker be stricken as a witness. While the jurors sat in the jury room, Lincoln Ashida countered by asking Judge Amano to exclude any testimony based on computer programs by the defense's expert, James Campbell. That simulation, which showed a purple Volkswagen hitting a bicyclist, would depict injuries and vehicular damage that hadn't been found on Dana Ireland's body or Ian Schweitzer's car. Its visual impact was bound to influence the jury more than the dry testimony of the state's own expert.

When either the defense or the prosecution wants to call an expert witness, that witness must be "qualified" by the court by answering questions under oath about his or her credentials and experience. The judge then decides whether to allow the expert to testify, and if so, the extent of that testimony. Such decisions can be crucial, as some juries put a lot of faith in expert witnesses. In this case, each accident reconstruction expert planned to give a different scenario about the vehicle–bicycle crash. Both the prosecution and the defense needed their expert's testimony to support their cases.

First Campbell and then Baker took the stand. They testified about their credentials and experience, and explained their techniques. After several hours of questioning by Lincoln Ashida and Cliff Hunt, the judge denied the defense motion for a mistrial. She ruled that both Campbell and Baker could testify as expert witnesses, but said Campbell couldn't present his computer simulation and Baker couldn't refer to it. "The court finds that it's unreliable," said Amano.

Lincoln Ashida breathed a sigh of relief. Charlene Iboshi squeezed his hand. "You did good," she whispered.

The next expert witness to qualify was forensic

odontologist and bitemark expert Dr. Norman
Sperber. The dental specialist was prepared to testify for the prosecution about the marks found on
Ireland's left breast. Sperber was the chief forensic
dentist for San Diego and Imperial counties, and
for the state of California's missing/unidentified
person system. He had developed a system for the
state to identify unknown persons based on dental
records, and had performed a similar service for the
FBI. Sperber had practiced his specialty for 35
years and had already been qualified five times as
an expert in Hawaii.

Under questioning by Lincoln Ashida, Sperber
explained that forensic odontologists use a four-
point scale when comparing bitemarks on victims
to dental impressions: "rule out," "consistent,"
"probable," and "reasonable dental certainty." He
testified that he'd used the fourth term in only two
of the 120 cases in which he'd testified. Under
cross examination by defense attorney Cliff Hunt,
Sperber said he'd originally ruled out all three defendants as persons who could have left the
bitemarks. He said after prosecutors returned to
him and suggested that Dana Ireland's bitemark
might have been distorted because her body was
bloated from fluids infused in the attempt to save
her life, he changed his opinion. He said Pauline's
dental impression was "consistent" with the
bitemarks on her breast. Sperber said he had arrived at that conclusion after looking at a photo of
the distorted body and comparing it to teeth im-

pressions from the suspects. Sperber had also compared teeth impressions of another early suspect in the case, Ray Harrison, and found that the man's sample was "highly consistent" with the bitemarks on the body.

Judge Amano questioned Dr. Sperber herself. She seemed concerned about the reliability of his comparisons, especially considering the bloated appearance of the body and its distorting effect on the bitemark. The fact that he'd changed his mind after a visit from prosecutors troubled her, too. Amano ruled that because both the photo and the body were distorted, "the conclusions of this expert . . . would not be of sufficient reliability." She disallowed Sperber from testifying.

This was a blow to the prosecution. Lincoln Ashida wanted all the evidence he could get and considered Sperber a "credible pro," one of the top five experts in the field of odontology. He knew it was problematic that Sperber had changed his mind about Pauline, but he wanted the option of putting the expert on the stand if it became necessary. Charlene Iboshi, who always liked to paint the entire picture for a jury, was even more upset than Ashida about losing Sperber's testimony.

But they didn't have time to dwell on the loss. It was time for automobile reconstruction expert Kenneth Baker to testify in front of the jury. Baker said he had reviewed the police report of the collision and photos of the scene, visited the site, and examined Ian Schweitzer's Volkswagen and Dana Ireland's mangled bicycle. The bike's rear wheel, he said, "had an indentation in it which broke the rim and some of the spokes" as well as scrapes to the paint and "other indications that perhaps it was run over." The object that hit the bike was approximately 12 inches high, about 4 inches wide, and "not flat but probably rounded in its profile," Baker said.

Schweitzer's Volkswagen bumper "was approximately 4 inches wide and when mounted on a Volkswagen would be approximately 12 inches off the ground," he testified. Baker said the vehicle involved in the collision could not have been a truck or van with a flat front as that would have caused more extensive damage to the bike and to Dana Ireland. Instead, the damage was consistent with a vehicle with a rounded front, he said, leaving the jury to picture the front of a Volkswagen Bug. Baker testified that after such a collision, "the car or vehicle that struck the victim's bicycle would catch up with her and she would be struck by the right fender of the vehicle." Baker was unable to examine the fenders of Schweitzer's Volkswagen, he said, because the car had none at the time he looked at it.

Under cross-examination by Hunt, Baker said that his consultation fee for helping prosecutors was $225 per hour and that he'd already spent about 25 hours on the case. He also conceded that he didn't have a degree in engineering. Hunt's cross-examination did some damage to the state's case. Pauline's attorney got Baker to admit that he should have asked for tire track measurements at the scene of the collision, but didn't. Hunt also elicited an admission that the damage to the bicycle was only "likely" to have been from a Volkswagen.

"In other words, you're not certain, are you, sir?" Hunt asked.

"That's correct," Baker said.

More important, Baker told Hunt he could find no marks on the bumper or the hood that might have come from a collision with a bicycle. That would have been expected had Dana been hit the way the state alleged.

The next day John and Louise Ireland got their first look at the other two defendants charged with killing their daughter. Although the Irelands were barred from attending Frank Pauline's trial, nothing prevented them from sitting in on a hearing for Ian and Shawn Schweitzer that just happened to be on the court calendar that day. (It was Friday, when no trials were scheduled so that Judge Amano could catch up on other matters.) Shawn and Ian Schweitzer were to appear in her courtroom for a hearing on a motion by their attorneys to hold separate trials for each brother. Although Louise Ireland had already gotten a good look at Frank Pauline when she had testified, she had never seen the Schweitzer brothers. If she'd been serious about her threats to shoot them, this would have been her chance. The portable security checkpoint in use for the Pauline trial stood idle and unmanned outside the courtroom door.

John and Louise entered the courtroom and took a seat in the second bench on the left side. Louise sat by the aisle. "I want to get a good look," she said. A side door opened and Ian Schweitzer, accompanied by a jail guard, walked into the courtroom wearing handcuffs, shackles, and a blue prisoner's jumpsuit. Louise's gaze followed the bewildered-looking 28-year-old man as he took his position in the courtroom. Ian had short curly dark hair, dark eyes, and a double chin.

Another door opened. This time Shawn Schweitzer, also in handcuffs and shackles but dressed in an orange jumpsuit, entered the courtroom and walked past Louise. "Oh, God," Louise said. Shawn was no longer the scrawny 16-year-old portrayed in family photos taken around the time of Dana's death. Tall and husky, the 23-year-old had obviously been lifting weights in jail. Even with his pitted skin, Shawn was the better looking of the two with more sharply chiseled features, dark hair, and dark eyes. Louise craned her neck to look at both brothers as they stood with their backs to her.

Their parents, Jerry and Linda Schweitzer, were in court as well to see their sons and to provide moral support. The Schweitzer parents and the Ireland parents sneaked peeks at one another but didn't exchange words.

The state planned to introduce evidence of incriminating statements allegedly made by each brother that would be inadmissible against the other brother if the trials were held separately. If the brothers were tried together, the jury would hear all the evidence and might assume both were guilty if a witness testified that one confessed. For that reason, both attorneys wanted to protect their clients from damning evidence that would prejudice a jury.

During the hearing, Amano granted the motion for separate trials. She said she would keep the November 15 trial date for one of the brothers but added that the other would have to waive his right to go to trial within 180 days of the May 20 indictment. Ian Schweitzer's attorney, James Biven, said his client was unwilling to waive that right. "He wants to go first," Biven said.

Amano questioned Shawn Schweitzer to make sure he was willing to wait until March 6 to go to trial. "You can't complain later on that somehow your right to trial within 180 days has been violated," Amano said. "It might be that you will be in custody until your trial."

Shawn Schweitzer said he understood.

Upon hearing that his son might remain in jail, Jerry Schweitzer rose from the gallery. "I have a question, your honor," he said.

Amano directed him to step forward.

"I would like to know about the severe conditions they have Shawn under," Mr. Schweitzer said, referring to Halawa Prison on Oahu where Shawn was incarcerated pending his trial.

Amano said she knew nothing about the prison

conditions. She suggested Mr. Schweitzer discuss the matter with his son's attorney, Keith Shigetomi.

After the hearing, Jerry Schweitzer told reporters that Shawn had been in "the hole"—solitary confinement—twice for two weeks at a time since being transferred to Halawa Prison from Hawaii Community Correctional Center, the Big Island's jail.

"In that kind of conditions, how can his mind function?" Jerry Schweitzer asked. "If they keep treating anyone in this manner they'll say anything you want him to say."

After the hearing, Louise stepped a little lighter as she walked back to her rented condominium. It somehow helped her to have set eyes upon the Schweitzer brothers. "It's a relief," she said. "They are guilty." It was enough to get her through another weekend.

Chapter 19

The Irelands and the lawyers had no time or energy for anything but the trial, but outside court there was excitement in the air. Hilo was hosting the World Indigenous Peoples' Conference on Education. Some 2,500 delegates and their companions traveled to the Big Island to exchange information about their struggles to preserve their unique cultures. Native Hawaiians shared their *aloha* with them all, welcoming delegates with a canoe regatta on picturesque Hilo Bay. That was followed by Hawaiian chanting, cultural dancing, and the sipping of the mildly intoxicating beverage, kawa, called 'awa in Hawaii. The historic event, which had begun the previous Sunday, would wrap up that Saturday.

On Monday, when automobile reconstruction expert Kenneth Baker resumed his testimony, prosecutors introduced a letter he had written to police that said a "small dent near the right end" of Ian Schweitzer's Volkswagen bumper "could have been the area of contact" with the bicycle that Dana Ireland was riding on Christmas Eve 1991.

Baker showed the jury some scratches on the bumper in court but testified that he wasn't referring to a small "dimple" on a vertical piece of the bumper. He said the area of contact wasn't necessarily the first place the car hit the bike. "There's no physical evidence that quantifies where on this bumper is the initial point of impact."

During cross-examination, Cliff Hunt showed Baker a police photo of Ian Schweitzer's Volkswagen with the fenders removed and stored inside the car. Baker testified that when he'd asked Detective Guillermo to show him the fenders, Guillermo told him that they "were not available when police recovered the Volkswagen." The statement helped bolster Hunt's theory that police had tailored their evidence to fit the suspects.

Baker testified that he believed that Ireland was still riding her bike during the moment of impact and that the vehicle was going less than 30 miles per hour. The car then ran over the bike, Baker concluded. The bike seat's support prongs could have caused the scratches to the Volkswagen's bumper as the bike began to fall to the left. "It's possible that the seat would have been exposed to the right end of the bumper," he said.

Under extensive questioning by Hunt, who continued trying to show that the vehicle that hit Dana Ireland was a truck or a van, Baker conceded that the woman's vaginal injuries could have resulted from the bicycle seat's prongs being driven into her crotch at impact. Although Baker had no formal training in medicine, he was an accident reconstruction expert, and was allowed to speculate on how injuries related to automobiles might occur. The prosecution didn't object to his speculation.

Special Agent Audrey Lynch, an 18-year FBI veteran, testified next. Before becoming an FBI agent, she'd worked for 13 years as a scientific researcher at several universities and was the author of a number of scientific publications. Lynch was a DNA specialist who analyzed bodily fluids at the FBI lab in Washington, D.C. She explained that she treated the evidence in the case with the RFLP method, which is used for comparing a blood sample from a known individual with fluid stain evidence. In the Ireland case, she compared 18 DNA samples from known individuals against 76 "questioned" items containing blood sent to her by Big Island police.

She found animal blood on the plywood taken from Ray Harrison's van. From the Waa Waa scene, where Dana Ireland was found, Lynch found human blood on a gauze pad used to treat the bleeding woman, a paper towel, a black shoe, a white athletic shoe, a pair of socks, and on the blue "Jimmy'Z" T-shirt.

"There was no DNA unlike that of the victim found on the T-shirt," Lynch said. "In other words, the blood on the T-shirt was consistent with coming from the victim, Dana Ireland."

Cliff Hunt's lengthy cross-examination revealed that Lynch had worked on the evidence from January 1992 until late April 1993. At that time the FBI wasn't using the PCR DNA test, which was a newer technology than RFLP. Lynch, an experienced expert witness who referred frequently to notes while on the stand, painstakingly defined RFLP and DNA and explained usage of the RFLP method. Lynch said that she wasn't qualified to use PCR technology, as she had not been trained in that method, but that others in the lab had been. Edward Blake, the defense DNA expert, had begun using that technology before the FBI had.

Lynch didn't remember recommending to Detective Guillermo that police ask Blake to do a PCR test, although Hunt produced a copy of a letter from her to that effect. Hammering at Lynch, Hunt wanted to know why she recommended the PCR test, why it hadn't been conducted, and why she couldn't recall specific telephone conversations with Guillermo or anybody else in Hawaii County. Lynch explained that in any given week she had hundreds of conversations with police investigators across the country.

Hunt's questioning progressed from polite to accusatory. The strategy might have worked with a stereotypical FBI agent concerned with maintaining an infallible image, but this short, bespectacled, middle-aged scientist did not rise to the bait.

Lynch testified that she ran several semen tests. She confirmed the presence of semen only on Dana Ireland's cervical and vaginal swabs made at Hilo Hospital, but was unable to detect a DNA profile "either because of insufficient and/or degraded

DNA." Because no profile could be detected, she had nothing to compare against the known DNA samples.

Despite having run the risk of losing the jurors' attention during this extended scientific testimony, Hunt seemed to keep their interest at least during the first hour. It was evident from his questions that he had studied DNA analysis procedures. The FBI's inability to conduct DNA analysis on the semen seemed helpful to the defense, even if it didn't immediately prove Hunt's contention that the FBI had botched the case.

On redirect examination, Lincoln Ashida elicited testimony that Lynch couldn't rule out multiple donors of semen in the evidence she examined. She also explained that at the time she had made her tests, the PCR DNA test had a lower probability of establishing a match than did the RFLP test.

The next day Charlene Iboshi presented the nuts and bolts of the state's case with testimony by its final witness, Detective Steve Guillermo. Looking fit and trim, the 41-year-old Guillermo swore to tell the truth in a sure tone that let jurors know he meant business. Then, with his hands folded in front of him and his body leaning slightly forward into the microphone he testified that the police report on the Dana Ireland case totaled more than 2,800 pages, including interviews with more than 300 witnesses.

Guillermo first testified about police activities

and evidence at the two crime scenes, Kapoho Kai Drive and Waa Waa. He identified evidence shown to the jury in enlarged police photos. Preliminary testimony dealt with tire impressions taken at Kapoho Kai Drive, providing a graphic representation to the jury of the first crime scene. Iboshi then broadened her direct examination by asking Guillermo where the evidence was analyzed. The FBI and Honolulu Police Department crime labs and Dr. Henry Lee's Connecticut State Police laboratory had all examined the evidence, Guillermo said. The Hawaii County Police Department had used the services of Dr. Lee, an internationally famous forensic scientist, in the past. In May of 1995 they again sought his services, forwarding to him hospital and autopsy records and photographs, as well as 14 pieces of evidence found at the Waa Waa crime scene, and asking him to examine them for the presence of hairs, fibers, blood, semen, and fingerprints. The Police Department asked several laboratories and individuals for assistance in the case, trying to find a link between evidence and the individual or individuals responsible.

Initial suspicion had focused on two men, Guillermo testified, not because of any physical evidence but rather because the two were reportedly seen by witnesses in the area shortly before and after the Kapoho Kai Drive collision. Both men were cleared when police confirmed that they had been at other locations at the time. The purpose of this foundational testimony was apparently to impress the jury with the thoroughness of the police investigation.

The restless jurors perked up when Guillermo testified about Dana Ireland's last few hours of life.

Charlene Iboshi then abruptly switched her questioning to the May 1994 telephone call from John Gonsalves, whom Guillermo described as "very forthcoming." That led to Guillermo's two interviews of Frank Pauline at the attorney general's office. Pauline seemed surprised at having been taken from prison for the interview, Guillermo said. The detective described the first interview as brief, and Iboshi asked only a few questions about it before moving on to the second interview.

Guillermo testified that Pauline had told him that on December 24, 1991, he was home in Hawaiian Beaches preparing for a party when Ian and Shawn Schweitzer stopped by in a purple Volkswagen. "Ian asked him if he wanted to party with them," Guillermo said. Although Pauline wasn't close to the Schweitzers, he agreed to join them "because he knew that 'party' meant to smoke cocaine." He relayed Pauline's story that as the three of them were riding in the Volkswagen, they saw Dana Ireland standing by the road. Ian Schweitzer said something like, "Ho!" and then turned the car around, sped up, and hit her, creating a sensation "similar to going over a speed bump twice. Once going forward and once reversing."

According to Guillermo, Pauline described the shirt Dana Ireland was wearing as a "tight-fitted top that exposed the stomach area." Pauline "couldn't clearly recall all of the details," Guillermo said, "and he attributed that to his drug use."

Guillermo repeated Pauline's story that Ian Schweitzer "had sexual intercourse" with Dana Ireland. "It was just for a short while, and Pauline further indicated that he had enjoyed watching Ian have sexual intercourse with the victim." Ian Schweitzer had asked Pauline to do the same, but Pauline had refused, Guillermo said.

Frank Pauline and Ian Schweitzer had gotten into a discussion and "Ian indicated that they had to knock her off," Guillermo said, "because she would be able to identify them, and they'd get busted."

Pauline walked back to the Volkswagen and got a tire iron "and at that point he approached the victim, looked at her, and swung the tire iron at her head," Guillermo testified. "He stated he did hit her but was unable to tell exactly where." Pauline didn't see any blood or hear any moans coming from the victim, Guillermo testified.

Frank Pauline believed that Ian Schweitzer had also hit the woman, but he wasn't certain. Pauline and the Schweitzer brothers then headed to the Schweitzer home in Hawaiian Beaches, where they washed the car and then Ian and Shawn changed

clothes. "Pauline was told by Ian not to say anything about it and if anyone asked to deny it,"
Guillermo testified.

Guillermo further recounted flying Pauline to
Hilo that same day for a reconstruction of the
crime. He also testified about Pauline's formal
statement to police, when Guillermo had asked
Pauline if he had touched Dana Ireland at any other
time than when helping to take her out of the
trunk.

"He stated that he did," Guillermo testified. "He
stated that prior to Ian Schweitzer having sexual intercourse with the victim he assisted in pulling
down her pants."

Guillermo had asked Pauline why he hit Ireland
with the tire iron, he said. "To make sure I killed
her," Pauline responded. "To make sure she died?"
Guillermo asked. "Yeah," Pauline answered.

After Pauline's formal statement, Guillermo testified, police had obtained a search warrant and recovered the Volkswagen from the Schweitzer
home, but "were unable to determine where the
fenders were." Police had also recovered a trash
bag containing clothing in a "heavily overgrown"
area on the Hilo side of the Schweitzer property, he
said.

Charlene Iboshi ended her direct examination after Guillermo identified the defendant for the
record. Cliff Hunt then began a cross-examination
that would drag on for the rest of the week. He
asked Guillermo why police had removed parts of

the bicycle during their examination and not replaced them, why they had made plaster impressions of a set of tire tracks that were unrelated to the case, and yet had failed to take impressions of swerve marks that prosecutors were now trying to prove were made by a Volkswagen. Guillermo said he didn't know why the bicycle parts hadn't been replaced because the examination was carried out by the Honolulu Police Department's crime lab. He explained the failure to take impressions of the swerve marks by saying they were far enough away from the collision scene that police didn't initially believe they were connected to the case. During the cross examination, Guillermo remained calm and professional, with curt but polite replies, while Hunt's sarcastic tone implied police incompetence.

Guillermo testified that police had recovered the trash bag next to the Pauline home and sent its contents to the Honolulu crime lab, where technicians had tested the items but found no blood. Hunt asked Guillermo to describe the contents of the bag, which included soda cans, a small soiled tank top, and scraps of cut cloth material.

Hunt's line of questioning then turned to the subject of the bicycle—or, to be precise, two bicycles. The police had obtained an "exemplar" bicycle similar to Dana Ireland's to use in their attempt to reconstruct the collision. Amidst frequent objections from the prosecution, Hunt attempted to highlight differences between the two bicycles.

He then held up two car fenders that police had

recovered from the Schweitzer property the same day they seized Ian Schweitzer's then-yellow Volkswagen. Guillermo said police had seized the fenders because there was a "possibility" they were connected to the Volkswagen. He said the fenders had been inside the Volkswagen when Kenneth Baker inspected it.

He also testified that three technicians from the Honolulu Police Department's crime laboratory had been unable to link the Volkswagen to the crime. For one thing, Guillermo said, black material on the bumper of the Volkswagen didn't have the same origin as the black paint on Dana Ireland's bicycle. The Volkswagen had three layers of paint, including blue paint. Blue transfer material found on the bike's rear reflector was compared to the blue paint from the Volkswagen but didn't match. The Honolulu lab also took samples of grease from the car's undercarriage and compared it with grease found on Dana Ireland's legs. Results of that comparison were inconclusive. Police had sent a strand of hair found on a tire iron allegedly used in Dana Ireland's attack for testing, but it didn't match her hair, Guillermo said. Neither did hair found on a piece of rope in the trash bag recovered from near the Schweitzer property. Hunt systematically picked away at evidence police seized, showing there was no physical evidence linking the Volkswagen to Dana Ireland or to the crime scene.

Cliff Hunt spent all of the next day and some of

the following day grilling Guillermo. He kept reiterating the fact that for years, police suspected either a foreign pickup truck or a van and that police had changed their focus only after Pauline implicated himself and the Schweitzer brothers. "I would have to guess possibly twenty-five different names of suspects came in," Guillermo said. The majority of them owned pickup trucks or vans.

Hunt asked Guillermo about the many tips police received and how Guillermo and his colleagues followed up on them. It wasn't clear what Hunt was driving at. Was he implying that the police had no real suspects until 1994? Or was he suggesting that one of those suspects was actually responsible for the crime but that police preferred to believe Frank Pauline because it was the easy way out? Either way, Hunt was helping the public learn how extensively police had investigated the case.

Hunt asked Guillermo whether police and prosecutors had waited three years from the time Pauline came forward to the time of his indictment to "try to substantiate the information or corroborate his story with the physical evidence?"

"Or interview other possible witnesses, yes," Guillermo responded.

Hunt also questioned Guillermo about the pressure John Ireland had put on police, including a letter from his Virginia senator to a Hawaii senator asking the lawmaker to speak to Hawaii law enforcement authorities about the investigation.

"Isn't that somewhat extraordinary, in your experience in law enforcement, to have a victim's family do something like that?" Hunt asked.

"Yes, it is," Guillermo said.

Hunt also revealed that Virginia Senator John Warner had written to FBI Director William Sessions asking about the FBI's assistance to the Hawaii County Police Department.

Hunt began to prepare the jury for his own argument by questioning Guillermo about the hospital sheet Edward Blake had examined at the DNA lab. Guillermo explained that the prosecution and defense had agreed in late 1998 to send various pieces of evidence that had previously been examined by the FBI to an independent laboratory headed by Blake, as well as the hospital sheet that had been under Dana Ireland from the time she was loaded into the ambulance at Waa Waa until she was wheeled into the emergency room of Hilo Hospital.

During the third day of cross-examination, the jury had some rare moments of comic relief. The laughter came after Hunt told Judge Amano that the battery in his microphone had run down. "Reflects maybe I talk too much?" Hunt joked. The comment prompted a big laugh from the jury box.

All the same, Hunt continued questioning the detective. Frequently referring to Frank Pauline as "Frankie Boy," Hunt pointed out discrepancies his client had made in different accounts of his story to police when he told them he was with Ian and

Shawn Schweitzer during Ireland's attack. Hunt was apparently trying to bolster the defense theory that Pauline had fabricated his confession to obtain something in return.

In one version, Pauline had said that he first saw Ireland near the intersection of Highways 137 and 132, known as "Four Corners," but in a reconstruction tour with police, Pauline told police he first saw Ireland more than a mile and a half down Highway 137 where it intersects Kapoho Kai Drive. Furthermore, Pauline had told police that Schweitzer ran Ireland down at the Kapoho Kai Drive intersection, which was almost a third of a mile away from where police had found her bicycle.

Another version had Pauline's brother, John Gonsalves, telling police that Pauline had told him he and the Schweitzer brothers were riding in a pickup truck during the attack on Ireland. Pauline had told police the vehicle was the purple Volkswagen.

In a line of questioning that would prove pivotal, Hunt asked Guillermo if police had used a dummy or a person Dana Ireland's size to see if she would fit in the trunk of a Volkswagen.

"We did not," Guillermo said. "Probably because we did not have anyone or anything that could replicate her fractured pelvis. So I don't know what position she'd be able to be placed in."

"Just because of that you didn't want to try to get a dummy or ask one of your secretaries or someone, a small woman, to get in there?" Hunt asked. "She could crawl into a ball or something or something smaller and see if maybe she would fit in there. You guys never even tried that, did you?"

"We did not try that," Guillermo said in the same calm, flat, convincing tone he'd used during direct examination.

Between questions, Hunt paced, his hands clasped behind his back and his head down. "You don't even know if a person Dana Ireland's size would fit in there, do you?"

"No," Guillermo said.

Hunt questioned Guillermo about his testimony earlier in the week quoting Pauline as saying that Ian Schweitzer had raped Dana Ireland and then Pauline had gotten a tire iron from the rear of the Volkswagen.

"You don't even know if this tire iron had anything to do with the assault on Dana Ireland, do you, sir?" Hunt asked, referring to the tire iron in evidence.

"We do not know," Guillermo said.

Guillermo's cross-examination was interrupted so attorneys could question FBI special agents who flew to Hilo from Washington, D.C.

Special Agent Joseph Dizinno testified for the defense that he did DNA testing on hairs found on Ireland's socks and underwear, the Jimmy'Z T-shirt, and the Volkswagen's trunk carpet. He said he had compared the DNA from the hairs to samples from the Schweitzer brothers, Frank Pauline, and Louise

Ireland. He said all were different from each other and none came from either Dana Ireland or the three defendants. Dizinno said the lack of hair transfers from the defendants didn't necessarily mean the men didn't come into contact with Dana Ireland; it just meant no hairs from them transferred to her body. Dizinno also compared hairs recovered from the scene to samples of hair from Herb Johnson and Ray Harrison, using conventional microscopic analysis, and found no matches to them, either.

Another FBI witness, Special Agent Richard Buechele, testified on behalf of the prosecution. Buechele said he examined "a thin white material" found on Dana Ireland's bike to see if it came from a vehicle. Buechele was able to determine that the material contained chemicals used in paint, but he didn't have a large enough sample to determine if it really was paint. Buechele also tested a blue substance found on the reflector of the bike but concluded that it wasn't paint. Prosecutors elicited the testimony to counter a defense suggestion that the substances on the bicycle came from a vehicle other than Ian Schweitzer's Volkswagen.

After the FBI agents left late that afternoon, Guillermo resumed the witness stand for the last time. "We're going to try to wrap it up today," Hunt told him. "The jury's already indicated I talk too much." The jurors, who were looking forward to another three-day weekend, smiled. Guillermo masked a sigh of relief. Despite his formidable performance, all these days on the witness stand had his stomach in knots.

Week four was over, but that didn't mean the prosecutors could relax over the weekend. This trial was taking its toll on Lincoln Ashida's routine. He had to forego his daily lunchtime basketball game. Instead, he lifted weights at home and ran in his neighborhood. During the trial he barely ate during the day. He lived on diet cola and a stomach relaxant. He'd try to eat when he got home, but it wasn't enough, and he was having trouble sleeping. Since the start of the trial, Ashida's weight had dropped from 165 pounds to 135 pounds.

On Saturday, Charlene Iboshi and Lincoln Ashida were working in the dilapidated prosecutor's office, situated immediately downstream from Rainbow Falls, a favorite tourist destination.

"Do you want to close?" Iboshi asked. Other people had already hinted that the case needed Lincoln to provide a strong finish. Although the closing argument was still more than a week away, this was the first time Charlene had broached the subject.

"Well, Charlene," Lincoln said cautiously, "what do you think? I can if you like."

"Lincoln, you've got the fire. You've got the energy," she said. "You do it."

On Monday, August 16, 1999, Lincoln Ashida was already seated when the jail guards brought Pauline into the courtroom. As Pauline walked behind the prosecutors, he squeezed Ashida's neck. "Morning, Ashida," Pauline said.

"Morning, Frank," Ashida replied, without missing a beat. Charlene Iboshi was appalled, but for Ashida, these things were never personal. Despite the adversarial nature of a trial, he could be friendly with opposing counsel and even with the defendant. Pauline apparently felt the same way.

When the trial resumed, Ashida played audiotapes of 1994 interviews by two television reporters, Jerry Drelling for KGMB and Nalani Blaisdell for KHON. Although it was difficult to make out the words on the KGMB tape because of audio distortion, Pauline's voice came through loud and clear on the KHON tape.

"My friends Ian and Shawn came down to pick me up. They wanted to go party down the beach, so I jump in with them and then headed down, went down to Pohoiki side," Pauline said on the tape. The three were smoking crack cocaine. "We came like towards an intersection area and there was one girl, she was like stand up and like walking the bike across, and then we passed."

"And then as we were going past like that, the driver, Ian, just stopped and he started to turn around and head back. And I kept telling him, 'Where you going,' and he told me, 'Oh, just shut up. Shut up,'" Pauline said on the tape.

Ian Schweitzer sped up and headed right for the girl, Pauline said. "Then I was trying for make him stop, and he wouldn't stop. I wen' for grab like the steering wheel, but he banged the girl. And then after he banged her, he ran her over several times, and then we stopped.

"Ian and his brother jumped out of the car, grabbed the body, and they tried stuffing her or something in the front. They got her in, and then they closed the car hood and then we left," Pauline said. They drove away on a back road. Pauline told them they were crazy. "I was trying to tell them to let me out and stuff. They wouldn't let me out."

They came to a side road with junk cars and "a big sand hill," and the brothers took the body out of the trunk, Pauline said. "When they pulled it out, I was trying for jump out. I wanted to dig out. They nevah like let me leave. They started having sex with the girl, and the guy Ian was biting her all over. It was a trip. She was half dead. I don't think she even felt it," Pauline said. He said he didn't see if Shawn Schweitzer had sex with her.

"After that, they wouldn't let me leave. It was either I stay in the car and live or I jump out of the car and die, so I just stood in the car." The car drove away and then "somewhere along the line they got rid of the body. And then we went to the brothers' house. The front part of Ian's Bug was like smashed and stuff and had blood like all over and he nevah like nobody know, so he started to wash it and stuff and then he opened the trunk part to shoot it down—blood inside and stuff like that," Pauline said on the tape.

"They went, they showered, threw their clothes in a bag, and threw it into the bushes there across from their house. And then after that all Ian told me was, 'No say nothing,' 'cause if I say anything he going come look for me, going make sure I'm not living."

In the interview, Pauline told the TV reporter that he had waited so long to report what he knew to police because he was afraid of the Schweitzer brothers. Pauline eventually went to the police, however, because he couldn't sleep.

"I had bad dreams of the girl coming to me, telling me help her so she can rest and stuff like that. I kept getting bad dreams. I could see her like laying on top of the ground . . . I just couldn't handle it anymore. If there was a way I could give my life to bring that girl's life back, I would," Pauline said on the tape. "Sometimes I get up in the middle of the night crying 'cause it hurts. It hurts a lot."

After playing the tape, the prosecution rested its case.

Chapter 20

Cliff Hunt began presenting the defense case by questioning the attorney who had represented Frank Pauline's brother, John Gonsalves, in a drug case at about the time Pauline went to police with his story in 1994. Cliff quizzed Joy Hutson about a plea bargain she had negotiated for Gonsalves in exchange for his cooperation with authorities in the Pauline case. Hunt established that prosecutors had originally charged Gonsalves with conspiracy to promote a dangerous drug, a class B felony punishable by up to 10 years in prison. After helping police in the Ireland investigation, Gonsalves pleaded no contest to third-degree conspiracy, served no jail time, and won the right to have the conviction wiped from his record.

Hunt grilled Hutson about letters exchanged between her and prosecutor Charlene Iboshi showing the progress of negotiations for the plea agreement. Hutson, who a week earlier had tried to quash the subpoena requiring her to testify, maintained that in negotiating the plea agreement she was just doing what was best for Gonsalves. "My job is to get the best deal for my client."

Hunt then began questioning one of his key witnesses, DNA expert Edward Blake. He was a professional-looking man with graying short hair, a matching mustache, and large rimless glasses. Blake said he had been the first person to testify about the PCR method of DNA in a court trial. He had since testified about the process "well over 100 times." He'd already collected $20,000 for his work on the Pauline case and would earn $1,200 a day while in Hilo.

Blake stated that he had been hired by the defense to review evidence in the case and locate portions of that evidence for DNA analysis, but that he hadn't been authorized to do the actual testing. "I inquired as to whether or not a sheet is normally covering a gurney—whether or not that sheet had been retained by anybody, and as it turned out, that sheet had been retained but not examined by any professional forensic scientists." He said he had looked at the sheet and found several stains. "Small pieces of fabric were cut out and—lo and behold— when that fabric was examined, there was a fairly large amount of spermatozoa that was tested." He explained the significance of the find, six years after Dana Ireland's attack: "From the perspective of a forensic scientist, a spermatozoa is nothing more than a little bag of DNA with a tail on it."

Blake said he examined a vaginal swabbing that

the FBI had used for its own tests, but "the actual swab portion of the swab was virtually gone because of the testing." All that was left were about 150 sperm, Blake said, explaining that one drop of semen contains 2.5 million to 5 million sperm. "That's why your mother tells you to be careful," Blake said. Several jurors snickered.

Blake obtained two more vaginal swabs and took the evidence to Lisa Calandro, a DNA analyst agreed upon by both the prosecution and the defense as an independent expert. When it was Calandro's turn to testify, she said she had tested the sperm cells from the swabs and the sheet and found that they were "consistent with the sperm originating from the same individual."

Calandro compared the DNA to samples provided by Pauline, the Schweitzer brothers, and 13 other people—including early suspects in the case—and Mark Evans, the man Ireland had visited before she was killed. All were excluded as donors of the sperm, Calandro said.

Under questioning by defense attorney Cliff Hunt, Calandro showed the jury a blowup of a document listing the "genetic profile" of the person who had deposited the sperm.

"But it ain't Frank Pauline?" Hunt asked.

"That's correct."

"Nor is it Ian Schweitzer? Nor is it Shawn Schweitzer?" Hunt asked.

"That's correct."

"Was there any indication that there was more

than one person as the source of the sperm that was found on the sheets or the swab?" Hunt asked.

"No," Calandro said.

Under cross-examination by Lincoln Ashida, Calandro said she wouldn't expect to find sperm if the person did not ejaculate. She also said it was possible for a "minor contributor" to leave such a small quantity of sperm that it would not be detected.

"It's possible that a minor contributor could exist," Calandro testified. "I did not detect any minor contributor." Calandro said she had found no semen on Ireland's panties, prompting a question by Cliff Hunt as to whether semen would leak onto underpants if a person had intercourse before riding a bicycle.

Ashida objected to the question, arguing outside the presence of the jury that it was improper because Calandro had not put such an opinion in her written report as required by the judge.

Hunt argued that the point was important because he expected that during closing arguments the prosecution would argue either that Ireland had consensual sex or that the sperm was left by an "unindicted co-ejaculator." The prosecution would have to explain why the DNA signature of the sperm found on the vaginal swabs and hospital sheet didn't match the DNA signatures of any of the defendants.

Amano nevertheless sustained Ashida's objection and disallowed Calandro's response to the question. Ashida didn't ask Calandro many more questions. He knew it was futile to try to wear down any of the defense's expert witnesses; it was better to just get them off the stand as quickly as possible.

Later in the day, James Campbell, the Pahoa engineer who had prepared the computer simulation that had been disallowed, testified that he had been hired by the defense for his opinion as to whether Ian Schweitzer's Volkswagen could have been involved in the collision with Ireland's bike.

"No. It's my opinion it was not involved in an accident with Miss Ireland," Campbell said. "There is no damage on the Volkswagen that matches anything on the bicycle."

Campbell testified that he would expect damage to the windshield of the Volkswagen if it had hit a person riding a bike. "We always find at twenty miles per hour or greater that the bicyclist goes through the windshield."

Campbell, who operated an accident reconstruction business, testified that the damage to Ireland's bicycle probably came from a small imported pickup truck with pipe bumpers. Under cross-examination, Lincoln Ashida established that Campbell had arrived at his opinion after reviewing only a few select pieces of evidence provided by the defense, including photographs, a police diagram of the accident scene, the bicycle, and Ian Schweitzer's Volkswagen.

Chapter 21

"The defense calls Frank Pauline Jr."

The courtroom was packed as Pauline made his way to the witness stand, wearing a pale blue shirt, brown slacks, and a tie with brown diagonal stripes. He had a tattoo the size of a quarter on the left side of his neck.

Hunt asked his client a few preliminary questions. Pauline testified that he was the second youngest in a family of seven children and had been raised "in the island of Hilo." He told the jury that he had attended Pahoa Elementary School and Pahoa High School but didn't graduate.

"Frank, did you murder or rape Dana Ireland?" Cliff Hunt asked.

"No, I didn't." Pauline's expression was one of defiance. His hands were clasped in front of him, his fingers intertwined.

"Tell the jury what happened that made you want to talk to the police like you knew something about Dana Ireland's murder," Hunt said.

Pauline said he was a heavy user of crack cocaine. "I think I started when I was fifteen," he said, adding that his family dealt drugs. "I'd steal for it. I'd take it by force if I had to."

When Pauline was sent to Halawa Correctional Facility on Oahu in February 1994 for the sexual assault of the passenger in a car he was driving, he first went into the Reception, Assessment, and Diagnostic Unit, where prison officials observe how new inmates interact with each other to "see if you're a menace to society," he said. After a month he was transferred to a medium-security module where he was able to obtain crack cocaine within two days.

"How can you get drugs in prison?" Hunt asked

"You can get drugs in any facility you like, long as you got money," he said. "Money talks." Pauline looked at the jury, testifying like an expert witness. He told them he obtained the drugs through a system called "fronting," whereby a user gets drugs but isn't required to pay until later. When it came time for him to pay, Pauline said, he had no money and the people to whom he owed money began to threaten his life. "The main thing at that point was for me to get my ass out of there before I get killed." He called his older brother, John Gonsalves, for help.

"How come you called John?" Hunt asked.

"He's the money man of the family," Pauline said.

"Why is that?"

"Selling dope," Pauline said. "John was known as the godfather with all the dope."

"When you say 'godfather,' what do you mean?"

"Supplies the whole Hilo and Puna districts."

"With what kind of drug?"

"Cocaine."

"So when John was up on the stand a couple weeks ago and he said he had nothing to do with it, was he lying?

"He was lying."

"Did you ever see your brother with big amounts of money?"

"Lots of times," Pauline said. "I even helped him count it."

"How much money?"

"In the thousands."

Around the time Pauline was having trouble paying for his drugs in prison, he said, his brother was having troubles of his own. Two men who allegedly brought in drugs from the mainland got arrested with about seven pounds of cocaine. Police linked them to Gonsalves and eventually charged him with conspiracy to promote a dangerous drug. "He told me he might be looking at time, stuff like that, prison," Pauline said. "He didn't want to pull no twenty years."

Gonsalves suggested that Pauline call a friend named Fred Perreira, whom Pauline identified as a psychic. When he did, Perreira asked Pauline if he knew anything about the Ireland case. Pauline testified that he had told Perreira that everything he knew was from rumors and information in the news media. "And then he asked me if I was involved in any way. I told him, 'You one psychic, you don't know I'm not involved?' "

Perreira thought about it for a moment and then said Pauline wasn't involved but that Pauline's brother, Wayne Gonsalves, and the Schweitzer brothers might be.

"I told him, 'You know what? I remember something about their Bug being smashed,' " Pauline said, and then it occurred to him: "I can make up one story . . . make a story up to help my brother, help myself before I end up getting killed."

According to Pauline, John Gonsalves told Pauline that if he went to police with his story, he could help himself at the same time he helped his brother avoid prison. "John said I got to say something or maybe he won't be there to help me," Pauline testified. John suggested Pauline call Detective Guillermo.

Pauline did call Guillermo, he said, but didn't want to talk to him on the phone because other inmates might hear his end of the conversation. He knew how they'd feel about him if they thought he was involved in the Ireland case. "Any sick pig that would kill one girl . . . they deserve to die."

Pauline testified that he later met Guillermo at the state attorney general's office and made up a story but told Guillermo he didn't remember the details because he had been high on crack cocaine. "The truth is, I couldn't remember 'cause I wasn't there. My story wasn't all put together, put it that way," he said. "I only knew bits and pieces from the news, from what I seen on TV, and from what people tell me."

Pauline wrapped up his testimony for the day with somewhat of an alibi for his whereabouts on Christmas Eve 1991. "Me and my brother Joe was up at his house—if I remember correctly," Pauline said.

The conclusion of Pauline's testimony would have to wait over a four-day weekend. That night, Cliff Hunt and Lincoln Ashida left on separate flights for Michigan to take video testimony of Dr. Werner Spitz, Macomb County's medical examiner, who had been called by the defense. Spitz is the author of a textbook considered a worldwide standard in the field of forensic pathology. A week earlier, at Ashida's request, Judge Amano had approved questions for Spitz prepared in advance by the prosecution and defense.

In a motion Hunt filed requesting funds to finance the trip to Michigan, Hunt indicated that he expected Spitz to bolster the defense theory that Pauline made up the stories he told police in 1994. "Dr. Spitz's testimony is exculpatory for the defendant because it will establish that Pauline's alleged admission that he struck Dana Ireland with a tire iron was false or fabricated," Hunt wrote.

The trial delay would give the jury four days to ponder Pauline's version of events. Privately, even skeptics were impressed by how Pauline had performed so far. Would it be enough to create a reasonable doubt?

Ashida wasn't happy about the trip. The Hawaii County Police Department had approached Spitz originally, but when Hunt had concluded that Dana Ireland's head wound wasn't caused by a tire iron, he latched onto Spitz as his own witness. Spitz was a busy man, however, and was unable or unwilling to leave Michigan to testify in Hilo. Hunt persuaded Judge Amano to let the attorneys fly to the mainland to take Spitz's deposition on video—a very rare practice in a criminal case.

When Ashida complained about it to Martha Rodillas, a secretary in the prosecutor's office who had married Detective Rodillas two months earlier, she told him it was a good omen. "You graduated college in Michigan," she said. "This is a sign. It's taking you back to where your law career started."

"Yeah, you're right," Ashida said, grasping at straws.

Ashida stayed in Ann Arbor, where he'd attended the University of Michigan 15 years earlier. He was discouraged by Frank Pauline's performance on the witness stand. "Not only was he planting seeds of reasonable doubt," Ashida said later, "but they were sprouting." In Ann Arbor, Ashida ate at all his old hangouts. He even made a special trip to the university campus and peered into the classroom where he'd studied American government. It gave him emotional strength.

The day of the deposition, Ashida arrived at Spitz's office wearing gray slacks and a blue blazer. While he waited for Spitz, the staff was lukewarm

at best. One member let it slip that Hunt and Spitz
were sitting in on an autopsy together; Ashida
would be odd man out.

When Ashida entered the conference room for
the deposition, he spotted a projector and screen.
Since Spitz was a defense witness, Hunt asked his
questions first. After he finished, Ashida noted that
the equipment hadn't been used yet. He realized it
was there for the answers to his own questions,
which Spitz had received in advance. He realized
they were setting a trap. Thinking on his feet,
Ashida asked Spitz one innocuous question from
the list and listened politely to the answer. "No further questions," he said.

"You can't do that," Hunt said.

"I just did," Ashida said.

Hunt insisted on placing a conference call to
Judge Amano, who answered her cell phone on the
golf course. "He outsmarted me," Hunt said. Both
lawyers made their arguments, but by the time they
hung up the phone, Hunt was the winner. Ashida
had to ask his prepared questions, and Spitz put on
his slide show.

Afterward, Spitz took Ashida and Hunt on a tour
of his "Hall of Shame" in the back room, where
glass cases displayed mummified body parts and
various foreign objects he'd removed from corpses
during his career. Spitz eagerly opened the cases
and fingered the hands, heads, feet, and internal or-
gans for his astonished guests. When the tour was
over, Ashida made a beeline for the MGM Grand

Detroit Casino, where he won a few dollars playing blackjack before heading back to Ann Arbor.

Monday, Pauline was back on the witness stand. He portrayed himself as a liar, a drug abuser, and a fighter, who had made up the story because he loved his brother.

Under questioning by his attorney, Pauline said he had placed himself at the scene of Ireland's attack because he was already in prison and knew that his brother, John Gonsalves, wouldn't be able to handle prison.

"I figured I could at least do that for my brother after all the stuff he done for me," Pauline said. "Love is powerful, Cliff. That's all I can say. Love is powerful, man."

Was this jury expected to believe that the same man who thought nothing of selling his girlfriend's engagement ring to buy crack cocaine would sacrifice himself for brotherly love?

Pauline testified about his phone call to Detective Guillermo and said he had asked Guillermo to work out a deal in exchange for information about the Ireland case. He told the jury about his meeting with Guillermo at the attorney general's office and the reconstruction tour. During the reconstruction, Pauline said, he took his cue from police when they repeatedly stopped at various locations and asked him if he remembered anything. "At first I was scared," Pauline said. He thought police would know that he was making up the story. But he had watched their facial expressions to determine what they wanted to hear. Pauline said he had told police he first saw Dana Ireland at the intersection of Highway 132 and Highway 137, " 'cause that's the pictures they were showing on TV."

Pauline said Guillermo had promised that after the reconstruction tour he could see his family at the police holding cell, but "I had to pull some stunts for get my visits." In the cell, Pauline tied a sweater around his neck and jumped when a guard came by to check on him. "I wasn't going to kill myself. I was playing one game," he said.

Police arranged for the visit with his family that night, Pauline said. After Pauline went back to Halawa Correctional Facility on Oahu, he was placed in protective custody. "I was considered one rat 'cause I was talking," Pauline said. "I felt like my pride was being hurt being put into a place like that." Guillermo arranged to get Pauline transferred to Maui Community Correctional Center, Pauline said, where "every day I was fighting—getting thrown into the hole." He called Guillermo and told him "more lies" in exchange for a letter to the warden asking to take him out of solitary confinement. While Pauline was at the Maui jail, he went to the news media because he didn't think authorities believed his story.

"Everybody considered me a liar because I am a liar," Pauline said. Pauline spoke to his brother's attorney, Joy Hutson, who told him she had made a deal for John Gonsalves. "I wen' shut up already.

My job was done," he testified. Pauline said officials transferred him back to Halawa Prison after he stopped talking to police, because he kept getting into fights at the Maui jail. At Halawa, three guards and a sergeant beat him, he said. He tried to get help from Guillermo when he was beaten up again. "I got beaten up, and stuff happened I no like talk about," Pauline said, adding that he had tried to hang himself in his cell, implying that this time it wasn't a stunt.

While Pauline was testifying about his encounters with Detective Guillermo, Steve and Trudy Guillermo were down the hall in Judge Greg Nakamura's courtroom adopting Alika. The weekend after their meeting in the park, the boy had paid a trial visit to the Guillermos' home, and he'd called Steve "Dad." The rest was just a formality.

Back in Judge Amano's courtroom, Hunt asked Pauline to explain the prior testimony claiming he'd enjoyed watching the rape.

"I told 'em something like this. I told 'em if I had one girl like that, I said, 'Would you be able for have sex with 'em?' I wouldn't be able to fuck something like that. It's sick. That's what I told 'em. They turned my words around, these people."

"Do you know anything about anybody who might have been involved in the murder and rape of Dana Ireland?" Hunt asked.

Pauline shook his head, his arms folded across his chest. "You hear so much stories, Cliff, you know. I get people who I can assume was . . . and I think my assumption is pretty good. But I could be wrong, too, eh?"

"You weren't there?"

"No."

"So you don't know for a fact?"

"No."

"You just heard stories."

Under cross-examination, Lincoln Ashida began to ask Pauline whether this was the first time he'd told this particular version of his story.

"So you calling me one liar, right?" Pauline asked before Ashida completed his question. Ashida immediately dropped his Mr. Nice Guy approach. This mutual hostility would characterize the rest of the cross-examination.

Pauline acknowledged that he had told his ex-girlfriend's grandmother, Louise Furtado, that he had been present during Ireland's attack but said he had been just testing her "for see if she would believe my story." Pauline denied that he was close to Furtado and said that, although he had once asked Judge Amano to let him out of jail so he could attend the funeral of Furtado's husband, he had really asked to be released "so I could do dope." As for Furtado's testimony earlier in the trial that Pauline had told her Dana Ireland had been punched, kicked, and hit with a rock, "she lied under oath." Prosecutor Lincoln Ashida asked Pauline how he knew that Ireland had been bitten since that information had not been in the news before Pauline's alleged confession.

"Guillermo brought it up," Pauline said. "He asked me if I bit her."

Ashida wanted to get Pauline off the stand as quickly as possible. He ended his cross-examination by asking Pauline about the motive for his testimony. "Isn't it true, the bottom line is you need this jury to believe that you're just a liar so they won't know that you're a murderer?" Ashida asked.

"I don't care if anybody believes me," Pauline said. "The main thing is I speaking the truth. That's all I care about."

After Pauline stepped down, the defense ended its case with the videotaped testimony of Dr. Werner Spitz, the forensic pathologist whom police had consulted early in the case. "My opinion is that Dana Ireland was not struck on the head by a tire iron," said Spitz, who had previously testified in such diverse inquiries as a U.S. House of Representatives assassination committee investigating the death of President John F. Kennedy and the Hilo murder trial of former police sergeant Ken Mathison. Spitz said he believed that Ireland had been hit in the back of the right hip by a "blunt flat area" and then thrown from the bicycle and run over. The undercarriage of a motor vehicle "is not a very friendly environment," he said.

Marks on Ireland's right hip, which a prosecution expert had identified as fingernail scratches, were likely caused by a rivet and seams on the inside of Ireland's shorts, Spitz said. "When I received these pictures of the shorts, the rivet jumped out at me because the injuries match it."

Also on this final day of testimony, the jurors—accompanied by the judge and a law clerk—spent 15 minutes inspecting the yellow Volkswagen that police had seized from Ian Schweitzer's backyard. The judge let reporters look at the car earlier, while the jury was on its lunch break. A picture of it would appear on the front page of the next day's *Tribune-Herald*.

Chapter 22

Tuesday morning, Mauna Kea glowed red as the sun's rays illuminated it from just above Hilo Bay. The lush lower third of the mountain was separated from its barren brown peak by a lei of clouds. Tiny white dots at the summit marked the observatories that housed some of the most sophisticated telescopes in the world. Lifelong residents and newcomers alike gazed at the spectacular sight.

Lincoln Ashida was primed for his closing argument to the jury. Wearing the "lucky" blue suit he'd bought in Washington, D.C., he walked into court feeling as prepared as possible. Then he got word that Cliff Hunt was asking for another mistrial. He glanced down at his yellow note with the word, "INTEGRITY."

"Charlene, you need to deal with this," he told Iboshi. "I have to stay focused."

"All rise."

When Judge Amano walked in, the jury was absent from the courtroom. It was clear to spectators that the judge was upset about something. Amano didn't like eleventh-hour surprises, especially surprises that kept jurors waiting.

Hunt complained to the judge that on the previous day—when the jury had viewed the Volkswagen—its gas tank had been missing from the trunk, thereby giving the jury the impression that the trunk was larger than it actually was.

James Campbell, the defense witness whose computer simulation had earlier been excluded from the trial, had noticed the missing gas tank when he had seen a photo of the Volkswagen in the newspaper, Hunt said. The gas tank had been in place during the five times Campbell had viewed the car at the Hilo Police Station.

"What's going on is a deliberate attempt by the prosecutors to misrepresent the evidence in this case," he said. "It shows they're desperate. It denies my client a fair trial."

Under questioning by Judge Amano, Charlene Iboshi said that Detective Steve Guillermo and the prosecution investigator, Billy Perreira, had made the decision to show the car to the jury in that condition because that was its condition when police recovered it.

"Were any prosecutors involved?" Amano asked.

"Judge, I was involved in terms that they asked if they could put the Volkswagen in the condition as it was," Iboshi said.

"As it was, meaning when?" Amano asked.

"As it was recovered," Iboshi said.

"Meaning the gas tank out of the front of the car?" Amano asked.

"That's correct."

"So, I'm going to take your representation as an officer of the court. May I do that?" Amano asked.

"Yes."

Amano told the attorneys that the jury would get a second viewing with the gas tank in the front of the car. She also said that Hunt could examine witnesses to explore his implication that the state made a deliberate attempt to mislead the jury. She added, however, that he wouldn't be able to argue that point to the jury unless the testimony provided a "good faith basis" for it. Hunt asked the judge to reopen the case and take the testimony in the presence of the jury.

"Your request is denied," Amano said.

Hunt called Billy Perreira as a witness. "Was there a discussion yesterday or any time before yesterday about whether or not the jury should see the vehicle with the gas tank inside the trunk compartment or removed from the trunk compartment?" Hunt asked.

"Yes, there was," Perreira said.

"When was that subject first discussed?"

"At the time that we were setting up the Volkswagen for the viewing yesterday."

"That was the very first time?"

"Yes."

"And who were the people that were discussing this question?"

"Myself, Charlene Iboshi, Steve Guillermo."

"And who raised the question of whether or not the gas tank should be in the trunk compartment or not?"

"I did."

"And what did you say?"

"I asked, 'Do we display this Volkswagen the way it was found at the Schweitzer residence or do we display it with the tank in as it came from the police evidence room?' "

"Who did you ask?"

"I asked Charlene Iboshi."

"What was Ms. Iboshi's response?"

"We asked Detective Guillermo to confirm the condition of the Volkswagen as it was found. And he said that it was found with the tank out and we decided that we'd show the jury the Volkswagen in the same condition as it was when it was recovered."

"And you were aware, were you not, sir, that one of the issues in this case was whether or not Dana Ireland would fit in the trunk compartment?"

"Yes."

"And you're also aware, sir, that a Volkswagen can't run without gas, correct?"

"Yes.' "

"And if it was to happen the way it's alleged to happen, according to Frank Pauline, the gas tank would have had to have been in place when Dana Ireland was placed inside the trunk, correct?" Hunt asked.

"A gas tank would have been in place."

"Well, the gas tank that was recovered with the vehicle, that gas tank fit the trunk compartment, did it not, sir?"

"Yes, it did."

"And isn't it true that at the five viewings at the police department that James Campbell did, that the gas tank was placed in the trunk compartment of the Volkswagen at each and every one of those viewings?"

"The tank was already in at the viewing, yes."

"In your opinion as an investigator on this case, would removing the gas tank on the trunk fairly and accurately depict the trunk compartment at the time Dana Ireland was allegedly placed inside the trunk compartment?"

"In my opinion, I don't know what kind of tank or which tank was in there at the time of this offense."

"Isn't it true, sir, that there is not any reference in any of the 2,800 pages of police reports in this case concerning the possibility or even the suggestion that a gas tank other than a stock gas tank, like the one that was recovered with this vehicle, was in the trunk compartment of this car when Dana Ireland was placed inside."

"Well, the fact that the tank was not in place—"

"Sir," Judge Amano interrupted, "did you hear the question?"

"Yes."

"Did you understand it?"

"Yes."

"Answer it—yes or no."

"Yes, there is."

"There is a suggestion that there was a non-stock gas tank?" Hunt asked.

"Yes."

"Please tell us about it," Hunt said sarcastically.

"The fact that the gas tank was not found in place and was found within the passenger compartment suggests that there's the possibility some other tank could have been in place when this Bug was running," Perreira said.

"Is that the only basis for your answer to the preceding answer, 'Yes'?"

"Yes."

"Mr. Perreira," Judge Amano asked, "the decision to remove the tank from the vehicle yesterday, was that made deliberately to make the trunk of the vehicle look bigger than it is supposed to look?"

"No," Perreira said. "It was made to show how the Bug was recovered."

"Any other questions, Mr. Hunt?" Amano asked, impatience apparent in her tone and expression.

"Well, what was your understanding of your purpose of the viewing of the thing?" Hunt asked Perreira. "To show how the Bug was recovered or perhaps to see whether this was the Bug that was allegedly involved in this murder and rape of Dana Ireland?"

"To show that this is the Bug that is involved."

"Well, then wouldn't it more accurately depict to the jury how the Bug would have looked at the time it was involved in the rape and murder of Dana Ireland to show, for instance, the gas tank in the front of the vehicle, sir?"

"If it was that gas tank that was used," Billy said.

"No further questions, Your Honor."

"Counsel will approach," Amano said.

After the bench conference, Hunt asked to call Detective Guillermo to the witness stand. "There's no reason I should take Mr. Perreira's self-serving answers. . . . I should be able to call Detective Guillermo and examine him," Hunt said. "What's going on is a deliberate attempt by the prosecution to misrepresent—the whole purpose of viewing the Volkswagen was to give the jury an opportunity to look at it, look for damages, size it up, consider whether or not a person could fit in the trunk. This is a deliberate tactical game by the prosecution. It shows their desperation. And, essentially, without being able to bring this to the attention of the jury, it denies my client a fair trial and a fair chance to challenge the evidence against him in this case."

Charlene Iboshi disagreed. "This was not a deliberate attempt to mislead the jury or the court," she said. "It was to put the condition of the Volkswagen as recovered for the jury. The photographs we stipulated into evidence earlier have the gas tank in there, Judge. It's clear that the tank was taken in and out during that process of the recovery and checking. The state's position, Judge, is we're going to have the Volkswagen available. We'll have another viewing as requested. We have the photographs in evidence, Judge."

Judge Amano announced her findings: "There is no evidence that there was a deliberate attempt by the prosecution to present the viewing of the Volkswagen in such a way that it would effectively make the trunk look larger," she said. "Yesterday there was a discussion about how the presentation should be made. The decision was to present it as found and I don't find that necessarily to be a decision that's made in bad faith." The judge said the jury would view the car again with the gas tank in place. "Insofar as you request to place this information before the jury," she told Hunt, "the court finds that it's not relevant and will reject that request as well."

She also told Hunt there was no need to call Guillermo as a witness. "Ms. Iboshi made an initial representation to the court of what decision was made, why it was made, and who made the decision. Mr. Perreira then came to the stand—he didn't hear that representation—corroborated exactly what she said. I don't feel the need to go forward any more."

"Your honor," Hunt said, "then the record should reflect this. Number one, I don't have to take the representation of a prosecutor on this kind of an issue. Number two, I called her office at nine o'clock this morning and spoke to Ms. Iboshi. And I gave her a heads-up. And, frankly, when I hung up I said, 'You've got one hour to make up your story on how to handle this thing.' And I'm sure that's exactly what they did, Your Honor. So for you to say that they didn't talk about it and he backed her up, it's because they conversed about it before they came to this courthouse."

"How do you know that?" Amano asked.

"Well, one thing that makes me believe it is that when we were in your chambers and you asked about who was here, she said, 'William Perreira's here.' She knew he was here. More than likely she had contact with him. She said that in your chambers."

"Okay," Amano said. "Ms. Iboshi, your response?"

"Judge, I did talk to Mr. Hunt. He asked me to get the witnesses here. I said, 'Okay, I'll have the witnesses here.' We said perhaps we can get the viewing done so I tried to make those arrangements from the time he made the call. So we've been trying to do all those things that were requested by counsel to accommodate the court."

"He is suggesting that there was some collaboration between yourself and Mr. Perreira about the explanation," Amano said.

"Judge, I did let Mr. Perreira know we would be talking about this area because it would be a basis for a mistrial. So I did tell him that we would be discussing this area, just so that he'd be aware of what was going to happen, Judge."

Amano sighed. "Okay. Is Guillermo outside?"

The detective came in and took the stand. This time the judge was the one who asked the questions. "Detective Guillermo, yesterday there was a viewing of a Volkswagen in the basement of this building. You were part of the preparation and setup of that, is that right?"

"I was aware of it," Guillermo said. "I didn't assist in setting it up."

"All right," Amano said. "And yesterday when we viewed the Volkswagen, the gas tank was outside of the trunk area. Are you aware of that?"

"Yes."

"And can you tell us whether or not you had any part in deciding whether or not the gas tank should be inside or out of the trunk?"

"When I was asked how the recovery was done, I explained to Ms. Iboshi and Mr. Perreira that the gas tank itself was within the passenger compartment area of the Volkswagen," Guillermo said.

"Did you discuss it with anyone else?"

"Just Mr. Perreira."

"And were you part of the decision to keep it outside of the car?"

"Yes."

"And why was that decision made?"

"That's how it was recovered and whether or not it was actually used at the time that the Volkswagen was running, we didn't know. So it was just recovered in that manner."

"Did you discuss with Ms. Iboshi or with Mr. Perreira the matters that we are talking about right now?"

"I received a call from Ms. Iboshi this morning requesting that I come here regarding the gas tank, how it was placed outside of the Volkswagen yesterday."

"Any further discussion with her?"

"No."

"Mr. Hunt?"

"What did you talk about with Ms. Iboshi this morning?" Hunt asked.

"She called me and indicated that she wanted me to appear at court as there was a motion being filed regarding the placement of the gas tank during yesterday's viewing."

"Did you discuss with her or did she discuss with you the discussion that was had yesterday about whether to place the gas tank in the trunk compartment or not?"

"What was brought up—"

"Yes or no, sir," Hunt said. "Did you discuss it? Yes or no."

"Not totally in that manner."

"Well, what did you discuss, then?"

"I explained to her how the recovery of the vehicle was made, including the gas tank."

"On the phone this morning?"

"Yes."

"Well, didn't you talk about it with her yesterday?"

"Yes, I did."

"Well, why did you have to talk to her about it again?"

"She asked about it. She inquired and I explained to her how the recovery was done."

"Well, she was, according to the testimony of William Perreira ten to fifteen minutes ago, she was a party to the discussion about how it was recovered yesterday. Was she party to that discussion?"

"Yes, she was."

"Then, why did you have to talk to her about it again this morning?"

"She asked."

"But didn't you discuss that with her yesterday?"

"Yes, I did."

"So she asked you that again?"

"Yes, she did."

"And what time did you get this call from her this morning?"

"Around nine o'clock."

"And did you discuss this matter with William Perreira this morning?"

"Briefly, outside of the courtroom. He just asked me or mentioned that there was a motion being filed regarding the viewing of the vehicle and the gas tank."

"And did you discuss with him the same things you discussed with Ms. Iboshi this morning?"

"I explained the same thing to him again."

"Well, why did you have to explain it to him if yesterday you, he, and she talked about it?"

"Because they asked."

"So he asked you this morning to tell him the basis for the decision that was made not to have the gas tank in the trunk compartment."

"He asked me how the gas tank was recovered."

"Well, I thought you guys talked about it yesterday when you guys were making the decision about whether or not to have the gas tank in the trunk compartment."

Judge Amano interrupted. "Do not answer the question," she said. "Mr. Hunt, we've gone over this area quite a bit now. It's asked and answered. Can you get to another area if you need to?"

"I don't have any further questions. Thank you, Judge."

Guillermo stepped down.

"Your honor," Hunt said, "based upon Detective Guillermo's answers to my questions and the conflict of the representation of the prosecutor and William Perreira and the reasons why they would have to ask these questions about him about the gas tank, I think there's a serious credibility problem here. And now . . . this should be presented to the jury on the issue of whether there was a fabrication or a deliberate attempt by the prosecution to misrepresent or tamper with the evidence in this case."

"What conflict are you talking about?" Amano asked.

"The conflict is very simple. Why would they

need to have this discussion about whether the Volkswagen was recovered with the gas tank in or out of the trunk compartment today if they had the conversation yesterday? Why would the prosecutor and the investigator, William Perreira, be asking Detective Guillermo these questions this morning when they talked about it yesterday, according to the testimony of William Perreira? There's a direct conflict in the testimony. It makes no sense, Your Honor, and I think it goes to the credibility of these witnesses and the issue of whether the state tampered with evidence in trying to show this jury the trunk compartment without the gas tank, because I think the truth in this case is they made the decision yesterday to do it that way and they're trying to cover their tracks this morning when they got together and tried to figure out some justification for not having the tank in the trunk compartment even though the five times the engineers came to look at it they stuck the gas tank inside the gas compartment."

"That's inaccurate," Judge Amano said. "I don't think there's any evidence, testimony today or at any other time, that the gas tank was stuck into the vehicle. I thought it was stored there. That's certainly what Mr. Perreira said this morning. And I don't hear anything to the contrary. Furthermore, any conflict that you refer to, I haven't heard. I understand what you're saying but I don't think that rises to the level of a conflict either between testimonies or a conflict of anything that was represented to the court. So I'm going to reject your request to present any further evidence to the jury. And, again, I believe we're taking whatever curative steps are necessary, if they are necessary. We're really erring on the side of caution to allow a reviewing."

The judge called in the jurors. "Ladies and gentlemen of the jury," she said. "Yesterday you were allowed to view the Volkswagen recovered by the police. This morning you'll be proceeding to the basement of the building to do a second viewing. This time the gas tank will be placed in the position that it would be in if the car were operating. You are once again instructed to consider the Volkswagen the same way that you consider all of the other evidence in this case. When we recess, you will be in the custody of the court's bailiffs, who will escort you to the basement and remain with you during the viewing. I remind you that you must remain together as a single body during the viewing. Do not talk about or discuss anything while you are doing the viewing. Do not allow anyone to approach you or speak with you. You will then be escorted back to the courtroom. Closing arguments should commence shortly afterward."

Following the viewing, Amano told the attorneys that the jurors had asked to see the car with its trunk lid on. After the request was granted, a juror gestured for the lid to be opened and closed, a move suggesting the jurors might have had a concern about the trunk space and its capacity to carry a

person. Lincoln Ashida was determined to deflect
that concern in his summation.

The courtroom was full again, and the Ireland
family was finally allowed in the courtroom. Jim,
Sandy, Louise, and John sat in the second bench on
the left, right behind the row reserved for the media.
The prosecution team's boss, Prosecuting Attorney
Jay Kimura, also sat among the roomful of spectators who had come to hear closing arguments.
Pauline's mother was in the courtroom as well, just
a few benches back from the Ireland family.

Lincoln Ashida took his position at the lectern
and recapped the prosecution's evidence against
Pauline, including the confession to police that he
hit Dana Ireland over the head with a tire iron. "On
June nineteen, nineteen ninety-four, Detective
Steven Guillermo asked defendant Frank Pauline
this question during the taking of the formal statement: 'When you hit her with the tire bar, what was
your intention?' The answer given by Frank
Pauline Jr.: 'To make sure I killed her.' Question, by
Detective Guillermo: 'To make sure she died?' Answer: "Yeah.' "

To counter expert testimony that a wound to Ireland's scalp couldn't have been caused by a full
blow to the head from a tire iron, Ashida said prosecutors had never said it was caused by anything
stronger than a glancing blow, something that
would be likely if Ireland moved her head while
"thrashing and fighting for her life."

Ashida reviewed Pauline's statement on TV that

he went public because he kept having images of Dana Ireland begging for help. He outlined the charges against Pauline and told the jury how the defendant's actions intersected with Dana's path to a bright future when she stopped to watch the surf at Shacks.

"Who are the last people to see Dana Ireland alive? The defendant and his friends take off in that direction. They were supposed to have that pre-arranged meeting up at Pahoa School with their friends, but Shayne Kobayashi told you that they never showed up. We know that as Dana Ireland took that path, which eventually ended her life, that as she was traveling on that westward direction on Kapoho Kai Drive on that red road, and as she sat riding that bicycle how she was struck from behind by that Volkswagen—by that Schweitzer Volkswagen that Mr. Pauline was a part of."

Ashida reminded the jury of the testimony about the repairs to the Volkswagen, "and as they take Dana Ireland in that vehicle and as they take her to that remote location after disabling her and after Mr. Pauline and his accomplices had their way with her, sexually penetrate her, how they take her to that shrub area near Ida Smith's house and just dump her body, discard it on the side of the road like a piece of trash because they were done with her."

Ashida then reminded the jury about efforts at the hospital to save Dana. "Shortly after midnight on December twenty-fifth, Christmas, nineteen ninety-one, Dana Ireland left this physical world," he said.

It was then, Ashida said, that Detective Guillermo entered the case. "Police did everything within their human and professional power" to gather evidence, he said. In 1994 they got a break while Pauline was in prison. Ashida alluded to a fourth partner in the crime. "His accomplices— some who he names, some who he chooses not to name—are not there," Ashida said. "He can lie through his teeth," Ashida said, "but he and no- body else can deny the forces of human nature." Those forces, Lincoln said, were Pauline's con- science and his understanding that "he who runs to the cops gets the best deal."

And yet, Ashida noted, after Pauline confessed, he changed his story. He told the jury he made up the tale to get transferred out of Halawa Prison. Sarcasm crept into Lincoln's voice. He walked to the jury box and placed his hand on the railing. "If his sole motivation was to get out of Halawa Prison," he said, "what is the number one way you guarantee that you spend the rest of your life in Ha- lawa Prison? Confess to a murder? Folks, it just doesn't make sense."

Ashida told the jury that Dana Ireland would be a witness in the case by way of her autopsy photo- graphs. He told them to look closely at those pho- tos, which hadn't been previously shown in court. "She was mauled by a pack of animals." Immedi- ately, Ashida realized his mistake. It's improper to call a defendant an animal. Without missing a beat, he kept going, hoping Hunt wouldn't catch his blunder. "Those photos are the most telling evidence that you have in this case," he said. Hunt never objected to the "animals" reference.

Now Ashida tackled his biggest challenge, the DNA. "We're not afraid of that DNA, we embrace it," Ashida said. "That same technology places Dana Ireland's blood on Frank Pauline's T-shirt." He said the DNA results of the semen didn't mean Pauline was innocent—just that he wasn't the contributor of that particular semen sample. Ashida stressed the small quantity of the DNA and that it could have become degraded or contaminated. "Don't allow the defense to make the DNA evidence any more than it really is, given its limitations."

Ashida told the jury that the car allegedly used in the crime was suspiciously painted a different color between Christmas and New Year's Day 1991. The Volkswagen was purple and in good condition before Christmas, Ashida said. "It ends up turning New York taxicab yellow."

Ashida now had to do damage control on the issue of the trunk space. Although Charlene Iboshi had said in her opening statement that Pauline had put Dana Ireland in the trunk, Ashida now suggested that Pauline had lied about that. Pauline was thinking, "If I say they put her in the trunk and not in the back seat that's better 'cause I'm sitting in the back seat," Ashida said.

Ashida asked the jury to find Pauline "guilty as a principal" of murder and "guilty as an accomplice" of kidnapping and rape. "There's a saying that goes, 'When you run with the pack you share in the kill.' On December twenty-fourth, nineteen ninety-one, Frank Pauline was part of that pack that shared in the mauling and killing of Dana Ireland." Ashida sat down feeling his closing had put the prosecutors back in the game.

Now it was time for Cliff Hunt to present closing arguments. "What happened to Dana Ireland was something that should never happen to a human being. And whoever did that should be convicted and punished very severely. But the person who did it was not Frank Pauline," Hunt said. "We've got a stupid story by Frank Pauline, a shoddy police investigation, and just about every witness the state calls has a reason to lie or to try to help the state. You think there's maybe some reasonable doubt in this case?"

The witnesses against Pauline included "a double murderer, a couple of convicted drug dealers, a probably very bitter mother-in-law, and an ex-girlfriend," Hunt said. "All of them had a motive and an interest in this case to lie." Pauline's brother, John Gonsalves "is a drug dealer" and "he got popped," Hunt said. "He had every reason in the world to try to get a deal for himself. And guess who's sitting in prison? Dumb, gullible Frank Pauline."

Pauline is "like the little pit bull in the family . . . really he's a loser . . . but he wants to be a winner," so he agreed to help his brother, Hunt said. According to Hunt, Pauline's account of the rape/murder is very stupid because according to Frank Pauline's story, they drive past a very attractive woman and turn around and run her over, [then] "stuck her in this trunk compartment that's barely big enough to hold a small suitcase."

Pauline sat listening, his chin propped up with his right hand.

Hunt told the jury that Pauline had made up the story to police, thinking if he got caught in a lie he couldn't be charged with anything more than perjury. "What Frank Pauline didn't figure was how desperate the prosecution was because of the pressure by the Irelands," he said.

Hunt displayed several items of evidence and then stacked them one by one in a pile he called "reasonable doubt."

"The prosecution seemed to be afraid to handle the evidence," Hunt said, showing the jury the large blue Jimmy'Z T-shirt that he said would not have fit Pauline in 1991 because Pauline was a lot larger then than during the trial. "This is reasonable doubt right here in my hand. That's why they didn't want to handle it," Hunt said.

Now it was Hunt's turn to raise the issue of the Volkswagen trunk. "Two viewings of the Volkswagen. Yesterday it didn't have a gas tank. Today it did. Why is that? Maybe so it would be bigger," Hunt said. "Reasonable doubt."

The FBI could find no paint from the Volkswagen on the bike, Hunt said. "What does that tell you? It ain't the vehicle."

Hunt said the very fact that Pauline and the Schweitzer brothers had hired a DNA expert to look for sperm indicated their innocence. "Do defendants who are guilty want to hire DNA experts to look for sperm?" he asked.

"I don't think Frank deserves a lot of pity," Hunt said. "What he did was wrong. Lied. Made up a story. That was very wrong. But that doesn't make him a murderer and rapist." Hunt finished with his strongest argument, the DNA results. "We know from the evidence in this case" he concluded, "that the person who raped Dana Ireland is not Frank Pauline, is not Ian Schweitzer, is not Shawn Schweitzer, and is not thirteen other people."

Because the prosecutors had the burden of proving Pauline guilty, Lincoln Ashida had one last chance to speak to the jury. Ashida warned the jury against "being led on yet another path by the defense, a path which attempts to put anybody else on trial but the person that you were sworn as the jury to consider, and that is Frank Pauline Jr., because what the defense attempted to do in those arguments is to lead you on that path as far away from Frank Pauline and Dana Ireland as possible, so as to confuse you and, well, let's blame the unknown fourth person, or fifth person, or the sixth person, for that matter."

He urged the jurors to consider only the culpability of Frank Pauline and reminded them of the painstaking investigative work done by the police. Ashida tackled the DNA problem by repeating his argument that it only proved that Pauline wasn't the contributor "of that particular semen sample." The DNA didn't and couldn't say anything about Pauline's other actions in the case. Ashida ended by saying, "We are gathered here today to look over there and say, 'You will be held responsible for your part in the kidnap, rape, and murder of Dana Ireland.'"

Judge Amano sent the jurors home for their final night before jury instructions and deliberations, thanking them for their attention and cooperation. "Please follow the rules, they still apply to you," she admonished. "Thank you very much, and you are excused for the evening."

As Lincoln Ashida walked out of the courtroom John Ireland approached him and grasped his right hand with both of his own. "I want to thank you and Dana wants to thank you for what you have done," John said. Ashida was deeply moved. He knew that even a guilty verdict wouldn't satisfy him as much as hearing those words.

* * *

The next morning Judge Amano instructed the jurors in the law. When she was done, they realized they wouldn't have the option of considering any lesser offenses such as manslaughter or assault. The judge then released the sole remaining alternate juror, 49-year-old Teresa Miller, who hugged her fellow jurors goodbye before they left to start deliberations. Amano met with Miller in chambers to debrief her and start her on a path toward closure from the experience of having served on a murder trial without being able to deliberate. It was a long session.

When Miller left the judge's chambers two hours later, a pack of reporters and TV camera crews chased her down the hall, where a television reporter fired off a question. "I felt like a scared animal," Miller said later. "In the back of my mind I thought I was going to fall off the stairs."

That night she told the *Tribune-Herald* that she would return to court for the verdict. "We were a team," she said. "We were a family. I want them to know that my heart is with them and I'm with them in spirit."

Miller said she cried in the jury box three or four times, including when Werner Spitz displayed autopsy photos during his videotaped deposition. "The tears were rolling down and I was trying not to let the jurors see," Miller said. "I thought, 'The jurors are going to have to hold those photos in their hands.'"

Miller said she was surprised after she was released from service to learn of the extensive media coverage. She said she was worried about the stress that deliberating this high-profile case would have on her friends on the jury. "My heart goes out to each and every one of them," she said.

Miller's tears flowed as she discussed the case after six weeks of silence. "It's such an unnatural state to be in, to be expected to listen to all this stuff and then to go into a little room and and not be allowed to discuss it," she said. Even so, Miller wouldn't reveal what her verdict would have been had she been allowed to deliberate the case. She said the only reason she spoke to the *Tribune-Herald* was that she wanted the public to know how seriously the jurors took their responsibility. "I just want people to know that they're dedicated to do the right thing, even if it's not what everyone would want," Miller said. "I don't want it to be like an umpire makes a bad call and they start booing the umpire. These people are doing a service. They have given up their summers."

Miller made an appeal for compassion from the reporters. "I hope that the media doesn't pressure the jurors to talk about the trial because I know I felt that pressure," she said. "This case is never going to go away. I'm changed by it. My life is changed by what happened."

Frank Pauline's mother, Pat Pauline, had been in the courtroom when Judge Amano instructed the jurors about the law. Pat Pauline was short, dark, and round. She told the *Tribune-Herald* afterward that she had "scolded Frank" after he testified that Gonsalves was "the godfather" of drugs in Hilo and Puna.

"I was hurt for a couple of days," Mrs. Pauline said, adding that Frank could have phrased it differently to say that Gonsalves "was maybe dealing or something."

Nevertheless, Pat Pauline didn't dispute the content of Frank Pauline's testimony—simply his choice of words. "When Frank took that stand, everything he spoke was the truth," she said.

The testimony by Pauline and Gonsalves was "not easy," Pat Pauline said, but she was supportive of both her sons. "They're brothers no matter what," she said. "I love them both."

Pauline's mother said Frank wasn't friends with Shawn and Ian Schweitzer. "I can name all of his friends, and the Schweitzers are not one of them," she said.

Although Pat said she believed that her son was innocent and that police and prosecutors had falsely targeted him, she said she wasn't completely disillusioned with the criminal justice system.

"I trust Riki May Amano and Frank's attorney," she said. Judge Amano had gone out of her way to make sure Pauline had a good attorney. Mrs. Pauline predicted a hung jury, but said she hoped her son would be acquitted of all charges. "There is a God," she said. "I just have to have faith."

Chapter 23

Jury service was nothing new to Lisa Kaneshiro. This was her sixth time as a juror and her third murder trial. An elementary school teacher, she had missed a job interview at a school near Hilo so she wouldn't disrupt the trial. She would spend the next three years commuting 58 miles one-way to Waimea because of it. She believed it was her obligation to serve her country.

The trial took its toll in other ways, too. Jurors were missing work and worrying about their jobs. And, although they weren't sequestered, some felt isolated by not being allowed to read newspapers, listen to news on the radio, or watch it on television.

"Once, when I was at physical therapy, the news came on and someone turned the volume up while the whole gym came to a standstill," Kaneshiro said. "I slapped my hands over my ears and yelled, 'Turn it off! Turn it off!' And they did."

Another time a juror had carried a *Tribune-Herald* with him to court. The bailiff had nearly panicked until the man explained that his wife was screening the newspapers for him. Being a Monday edition, the paper had no stories about the trial.

Now that the jury could finally discuss the case, they quickly elected Kaneshiro as the jury fore-woman and got to work. It was serious business. The 12 people who'd shared the jury room for all this time were suddenly strangers.

"For many weeks, we had been sitting there smiling at each other and getting acquainted and sharing family photos and recipes and jokes and becoming good friends," Kaneshiro said years later. "Now suddenly, we could talk about the real reason we were there together. And lo and behold, we hadn't all reached the same opinions and conclusions.

"Some had reached a decision before the doors closed, and wanted to have a vote and end it all then and there. Some weren't sure what they thought yet. Many still had questions and wanted to talk. A few were afraid and unsure and suddenly didn't want to be involved at all. 'Whatever the rest decide is all right with us,' they told us, 'I just don't want to make a decision.' The more the group talked among itself, the worse it got. Voices got loud; feelings got hurt. I think most of us had a sleepless night after that first day of deliberations.

"On the second day, we began by talking not about the trial, but about our own selves and feelings," Kaneshiro said. Amazingly, our emotions eventually started to settle down and we began to listen to each other and find things that we could agree on. We asked each other questions. We sorted through the evidence and looked at it all up close. We discussed and discussed and discussed. We took a little bit more care in the way we voiced our opinions. We went over and over the instructions. We looked at more evidence and discussed some more. We took little temperature checks along the way. We'd found a way to work with each other, and we started to like each other again. By the end of the day we were exhausted but hopeful."

Most of the jurors tossed and turned in their beds during deliberations.

"We'd all been dealing with sleeplessness, nightmares, loss of appetite, stomach problems, and crabbiness," Kaneshiro said. "This was a particularly horrible and shocking crime, and, as jurors, it was our duty to see, hear, and think about things that no one in his right mind would ever want to know about, much less dwell on. You could see it in the morning when we met on the bench downstairs and waited for the bailiff to take us to the jury room. We were starting to not look so good.

"The day before we brought in the verdict, we all knew that we were almost there," Kaneshiro said. "That, for sure, was a sleepless night. I remember putting Visine in my eyes on Friday morning, as I got ready for court, then putting the bottle in my purse to bring along. My eyes felt like little red coals.

"We quickly got down to business," Kaneshiro said. "Whatever had been unresolved the day before had been hashed over and over by twelve sleepless minds all night long. We read and re-read the instructions just to be sure. Our temperature checks became final votes. Voices were firm and sure. As we went around the table, you could just feel relief flooding the room, and making us almost giddy. People were smiling and talking to each other about inconsequential things again."

Kaneshiro filled out the jury verdict form and sent for the bailiff.

Just before lunch, the word went out that the jury had reached a verdict. Judge Amano held the return of the verdict until after lunch to allow everyone time to make it to court. All three of the television network affiliates in Honolulu planned to interrupt programming to broadcast the verdict live.

Reporters at the two Big Island newspapers, the *Hawaii Tribune-Herald* and *West Hawaii Today*, had been crossing their fingers that the verdict wouldn't come on Friday. Neither newspaper published on Saturdays, which meant the Honolulu newspapers would have the story a full day earlier than the local papers. The *Honolulu Star-Bulletin*, a morning newspaper, decided to publish a rare special afternoon edition just because of the verdict. The case had always been bigger in Hawaii than the O.J. Simpson trial.

* * *

The bailiff delivered lunch to the jurors and told them it would be some time before they could enter the courtroom to report their verdict. While waiting, the jurors began to speculate about what would happen next. As they chatted, they became aware of an increasing roar in the hallway outside. One of the jurors asked what it was. Kaneshiro explained that it was a growing swarm of spectators arriving for the reading of the verdict. "After that, no one had much appetite for lunch," she said. "Conversation pretty much died out as each of us sat there listening to the roar and feeling miserable. As it got louder and louder outside, it got quieter and quieter inside.

"Then we heard the courtroom doors open and the people filing in," Kaneshiro said. "I felt cold and shaky and, from the pale faces, I'm sure every other juror felt the same. I asked them to stand in a circle around the table and we joined hands to give each other strength and to say our parting words to each other.

"Then it was time."

Chapter 24

Security was tight inside the courtroom on Friday afternoon, August 27, 1999, as members of the Ireland and Pauline families filed in along with other spectators to hear the verdict. Louise Ireland wore the same white blouse she'd worn on the witness stand. Pinned over her heart was a framed picture of Dana. She and John looked tense, as did Sandy and Jim. They sat in the second row, with victim/witness counselors from the prosecutor's office bracketing them on both ends of the bench. Three members of the Pauline family—Joey Gonsalves and his wife, and Frank Pauline's sister, Marlena—were in the fourth row. Frank's mother, Pat, wasn't in attendance.

When the jurors walked into the packed courtroom, their hearts were pounding, Lisa Kaneshiro said later. Observers noted that the six men and six women, who had deliberated more than 14 hours over two and a half days following the five-week trial, looked grim but satisfied when they entered the room. They nodded at the sole remaining alter-

nate juror, who hadn't been with them in deliberations but had sat with them throughout the entire
trial and returned to court for the verdict.

Pauline was flanked by four jail guards. Two
other guards and two state sheriffs guarded the exit
doors. Pauline was wearing a white shirt with blue
pinstripes.

Across the state, people stopped in stores and in
their homes to watch live TV broadcasts of the
verdict.

Tensions ran high as Lisa Kaneshiro handed the
verdict forms to Judge Amano's clerk, who passed
them to the judge. Amano looked over the forms
carefully before passing them back to her court
clerk. Lincoln Ashida kept his eyes focused on his
pad, his pen ready to write down the verdict. He
knew it was unnecessary, but he needed something
to do with his hands.

The judge addressed the spectators, telling them
that the jury had deliberated for 14 hours. She admonished them to make no sounds or comments
upon the reading of the verdict, adding that anyone
who felt they couldn't remain silent should leave
immediately.

Pauline stood while Amano's clerk read from the
jury's verdict forms: "We the jury in this case find
the defendant guilty of murder in the second degree. We the jury in this case find the defendant
guilty of sexual assault in the first degree. We the
jury in this case find the defendant guilty of kidnapping." Pauline stood facing forward and showed

no emotion. His sister, Marlena, broke down in tears.

John Ireland buried his face in his hands and made a sound that was somewhere between a sigh and a sob, but quickly regained his composure. Louise Ireland looked momentarily stunned. Sandy squeezed her husband's hand as he began to cry. Moments later Louise and Sandy Ireland had tears in their eyes, too. John Ireland hugged his surviving daughter.

Lincoln Ashida felt a jolt of relief and then went numb. Although he and Charlene Iboshi had never discussed it, they both knew better than to pat each other on the back. This wasn't about them; it was about justice.

The judge polled the jury. "Do you agree with each of the three guilty verdicts?" she asked each juror individually. They all answered yes.

Judge Amano ordered Pauline to appear in court October 14 for sentencing and told the jurors that their duties were completed, asking them to return to the jury room so she could talk to them. The courtroom was absolutely silent.

When the families and spectators left the courtroom they encountered a crowd of state workers who had taken a break to watch the event, and cameras wielded by members of the press. The press wanted interviews with family members, prosecutors, defense counsel, and even those spectators who had sat through the entire trial. The jurors, however, were spared the chaos.

"When we went back into the jury room to wait for the judge, everyone just broke down and cried just from the release of all the tension," said Lisa Kaneshiro. In a few minutes Judge Amano joined them in the jury room. Amano made it her practice to debrief all her juries after a trial, but she knew it was especially important in this case. She thanked each member for working so hard, for paying attention and for deliberating carefully.

The judge explained that she'd taken unusual steps to shelter the jury from the reporters congregated outside the courtroom. After the first week of trial, Amano's bailiff had begun meeting the jurors on the ground floor of the state building each morning and then escorting them up the elevator and along a private route to the jury room. Amano now told the jurors about the video recording equipment hidden behind the portable wall down the hall from their room. During most of the trial the only indications the jurors had of television coverage was the single TV camera inside the courtroom.

The judge talked to the jurors about how they were feeling and told them she knew they'd been through an emotional experience and might suffer some post-traumatic stress. "It really helped to kind of bring us back down again to a point where we could gather our poor scrambled emotions and hopefully go on and lead normal lives again," Kaneshiro said. Amano told the jurors the media would probably want comments from them but said the decision to provide them was their own. "The jury was generally horrified by that," Kaneshiro said. To ease their fears, Kaneshiro volunteered to be the spokeswoman. After the debriefing, the bailiff escorted the jurors out a back door. Meanwhile, the Irelands were participating in a press conference on the first floor, directly below the courtroom.

The Ireland family was relieved at the verdict, but the conviction was bittersweet. No verdict would ever bring Dana back. "I don't feel any closure," said John Ireland. "I just feel relief that they've got him. I'm not happy or anything."

Louise Ireland echoed the sentiment. "I still think about her all the time," she said. "There is no closure and there will never be."

"That six weeks was quite an ordeal for us," John said. "We still realize we have two more trials to go through, and there's always some apprehension about what's going to happen there. We've won one fight out of three. In other words, one down and two more to go."

John Ireland praised Judge Amano for keeping the trial dignified. "I was concerned for quite a while that the trial would turn into a three-ring circus." As for the verdict, "I don't think Dana would be happy," John said. "She was the type that would feel for the convict's family and probably for him, also."

Sandy said she felt "great relief" from the verdict. "I feel that a weight's been lifted off our shoul ders." Louise Ireland said she had been prepared for a less satisfactory verdict. "I'm glad he was convicted of all three charges, that's for sure," she said. "He was a bad guy and I'm glad that his mouth got him in trouble."

Louise said the verdict had given her a new appreciation for the Aloha State. "I didn't want to go back to Virginia with the frame of mind I had about Hawaii," she said, "but the trial and the people here changed my whole attitude about Hawaii."

Since Frank Pauline's mother wasn't in court for the verdict, his older brother, 34-year-old Joe Gonsalves, made a comment on behalf of the family. "It was unanimous," Gonsalves said. "I don't think from my opinion it was good but the law is the law."

Frank Pauline's attorney, Cliff Hunt, said he would appeal the verdict on some legal aspects of the case, but he accepted the jury's decision. "The jury, I think, considered the case carefully, so we'll have to just move on from here." Hunt said Pauline took the verdict "pretty well under the circumstances." The hardest part for Pauline was "perhaps listening to family members testify against him," while the most difficult obstacle to overcome as a defense attorney was "Frank's so-called confession."

Hilo attorney Brian De Lima, who had been Pauline's attorney before Judge Amano had bumped him over the possible conflict, said he had problems with the verdict. "The question that this verdict does not answer is whose sperm was found on Dana Ireland? Who is that person? And if you are to believe Frank Pauline's confession, it should belong to one of the Schweitzers and they were excluded. So whose is it? We may never know," De Lima said. "This question is not answered by this verdict and frankly, no one knows whose DNA that is."

Prosecuting attorney Jay Kimura praised his staff for the "arduous preparation and teamwork." Kimura called the verdict "a reaffirmation that the jury system works," especially in the wake of the O.J. Simpson verdict. "That case saw a lot of erosion in faith in the system," Kimura said. "We're obviously happy with the verdict."

Lincoln Ashida told reporters the jury had reached its decision with all of the facts available. "This wasn't a case where any evidence was excluded," Ashida said. Charlene Iboshi said prosecutors would seek extended terms at sentencing that she hoped could result in three life sentences.

Lincoln Ashida drove back to the prosecutor's office. Waiting at the entrance were the entire staff, equipped with makeshift pom-poms crafted from shredded computer paper. "Give me an L," they cheered. "Give me an I. Give me an N. Give me a C. Give me an O. Give me an L. Give me an N. What does that spell? Lincoln!" After getting some enthusiastic hugs, Ashida left the exuberance and sat quietly in his office. Now that it was over, he just wanted to go home and be with his family. He politely refused Detective Guillermo's invitation to go out and celebrate.

"To this day, I've never celebrated," Ashida said years later, "because relief was just too strong a feeling and there's just no room for anything else."

That night the Irelands ran into the jury forewoman, Lisa Kaneshiro, while having dinner at Pescatore, an Italian restaurant in Hilo. Kaneshiro hugged John Ireland and complimented Louise on her pin. "I loved that juror," Louise Ireland said later.

Now that the verdict was public, Kaneshiro could explain the deliberation process.

She said the jurors talked about all the witnesses and made a list on a blackboard of what parts of their testimony they believed, what they didn't believe, and what they questioned. One of the things they agreed on quickly is that the T-shirt found near Dana Ireland's dying body belonged to Frank Pauline. Although Pauline's attorney, Cliff Hunt, had tried to persuade the jury that the size large shirt would have been too small for Pauline, the jury didn't buy it. "You like your shirt to fit snugly across your torso—a lot of local guys do that," Kaneshiro said.

The jury was convinced that the purple Volkswagen was the vehicle that ran over Dana Ireland, believing testimony that the car had a basketball-size dent and had been painted yellow shortly after the attack.

"It was a gorgeous little number," Kaneshiro said. "And for somebody to take that and just suddenly strip it . . . why would you go to all that major problem to make it really different? It was very believable to us that the Bug was the actual vehicle that was involved."

Ironically, Dr. Werner Spitz, the defense expert who had testified that Dana's injuries were caused by a truck, helped persuade the jury that she had died from being hit by the Volkswagen. "We believed the part about how he believed she was injured by a car running over her," Kaneshiro said, "but yet we didn't buy the part about a pipe bumper on a small truck."

The jury had the Volkswagen's bumper and Ireland's mangled bicycle in the jury room. They were able to fit the bumper into a bend in the bike's tire rim, Kaneshiro said.

The jury also believed it was possible to put a person Ireland's size into the trunk of a Volkswagen, she said. "But even if she wasn't put into the trunk, the fact that the entire car was stripped and all the fabric was out of it, we figured that she was either in the trunk or she was put in the back seat."

According to Kaneshiro the jury wasn't swayed by the fact that the DNA didn't match Pauline or the Schweitzer brothers. "We think there's another person involved," she said. The jury didn't believe Pauline's testimony that he made up the story of his involvement to get transferred out of Halawa prison. "He's canny and crafty, but he just was not believable to us on the stand."

But they did believe the testimony of Pauline's brother, John Gonsalves, on Pauline admitting his involvement. "His testimony was very, very compelling. It just rang true." Kaneshiro said Detective Guillermo made a good witness. "He was very impressive," she said. "He seemed reasonable. He seemed honest. He seemed forthright and very intelligent. He was believable." But she said the jury was sorry that police hadn't videotaped the reconstruction tour with Pauline or tried to put a person Ireland's size into the trunk of the Volkswagen. "It would have made it easier for us," said Kaneshiro.

Only after examining all the evidence and testimony did the jury vote on the charges against Pauline. "I told them that even though I hated the thought of a hung jury, I would rather have a hung jury than a jury that was not in complete agreement and at peace with the verdict," Kaneshiro said. They voted and everyone agreed. "That was when you could feel this huge wash of relief. It was almost like a physical thing."

Kaneshiro was surprised and somewhat troubled when she went out in public the day after the verdict was announced and strangers who had seen her in a televised press conference approached her and thanked her for the verdict.

"I'm glad people agree with our decision," Kaneshiro said, "but it's important for them to know that we would have gone the other way if there was a reasonable doubt."

The Irelands decided not to return to the Big Island for Frank Pauline's sentencing hearing on October 14. Although John Ireland had spent years working on a statement to read at the sentencing, he decided to send Sandy in his place. "I don't think we can take another trip," he said. "It was a tough six weeks."

Reaction to the verdict was mixed. Most Big Island residents were happy about the conviction. But one of the DNA experts who had testified at the trial said he was "stunned" by the guilty verdict. Edward Blake, the California forensic serologist who testified on behalf of the defense, said he didn't understand how the jury could have convicted Pauline when the DNA from the sperm found on Dana Ireland's hospital sheet didn't match Pauline or the Schweitzer brothers.

"The physical evidence doesn't support this verdict because the physical evidence proves without any doubt that Dana Ireland was raped by an as yet unidentified man, and until that man is revealed no one can understand what happened to Dana Ireland," Blake said. "I honestly just don't understand how the citizens of Hawaii can be happy with that verdict knowing the source of that spermatozoa is walking the streets to rape and murder again."

Meanwhile, Pauline's attorney, Cliff Hunt, confirmed reports that Pauline had offered to testify on behalf of the Schweitzer brothers at their trials scheduled for November and March. "He's decided that he's basically screwed up their lives. Now he's decided that because he was convicted, they're going to go down with him," Hunt said, explaining that Pauline had passed a note containing the offer to one of the Schweitzer brothers in prison. "Frank's not conditioning the offer on anything," Cliff said. "He's doing it because he believes it's the right thing to do."

In the end, the Schweitzer brothers' attorneys would reject Pauline's offer because Pauline had already testified that he was a liar. His testimony couldn't help the Schweitzers.

Chapter 25

On October 14, 1999, Pauline was back in Judge Amano's courtroom, this time wearing an orange prison jumpsuit. "CR 97-256 State of Hawaii versus Frank Pauline Jr. for sentencing," the judge's clerk said, reading from the court calendar.

Pauline took his old seat at the counsel table. His goatee and mustache were back. He nodded at the judge's law clerk and at Lincoln Ashida.

Once the hearing got under way, Charlene Iboshi told the judge that Sandy Ireland wanted to read a statement prepared by her parents and one of her own.

"Please come forward, Ms. Ireland," Judge Amano said.

Jim approached with Sandy and stood to her right while she read her father's statement.

"We remember a physician telling us early Christmas morning that our daughter had died," Sandy read. The statement went on to describe how Dana Ireland had been born when John and Louise Ireland were nearly 45 years old. "Her birth took years off our ages, and we felt years younger than our biological ages," Sandy Ireland read. "Dana's violent death has aged us considerably."

After their daughter's murder, the Irelands became "bitter and angry," the statement said, "because the law does not permit the ultimate penalty—execution. It has had a detrimental effect on us mentally."

Sandy continued: "We have not had a good night's sleep since Dana's death." She noted that the Christmas season for the Ireland family had become a time of grief. "December twenty-fifth is the day we visit Dana's grave," Sandy read. Sandy told the judge a small measure of compensation for the Irelands would be to see Pauline receive the maximum penalty.

She then read from her own statement. "Dana was my only sister and best friend." She recounted Dana's coming to Hawaii in 1991 to spend time with her and to contemplate her future. Dana loved it on the Big Island, Sandy said. "All of her joy, all of her possibility, and all of her sweet being were destroyed by Frank Pauline on Christmas Eve nineteen ninety-one," she said. "Now it is time for Frank Pauline to bear the responsibility for his actions."

In Hawaii, a judge has little discretion in sentencing someone for murder. Second-degree murder carries a mandatory sentence of life in prison with the possibility of parole. Kidnapping and sexual assault each require 20-year terms. But the law allows for extending kidnapping and sexual assault convictions to life terms for career criminals, and that's what Charlene Iboshi asked Judge Amano to do, noting that Pauline's criminal record had begun at age 10. "Unfortunately, the wheels of justice grind very slowly," Charlene said. "I think in this case the defendant thinks he can get away with a lot of things—including murder."

Iboshi also asked the judge to require that Pauline serve the terms back to back rather than at the same time. The question of consecutive rather than concurrent prison terms is one of the few issues left to the discretion of a judge at sentencing in a case where probation is not an option.

Pauline's attorney, Cliff Hunt, called the proposed extended and consecutive sentences "draconian."

"At the time of these offenses, Mr. Pauline was only eighteen years of age," Hunt said, claiming that Pauline had been a reluctant participant in Ireland's death and that Pauline's statements to police led to his own arrest and to the arrests of the Schweitzer brothers. "What reward does he get for confessing to the crime? According to their theory, that's what he did," Hunt said.

Before the judge imposed her sentence, she told Pauline he had the right of allocution, a chance to be heard one final time.

Pauline rose to address the court, then turned around to face Sandy Ireland. Pauline denied his guilt, but said he was sorry for the Ireland family and sorry that he'd lied. "I'm sorry, and I hope that these people do catch the real person who did 'em," Pauline said.

Pauline looked Sandy right in the eye and said if Dana Ireland were in the courtroom, she would say the jury convicted the wrong man. He said he had lied when he implicated Shawn and Ian Schweitzer. "I feel sorry that I lied about the brothers. They were not involved. I just made it up," Pauline said. "Whatever punishment comes on me, I feel God is doing this to me for my lies."

Pauline told Sandy that her father should pursue his original theory about who killed Dana Ireland. "Tell your dad no give up," he said. "He was on the right track."

When Pauline was done, Judge Amano told him it was "necessary for the protection of the public" to extend Pauline's terms. She sentenced him to three life terms, but said the sentences for the sexual assault conviction and the kidnapping conviction would be served at the same time. The murder conviction, she said, was to be served consecutive to the kidnapping and sexual assault conviction and tacked on to the prison term Pauline already was serving for unrelated theft and sexual assault convictions.

A parole board would later determine the minimum amount of time Pauline would have to serve before becoming eligible for parole.

Outside the courtroom, Iboshi said prosecutors would ask the parole board for "the maximum that we can get." She said she wasn't concerned by Pauline's contention that he was innocent of Ireland's murder. "We're taking the position that we have the right man, and we're going to trial on the other two," Iboshi said.

Those trials were still months away.

A month later, on November 18, 1999, Frank Pauline's attorney asked Judge Amano for a new trial. In documents filed in Circuit Court, Cliff Hunt argued that Pauline's constitutional rights had been violated because Hunt and Pauline weren't present when the jury had viewed the Volkswagen. Furthermore, Hunt argued, it was improper for detectives to place the trunk hood on the Volkswagen and close it and open it for the jury without Hunt present.

In his motion, Hunt wrote that the Volkswagen was never entered into evidence and that the "experiment" with its trunk wasn't conducted as part of the official court record. Hunt cited several higher court decisions in which "the courts have condemned juror experiments."

At a hearing the following Monday, Judge Amano denied Hunt's motion.

The Hawaii Paroling Authority set Frank Pauline's minimum prison term at 180 years. The parole board said he had to serve at least 90 years for the kidnapping and rape convictions and another 90 years for the murder conviction. That meant, technically, Pauline would be eligible for parole only after serving 180 years behind bars. What it really meant, of course, is that he would never get out of prison.

John Ireland said that he was surprised at the length of the minimum term set by the parole board, but that his daughter's killer deserved it. "He'll never see anything but prison walls."

Louise Ireland said the length of Pauline's time in prison didn't matter much to her. "I wish they had the electric chair. If he got a thousand years it wouldn't make any difference."

Chapter 26

Another Christmas passed for the Ireland family without any closure. Again, no presents. Again, just pain. The Irelands' only comfort was that Frank Pauline was locked away in prison and that Ian Schweitzer was about to go to trial.

On Monday, January 24, 2000, Ian's trial began. In this one, Lincoln Ashida would question most of the state's witnesses; Charlene Iboshi recognized that Ashida was better at courting a jury than she was. Although Iboshi had built the case, she was content with her lower-profile role in the courtroom. To her, results were more important than ego. Since she was more familiar with the details of the investigation, she would question police witnesses and a few others.

James Biven, the lawyer representing Ian Schweitzer, had dark brown wavy hair and wore glasses. The 43-year-old Biven wasn't as big a challenge to the prosecution as Frank Pauline's attorney had been. A former prosecutor in Kona, he was a low-key trial lawyer, not given to flamboyant orations before a jury. Ashida had a social relationship with Biven and knew it would be easy to fall into a false sense of complacency. But he was determined not to let his guard down and to put as much energy into this trial as he had into Pauline's.

Biven knew the excessive publicity in this case hadn't helped his client. During jury selection, he'd asked them point blank what they thought about Ian Schweitzer's newspaper photos. At least one prospective juror admitted to thinking Ian looked like "a thug."

The trial itself failed to generate the tension that had permeated Frank Pauline's trial. The testimony was essentially a rerun of the first trial, with a few exceptions. This time, prosecutors never told the jury Dana Ireland was put in the Volkswagen's trunk. More important, the jury didn't hear any testimony from Frank Pauline.

Pauline's brother, John Gonsalves, took the stand briefly, but his testimony didn't last long because Judge Amano had ruled that prosecutors couldn't ask him about Pauline's confession. Hearsay testimony about alleged confessions by accomplices typically is barred from trials because it is unduly prejudicial to the defendant, who has a constitutional right not to testify and therefore can't refute the testimony. Gonsalves's statements, therefore, were limited to his recollections about Christmas Eve 1991, when he said he saw Frank Pauline, the Schweitzer brothers, and a fourth person standing by the dented Volkswagen. Gonsalves also acknowledged that he had sent a letter to the Ireland family asking for $25,000 in reward money after testifying in Pauline's trial the previous summer.

While the prosecutors couldn't present the incriminating statements by Frank Pauline and his brother, they did have a new star witness to testify against Ian Schweitzer. Michael Ortiz, whom Ian had befriended in jail, gave yet another version of what happened to Dana Ireland. He testified that Ian had admitted to ramming her with his car but said it was an accident.

The 31-year-old Ortiz said that while he was in jail in August 1998 during a theft trial in Hilo, Ian had asked him what it was like in court. As the discussions progressed, the two men developed a close relationship, and Ian had confided in Ortiz about his own case.

"My thought was, he needed somebody to tell," Ortiz said. "He could trust me." Ortiz said Ian Schweitzer had told him that on Christmas Eve 1991, he and his brother, Shawn, drove in Ian's purple Volkswagen to the beach at Pohoiki, where they joined friends. When it was time to leave, Ian drove his brother and Frank Pauline in the direction of Kapoho. They saw a "pretty *haole* girl on a bike," Ortiz said. "Frank whistled at her, and she flipped him off. Frank told him to turn around the car."

Ian drove toward Ireland just to scare her, but "the Volkswagen slid in the gravel and hit the back of the tire," Ortiz said. "She flew off the bike to the short bushes." Ian noticed that the rim of the girl's rear tire "was smashed in, shaped like an egg," Ortiz said. He testified that Ian had told him that Pauline had jumped out of the car and grabbed the girl by her long blond hair. Pauline had thought it was funny when a clump of hair came out in his hand. Ian was frightened.

Pauline had dragged the girl into the car and put her on his lap in the front passenger seat, Ortiz said. As Ian Schweitzer drove away, Dana Ireland was hitting Frank Pauline and yelling, while Pauline held her down. Ireland bit Pauline on the arm, Ortiz testified. "Ian wen' seen Frank rip her shirt off and bite her on the breast," Ortiz said. Ian drove to a side road.

"Frank got out, started hitting on her and took her in the bushes,"Ortiz said. When Pauline returned to the car, he was covered with blood. Shawn Schweitzer was "real scared," so Ian Schweitzer drove him home and then drove with Pauline to another man's house. When Ian dropped Pauline off, he told Pauline, "We have to stay away from each other for a while so nobody knows," Ortiz said.

"Ian told me that the front bumper had one dent in it," Ortiz said. "He had to change things on it, and he cleaned it up. Had it painted." Ian allegedly had told Ortiz that he had raised the height of the front of his Volkswagen so it "wouldn't match the bike where it banged."

According to Ortiz, Ian Schweitzer had told him that no one would find his or his brother's sperm on

Dana Ireland's body " 'cause they never did nothing to her."

Ortiz said that he had never talked to Shawn Schweitzer, but that the younger Schweitzer had been at the jail at the same time Ortiz and Ian Schweitzer were there.

"The brother's window is facing the rec yard . . . and he taps the window and tells his brother, 'Hang in there,' " Ortiz said, adding that Ian Schweitzer had been upset with his brother and Pauline. "Felt like they was opening their mouths too much to everybody." Ortiz told the jury he had received nothing from prosecutors in exchange for his testimony. "I'm coming forward 'cause I got sisters," Ortiz said. "If someone were to do something like that, I would like someone to come forward."

When court ended for the day, Lincoln Ashida paid a visit to his son's school to find out how the kindergartner was doing in class. The teacher, Karen Coon, said Scotty had been "acting out" recently—having temper tantrums, hitting other children. When she asked the boy the reason for his anger, he began to cry. "My daddy goes to work before I wake up in the morning," Scotty said, "and I have to go to sleep before he comes home at night."

Ashida felt his guts being ripped from his belly.

"But we understand why you have to work late," Coon told him. "We appreciate what you're doing."

Ashida returned to his office with a heavy heart. As much as he wanted to drive straight home, he knew he had to prepare for the next day's court session.

In this trial, prosecutors ended their case with their most powerful emotional witness. Sandy Ireland testified that she had kept her mother away from the ambulance that delivered Dana Ireland to Hilo Hospital on Christmas Eve 1991.

"I kind of held my mom back because I didn't want her to see Dana," Sandy said. Sandy later regretted it, she said, because neither woman ever saw Dana again.

Defense attorney James Biven presented three witnesses who contradicted the state's claim that Ian Schweitzer had painted his Volkswagen Bug yellow within days of Dana Ireland's slaying. Jerry Francisco*—the "Filipino kid"—testified that he had bought the car from Frank Pauline's cousin, Marco Salvador Jr., for two pounds of marijuana, and had traded it in early December 1991 for another Volkswagen that Ian Schweitzer had owned. Sometime in mid-January—three weeks after the Bug supposedly rammed into Dana Ireland—Ian drove to Francisco's girlfriend's house and asked Francisco for title papers to the car. Ian Schweitzer's Volkswagen was still purple and had no dents, Francisco said.

Another witness, Ian Schweitzer's ex-girlfriend,

*Not his real name

testified that the car was still purple when she had first met Ian in March 1992. Sandy Pacheco, who avoided making eye contact with Ian during her testimony, said she remembered the date because she had started a new job the next day.

During questioning by James Biven, Pacheco said she saw Ian and his father painting the car yellow in April of that year—four months after Dana Ireland's attack. She said she knew it was in late April because she had paid for the paint with settlement money from her divorce, which had become final on April 23, 1992.

Following Pacheco's testimony, police Lieutenant Paul Ferreira testified that he had interviewed Pacheco at her home in 1994. During the interview, Pacheco had showed Ferreira remnants of the yellow paint that was still sprayed on the right side of her garage.

Testimony in this trial ended without Ian Schweitzer's taking the witness stand.

Families of both Dana Ireland and Ian Schweitzer sat in the half-filled Hilo courtroom while attorneys made closing arguments to the jury. As with the Pauline trial, the families had been barred from the courtroom throughout the earlier part of the trial because they were listed as possible witnesses.

Lincoln Ashida wasn't as pumped up for this closing as he'd been for the previous one. He was just numb. Although he had no doubt about Ian

Schweitzer's guilt, he knew that he had even less evidence against him than he'd had against Pauline. He hoped this jury wouldn't feel it was off the hook because someone was already in prison for Dana Ireland's slaying. At the same time, Ashida hoped the momentum of the Pauline conviction would spread to the deliberation room and he believed that Michael Ortiz had been an effective witness.

After taking his position at the lectern, Ashida returned to the familiar theme of Ian Schweitzer and his "pack of friends" who ran over Dana Ireland and then drove her to a remote area where she was "raped and beaten and raped and beaten" and left to die. He used the new testimony about the April painting of the Volkswagen to his advantage. In March, he said, police went to the Schweitzer house and left word that they wanted to talk to Ian. "Exactly around that time" Schweitzer painted the car yellow, Ashida noted. He didn't remind the jury that in opening statements he'd told them the car was yellow by the beginning of 1992.

About halfway through his argument, Ashida began to lose confidence. He complained during a court recess afterward that he'd tried to read the jurors' faces but had seen only blank stares. "I started with the emotions but the jurors weren't reacting," he said. "So I decided to switch to the facts. Then I realized, fuck, we don't have the facts."

Later, Ashida said he'd meant it as a joke.

In any case, Ashida's confidence fell even more during James Biven's closing argument. Biven, who had maintained an unassuming presence throughout the trial, delivered a surprisingly powerful, highly organized argument. He asked the jury to pay attention to the physical evidence—none of which linked his client to the crime. "The scientific evidence has no motive, has no bias, and doesn't make deals with the prosecution," he said.

Biven asked why police hadn't followed up on Lieutenant Ferreira's observation of yellow paint in Ian Schweitzer's girlfriend's garage. "Probably 'cause it was inconsistent with the prosecution's theory," he said. "The prosecution in this case was not concerned about the truth."

When Lincoln Ashida's rebuttal argument time came, he was determined to end strongly. Using a toy purple Volkswagen and a toy bicycle he acted out the state's theory. "This vehicle was aimed at that bicycle," he said, the passion rising in his voice. He pointed at Ian Schweitzer. "There is guilt in this courtroom and he is sitting right there."

As everyone waited for a verdict, the first hint of the jury's perception of the case came from a juror who'd been replaced at the last minute for health reasons. The juror, who had sat through most of Ian Schweitzer's trial, said she would have voted to acquit if she'd been able to deliberate. Marcie "Bunny" Greenwell, 33, had been in court until the last day of testimony, when she had been hospitalized with pneumonia and replaced by an alternate juror.

"It's not black and white enough for me to vote for a conviction," said Greenwell, an escrow assistant. She told the *Hawaii Tribune-Herald* that DNA results played a large role in her conclusion. "Looks like there's someone still out there that the DNA belongs to."

Greenwell said she had enjoyed serving on jury duty but was "a little intimidated" when she realized she'd been called for the Ireland case. She said she knew there was a lot of pressure from the community for a conviction but hoped the jury would make its decision based on the evidence. "It's going to be really, really hard for me to deal with if this jury finds him guilty," Greenwell said, "knowing I could have been the one who made a difference for this guy."

The next day, Tuesday, February 15, started as a typical Hilo morning, with clouds and a few warm showers. At 1:30 P.M. the forewoman notified the court that the jurors had reached a verdict. A chill gusted through the courthouse and then the air stood still. In a courtroom whose spectators included reporters, judiciary employees, curious citizens, and members of the Ireland and Schweitzer families, Judge Amano asked Ian Schweitzer to rise as her clerk read the jury's verdict: "We the jury in this case find the defendant guilty of murder in the second degree," the clerk read. "We the jury in this case find the defendant guilty of sexual assault in the first degree. We the jury in this case find the defendant guilty of kidnapping." A deputy sheriff slapped handcuffs on the 28-year-old Schweitzer, who stood with his head bowed, his somber expression unchanged.

Amano ordered Schweitzer, who had been in jail since his indictment the previous May, to return to court on April 11 for sentencing.

Immediately after the verdict, Schweitzer's father, Jerry Schweitzer, leaned forward in his seat, his tear-stained face buried in his hands. Schweitzer's mother also broke into tears. The family had always insisted that prosecutors had wrongly targeted Schweitzer and his younger brother, Shawn.

In contrast, Louise Ireland said she was relieved by the verdict. "I feel like I'm glad it's behind me so I can maybe go on and try to live a little of my life," said Dana Ireland's 75-year-old mother, who clung to a bouquet of roses, again wearing the pin bearing a photo of her dead daughter.

As the Ireland family exited the courtroom, John Ireland bent down and spoke briefly to Jerry Schweitzer, who was still seated on a courtroom bench.

"I just told him that he has my sympathy," John said later.

Jerry Schweitzer responded by telling John's wife, "I wish you a long, long life."

"Thank you," replied Louise. "But I can't see my daughter anymore."

The Schweitzer parents left court without speaking to anyone else.

* * *

During a news conference in the courthouse, John Ireland said he was pleased with the verdict but noted that Shawn Schweitzer still had to stand trial. That trial was on the court calendar for the following month; Ireland told reporters he'd already learned the case would be postponed. "The last eight years for us have been hell," John said. "We still have a long way to go."

John, who was now 76, had met dozens of families of murder victims and learned about many murders since Dana Ireland had died in 1991. "They did everything to my daughter except cannibalization," John said. "I know very few cases that were that brutal."

Louise told reporters she was comforted knowing Schweitzer was facing life in prison. "I hope he will never see daylight," she said. "Then I can go to bed at night and think, 'Okay, you're going to suffer for what you did to my daughter.'"

Chapter 27

Ian Schweitzer appeared in court for sentencing on
Tuesday, April 11, 2000, but prosecutors unexpect-
edly asked for a delay. Lincoln Ashida told Judge
Amano that earlier in the morning prosecutors had
received written information about the Ireland case
from the Hawaii County Police Department. "We
believe that this information is germane to this
case," Lincoln said in asking for a short postponement of the sentencing hearing. He didn't explain
further.

James Biven didn't object to the delay. "We
would like to see that information," Biven said,
asking the judge to continue the hearing until sometime after April 21. Biven explained that he would
be on Oahu on that date "so I can meet with my
client and have a face-to-face." Ian was being held
at Halawa Prison on Oahu pending his sentencing.

Judge Amano asked Ian to rise and then offered
a vague explanation for the sentencing delay:
"There is additional information that will affect
your sentence."

After the hearing, Lincoln Ashida wouldn't pro-

vide any clues about the nature of the new information. "I'm not going to discuss the details of whatever information was provided to us until Mr.
Biven has the opportunity to review it privately
with his client," Ashida said. He wouldn't confirm
or deny rumors that prosecutors were working out
a plea bargain with Ian's brother, Shawn. "Plea discussions are generally confidential and private, so I
cannot answer that," Ashida said.

Ian's father, Jerry Schweitzer, was surprised and
puzzled by the latest twist in the case.

Sandy Ireland, who now lived on the island of
Kauai, was on the Big Island, prepared to read a
statement on behalf of her family. But she left the
courtroom before the hearing began after speaking
with prosecutors.

John and Louise Ireland were participating in a
candlelight vigil for homicide victims in northern
Virginia at the time of Ian's hearing. They told the
Tribune-Herald that night that they had spoken to
prosecutors after Sandy told them the sentencing
had been postponed. "All I know is that they got
information from police," John Ireland said.
"That's all I know."

"We're as puzzled as you are," Louise Ireland
added. "I don't think this will ever end."

A plea bargain was indeed in the works. After
Ian Schweitzer's verdict, Shawn Schweitzer's attorney, Keith Shigetomi, had called Lincoln Ashida.
"You like deal or what?" Shigetomi asked, using
pidgin. Ashida agreed, but only if Shawn came

clean with what he knew. He felt that was important for the community. In addition, getting Shawn on record would make him a valuable witness in any retrial if one of the other verdicts were overturned on appeal.

Six days later, Shawn Schweitzer pleaded guilty to kidnapping and manslaughter for his role in the Christmas Eve 1991 slaying of Dana Ireland. In the plea agreement with prosecutors, the 24-year-old Shawn would be sentenced the following month to five years probation and one year in jail, but would get credit for the time he'd already served. As a result, Ian Schweitzer's kid brother would be released from Oahu Community Correctional Center as soon as he posted $4,000 bail to ensure that he'd appear for sentencing.

Judge Amano ordered Shawn to stay away from the Big Island until his sentencing hearing on May 9. She also ordered that he have no contact with any of the witnesses who'd testified against his brother and Frank Pauline.

In court, Lincoln Ashida read a brief statement, which said that Shawn Schweitzer was present during Ireland's attack, that he had failed to take action to prevent it, and that he had hindered prosecution of the case.

"Is it a true statement?" Amano asked Shawn.

"Yes," Shawn said. He indicated under further questioning that he was aware of the implications his statement might have on his brother's sentencing, scheduled for the following Monday.

Prosecutors were asking for consecutive extended sentences for Ian Schweitzer. Without the plea agreement, Shawn Schweitzer faced the same sentence. Although the maximum sentence for kidnapping and manslaughter was 20 years in prison and a $20,000 fine, Judge Amano told Shawn that she would honor the agreement with prosecutors for five years probation. "I've committed—or promised—that I will go along with the deal," Amano said before ordering Shawn to return to court for sentencing on May 9.

Sandy Ireland was in court for Shawn's change of plea; she said nothing.

Shawn's father had attended all of Shawn's other hearings but was absent for this one. He told the *Tribune-Herald* later that afternoon that he didn't attend because "it's a kangaroo court." Jerry Schweitzer said that he still believed his son was innocent and that he didn't trust polygraph tests. "The polygraph's nothing. It's a joke."

John Ireland expressed relief that there wouldn't be a third trial but said he wished Shawn Schweitzer had confessed sooner. "He owes everybody an apology for what he put us through." John said Shawn's confession was good for the Ireland family and for the Big Island community because finally they all knew what had happened. "I think that if he passed the polygraph test he's telling the truth," he said. John's wife was unhappy that Shawn wouldn't stay in jail. "I don't have no sympathy for him at all," Louise Ireland said. "He had a chance to save Dana and he didn't do it."

In a press release issued after the change-of-plea hearing, Lincoln Ashida said Shawn Schweitzer had made a detailed confession to police on March 23 and had passed a lie detector test administered by the state attorney general's office.

"Shawn Schweitzer, while present during these crimes, didn't have any physical contact with Ms. Ireland," Lincoln Ashida wrote in the press release. Schweitzer was criminally culpable, Ashida added, because he had failed to aid Ireland or call for help and because he had lied to police and "furthered the 'conspiracy of silence' with his brother and Pauline." Prosecutors never explained whether Shawn's confession answered the question of a fourth suspect. Their silence on that subject suggests that it didn't.

Ashida later met with reporters and played them Shawn Schweitzer's taped confession to Detective Guillermo:

SHAWN: Well, we left our house around twelve and we went up to see Wayne, Wayne Gonsalves. And he wasn't home and Frank came out. He asked us where we was going. And we told him that we was going to the beach and he said that if he could come.

So my brother said it was all right and he got his stuff and we went up to Pahoa and we went to the store, bought some chips and beer and stuff like that and we hung out around Pahoa for a little while. And then we went down to the beach and while we was down there my brother, them, was over by Shacks and I went by.

I walked to Pohoiki maybe hour, maybe little bit more. Then I walked back over to Shacks and hung out around there for a while and then we left. And Frank wanted to go see somebody in Kapoho so we was going down towards Kapoho.

And I wasn't really paying attention. I was just kinda looking out the window. And then I heard Frank say, like, "There is that girl, that fuckin' bitch," and told my brother for bang 'em. And the next thing I knew that he then bang her and I felt the car like run her over, and the car lift up. And then he turned around, turned the car around. They got out of the car and they was looking at her and I told them, "We gotta get help for her." And they told me for shut up and for stay in the car.

And then Frank wen' pick her up and he put her in the front seat, the passenger seat, where he was riding and we got into, they got into the car and drove. I told them, "No. What you guys do- ing?" And they just yell at me and tell for shut the fuck up and keep my mouth shut. And they kept driving until we got to the spot where she was found. And I guess they was planning on throwing her off the cliff, I guess.

And then Frank started doing sick stuff to her, started taking her clothes and trying for rape her I guess. Before they got out of the car she was started to come to, and when he got out of the car he was doing that stuff to her. And then my brother got back in the car and I told him, "You better get me the fuck outta there," or else I going tell. And he did.

He start up the car and we started reversing out. And then Frank came running after the car and he jumped back in the car and he said, "What the fuck you guys doing?" And my brother's telling him that he sick and why he was doing that. And then we took him home.

And then we went home and Ian wen' shoot the car down. And I went in and took a shower and I went to my room.

I dunno. I not sure what he did with the seats that was in the car, but the seats, the passenger seat had a lot of blood on it. It was like a cloth seat so it's pretty soaked. I dunno what he did with the seats or the carpet.

And they just told me for be quiet and everything would be all right. Nobody would find out.

GUILLERMO: Okay, going back to the beginning, you said "we" left the house. "We." Who is the other person that was with you or the other people that were with you?

SHAWN: Ian.

GUILLERMO: That's your brother Ian.

SHAWN: Yeah.

GUILLERMO: Okay, and what kind of car was you guys in?

SHAWN: His Volkswagen Bug.

GUILLERMO: Do you know which, can you describe the Bug for me?

SHAWN: Was purple, had one gray graphic in the back. There's a baby window bug, it's you know lowered and had rims on it.

GUILLERMO: Is that a center line rims or—

SHAWN: Yeah.

GUILLERMO: You also talked about the seats that were in the car.

SHAWN: Uh huh.

GUILLERMO: You remember what color seats those were?

SHAWN: Think they were gray.

GUILLERMO: Gray-colored seats?

SHAWN: Like high back seats.

GUILLERMO: Do you know who put the seats in? It was something that your brother bought or it came with the car or . . .

SHAWN: He put the seats in.

GUILLERMO: Yeah? Were they Volkswagen seats?

SHAWN: No. They were like I think they were like Scat seats or something.

GUILLERMO: What are Scat, tell me, I'm not familiar with that.

SHAWN: It's a company that sells Volkswagen seats, products.

GUILLERMO: Okay, to put in those seats, did he have to do anything as far as changing the brackets on the floor, you know, where you mount the seat itself?

SHAWN: Uh, huh?

GUILLERMO: Did he have to do anything like that, do you recall?

SHAWN: I no think. No. Nevah have brackets.

GUILLERMO: So, how did he mount the seats? Did he have to drill the floor on his own or—

SHAWN: Yeah, think so. He bolted 'em to the floor.

GUILLERMO: Okay. Prior to going to, I guess, the Pauline residence to hook up with Wayne, was there any drug use and drinking between the two of you?

SHAWN: No.

GUILLERMO: None? And, the person that you guys pick up at Pauline's residence again is—

SHAWN: Frank Pauline.

GUILLERMO: Frank Pauline Jr.?

SHAWN: Yes.

GUILLERMO: Okay. You talked about the store that you guys stopped at in Pahoa. Do you recall what store that was?

SHAWN: Cash and Carry.

GUILLERMO: Okay, and what kind of items did you guys buy again?

SHAWN: Beer and chips.

GUILLERMO: What kind of beer, do you remember?

SHAWN: I not sure, but think was Coors.

GUILLERMO: Coors Light or regular Coors or—

SHAWN: Regular Coors and Coors Light, I think. I not sure.

GUILLERMO: Do you recall who paid for the beer?

SHAWN: Ian and Frank.

GUILLERMO: They both had the money? I guess you didn't have any money at that time?

SHAWN: Yeah.

GUILLERMO: Where did you guys hang out?

SHAWN: We went by Akebono.

GUILLERMO: In the parking lot area?

SHAWN: And then we went up to the top of Pahoa and then we went down to the beach.

GUILLERMO: The top of Pahoa, meaning?

SHAWN: The school.

GUILLERMO: Above the school?

SHAWN: Yeah.

GUILLERMO: And that's an area I guess a lot of guys gather and what not, too?

SHAWN: Yeah.

GUILLERMO: Do you recall about how long you guys spent there before heading down to the beaches?

SHAWN: About an hour. About an hour.

GUILLERMO: Okay.

SHAWN: Maybe more.

GUILLERMO: So when you guys arrive down—I guess it's Shacks first—it's where they parked, is that right?

SHAWN: Yeah.

GUILLERMO: You recall who was there?

SHAWN: Had some of Ian's friends over there, Alex and Jim.

GUILLERMO: Alex's last name is?

SHAWN: Frenchy.

GUILLERMO: Okay.

SHAWN: Alex Frenchy and Jim Orlando. It's the only two guys I remember.

GUILLERMO: Okay, and you told me from there you walked over towards Pohoiki and that's where the ramp is at. Is that where you swam?

SHAWN: Yeah.

GUILLERMO: Okay. When you returned, how long after you get back to Shacks before you guys leave there?

SHAWN: Maybe about another hour, around there.

GUILLERMO: Okay, do you recall what or do you know if Frank or Ian were doing any drugs at that time?

SHAWN: Not to my knowledge.

GUILLERMO: But for sure you know they were drinking?

SHAWN: Yeah.

GUILLERMO: Okay. Did you at any time see a Caucasian female riding by on a bicycle while you were there?

SHAWN: No, I nevah seen her.

GUILLERMO: Okay, when you guys leave, first of all, what direction do you guys travel from Shacks?

SHAWN: From Shacks we went left towards Kapoho on Red Road.

GUILLERMO: Towards Kapoho?

SHAWN: Yes.

GUILLERMO: And is Ian driving the car at that time?

SHAWN: Yes.

GUILLERMO: Frank is sitting where now?

SHAWN: In the front passenger.

GUILLERMO: And your seat is where?

SHAWN: In the back.

GUILLERMO: In the middle or in the back of either Frank or Ian?

SHAWN: In the back of Ian.

GUILLERMO: In the back of Ian. Did you remember mentioning something about Frank talking about the female that was there?

SHAWN: Uh huh.

GUILLERMO: "There is that bitch" or something like that?

SHAWN: Yes.

GUILLERMO: Did you get to see her at all where you were seated?

SHAWN: Not until they hit her hard.

GUILLERMO: Do you recall if she was walking? Standing?

SHAWN: She was kinda flipping over.

GUILLERMO: That's all you see?

SHAWN: Yeah.

GUILLERMO: And you mentioned Frank saying something to Ian about "run her over" or something like that? You remember the words he used?

SHAWN: "Run that bitch over." Might have been more, like swearing. "Run that fuckin' bitch over." And he was calling her "one fuckin' cunt" and stuff.

GUILLERMO: Is he the only one that gets out of the car after she is run over?

SHAWN: No. Ian, they both got out of the car.

GUILLERMO: Did Ian say anything as he left the car or as he got back into the car to you?

SHAWN: Not that I recall.

GUILLERMO: 'Cause you were already yelling some stuff at them?

SHAWN: I told them, well, I thought we woulda gone, going get help, but I dunno. I guess they stuck with what they had in mind.

GUILLERMO: Okay, so how was she loaded into the car again, now?

SHAWN: Frank wen' pick her up and put her in the car. She was, they was both on the front seat.

GUILLERMO: Can you describe like how he carries her in the car, I guess you're familiar with like carrying children and you put them in your arms, your arms are under them or is it over your shoulder or—

SHAWN: He grabbed her like under her arms, on her chest.

GUILLERMO: From the front or from the back?

SHAWN: Back. And she was laying down on the ground. He just kinda grabbed her and dragged her to the car, threw her like in the middle, kind of on the passenger seat.

GUILLERMO: Partially on him and on where the gearshift is at?

SHAWN: Yeah.

GUILLERMO: Is she moaning or anything at that time while you told him that?

SHAWN: No.

GUILLERMO: No movements or anything like that? So from there, once she's loaded into the car and she's seated on Frank, do you recall what direction you guys headed?

SHAWN: Headed out, back out towards the main road. And when we got to the main road, took one right, and we kept going straight. We got to that spot. I don't remember too much. I was kinda crying and in shock. I nevah understand what was going on.

GUILLERMO: So when you pull off, off of the roadway to where eventually she was found, are you able to see who carried her out of the car and takes her down to wherever she is found?

SHAWN: Frank wen' pull her out of the car.

GUILLERMO: By that time she was already, you said, coming to or something like that?

SHAWN: Yes. She started moaning like in pain, I guess.

GUILLERMO: Uh huh.

SHAWN: And Frank, he wen' put her like on the front fender and—

GUILLERMO: Do you know which side?

SHAWN: The same side she got bang. The passenger side. And then they started taking off her clothes. And my brother was standing just outside his door and I told him for get me out of there. And I guess, he, we just left and I dunno what he did with her or what. But he was like kind of holding her when we left and then I seen him chasing after the car.

GUILLERMO: While you guys were on this roadway, try to describe for me the position that the Volkswagen was at on that road where she was found.

SHAWN: Just in the middle of the road.

GUILLERMO: Was the—

SHAWN: Stopped in the middle.

GUILLERMO: Was the Volkswagen facing the direction of the ocean?

SHAWN: Yeah.

GUILLERMO: Or was it turned sideways to the ocean?

SHAWN: It was kinda facing the ocean and little bit sideways.

GUILLERMO: Did any cars pass by while you guys were there or while you guys were driving from Kapoho to that street where she was found?

SHAWN: No cars.

GUILLERMO: How long were you guys at the small roadway where her body was found, about? I know you have to estimate.

SHAWN: Not that long. When Frank started doing that to her, then I guess Ian was kinda tripping out, too, like pretty sick to do something like that, I guess. And I started yelling at him, "Get me the fuck outta there." Maybe I miss what you like from how long took us to get into the road?

GUILLERMO: Did it take you guys long to get down that road?

SHAWN: No, couple minutes.

GUILLERMO: Once you guys pull off what I guess everybody refers to as Beach Road, right?

SHAWN: Yeah.

GUILLERMO: You guys turn down and then you guys driving a long distance or just a short distance?

SHAWN: I don't think we went all the way down to where the road ends. Wasn't that far, maybe halfway through.

GUILLERMO: Did the Volkswagen bottom out as you guys went onto that road or came out of that road?

SHAWN: Little. Wasn't too bad. It was like Ian was kinda driving on the rocks, yeah? The high spots.

GUILLERMO: So it was okay?

SHAWN: Yeah.

GUILLERMO: So as far as, if someone was to be walking by, driving by, they wouldn't be able to see the Volkswagen right away? They would have to kinda look down this roadway?

SHAWN: Yeah.

GUILLERMO: You mentioned Frank was doing some sick things to her. Can you be more specific about what kind of things you saw?

SHAWN: Well, I saw him started taking off her clothes and I saw him take off his clothes and he just like kissing her breast and stuff, if you call it kissing or what, but that's what I saw. Couldn't watch that.

GUILLERMO: If you can recall, do you remember what she was wearing?

SHAWN: She had on one small white top and one denim shorts.

GUILLERMO: Okay, that's all you can remember? You know if she had on shoes, slippers, anything like that?

SHAWN: I no recall if she had shoes on.

GUILLERMO: How about Frankie, how was he dressed?

SHAWN: In shorts and shirt.

GUILLERMO: Okay, how about your brother, how was he dressed?

SHAWN: In shorts, tank top, shirt. I think he had on surf shorts and one gray tank top.

GUILLERMO: The T-shirt that was found at the scene, you know where body was found?

SHAWN: Uh huh.

GUILLERMO: You know whose T-shirt that was?

SHAWN: That was Frank's shirt.

GUILLERMO: When you saw him taking off his clothes, do you recall him having any underwear on?

SHAWN: No.

GUILLERMO: You don't recall? Or you don't know?

SHAWN: Once I seen that, I looked away. So I didn't really get to see if he had underwear on or not.

GUILLERMO: There was a small black basketball type shoe that was found there. Would fit a child. Do you know whose shoe that is?

SHAWN: No, I don't.

GUILLERMO: You've never seen it in your brother's car or anything like that before?

SHAWN: No. I don't recall seeing those shoes in the car.

GUILLERMO: Do you have any idea where that came from? After I guess Ian gets back into the car and you guys start heading down the road, how far you guys drive before Frankie catches up?

SHAWN: We was like almost to the top when we got back on that—

GUILLERMO: On to that main road?

SHAWN: Beach Road.

GUILLERMO: On to the Beach Road? You guys had reversed out already? You guys were reversing out?

SHAWN: Yeah, we was reversing out. Wasn't like we wen' reverse right out. Was kinda slow so by then he run up to the car and jump back in the car.

GUILLERMO: Did you tell Ian anything as he got back into the car?

SHAWN: He was telling us where we going. And I told 'em think Ian told 'em that he wasn't going sit there and watch him do that to the girl, then—

GUILLERMO: Shawn, as we were discussing this, Frank had just gotten back into the car and there

was some swearing going on between Frank and
Ian and I asked you like what was happening
with you. Were you also involved in that conversation? Were you trying to tell them to get help?
Or how did it go?

SHAWN: I was in shock. I was just kind of in disbelief what was going on. I nevah know what for
say, how for handle the situation so I don't think
I said too much.

GUILLERMO: Okay, so as you guys were driving
back towards Hawaiian Beaches, where did you
guys go first of all, once you get back into the
subdivision?

SHAWN: Which subdivision?

GUILLERMO: The Hawaiian Beaches subdivision,
once you guys get back there?

SHAWN: We went when we came out over there get
one road that goes up, and we turned up there
and now one dead end road. Ian got out of the
car and he was looking at the car.

GUILLERMO: Did you look at the car also?

SHAWN: No, I stayed in the car. And then when he
got back in we went back to Pauline's house.
Dropped him off.

GUILLERMO: Did it, when you went to Pauline's
house, was there anybody there that came out to
see you guys and talk to you guys?

SHAWN: They nevah talk to us. They wen' talk to
Frank I guess.

GUILLERMO: Do you recall who came out?

SHAWN: It was John I think, Joey. I not sure. Right

after we was leaving already, just reverse and left so I don't know what they talked about.

GUILLERMO: So Frankie returns home, he doesn't have his shirt on?

SHAWN: No.

GUILLERMO: And the time that you or all of you left and rode where she was found to the time you get to Frank's house, did he wipe up blood? I guess he had a lot of blood on him too, right?

SHAWN: Kind of, on his shorts.

GUILLERMO: Did you see him wipe off at all?

SHAWN: No, no. Had planny blood on the seat. How she was in the car and her head was like on the seat. I guess that's where she was bleeding planny from. So most of the blood was on the seat.

GUILLERMO: But there was some on his clothes. You saw that?

SHAWN: There was some on like his skin.

GUILLERMO: So from there you guys head straight home? Is that correct?

SHAWN: Yeah.

GUILLERMO: And did you help Ian wash the car?

SHAWN: No.

GUILLERMO: Why did you go to wash up when you up until now you haven't told me that you touched her or anything like that?

SHAWN: Why I took a shower?

GUILLERMO: Yes, was there any blood on you?

SHAWN: No. I wen' freshed up and 'cause the salt water and stuff.

GUILLERMO: Couldn't you have, I'm assuming you would help your brother clean up the car right? I mean there was all this blood possibly on the fender or alongside the fender, wiping the car. I'm assuming, I don't know if you helped your brother, guys, is why I wen' ask.

SHAWN: No, I nevah.

GUILLERMO: You didn't help them at all?

SHAWN: No. I was still yet pretty shaken.

GUILLERMO: Was there anyone else at your home when the two of you got there?

SHAWN: My parents was home.

GUILLERMO: Did they notice how shaken you were?

SHAWN: No, just told 'em that I felt sick.

GUILLERMO: Your mom didn't ask you why? Your dad asked you why?

SHAWN: My mom wen' ask, you know, what kind sick? What's a matter?

GUILLERMO: Uh huh.

SHAWN: I just told her that I felt sick and then I took a shower.

GUILLERMO: Did you go back outside afterwards to go check on Ian?

SHAWN: No.

GUILLERMO: You guys didn't talk about it the rest of that night?

SHAWN: He came in after and he talked to me and he told me for just be quiet. No tell anybody nothing.

GUILLERMO: And your response to that was what?

SHAWN: I didn't have a response at the time. Just told 'em get out of my room. The last time I talked to 'em about that.

On April 24, 2000, Shawn's older brother, Ian Schweitzer, again appeared before Circuit Judge Riki May Amano for sentencing.

Sandy Ireland asked Judge Amano to impose the stiffest sentence possible on her sister's killer. Sandy said that although she found it painful to be in court, she considered it her "moral responsibility" to speak on behalf of her family. "Ian Schweitzer made a terrible and evil choice," Sandy said, adding that he'd shown no remorse. According to Sandy, Ian was just as culpable in her sister's death as Frank Pauline. "They acted like immoral monsters."

Prosecutor Lincoln Ashida asked Amano to sentence Ian to the same sentence Pauline had received. "If not for his actions, I think the madness of Frank Pauline may have never been unleashed on Dana Ireland," Ashida said.

Ian Schweitzer spoke briefly before his sentence was imposed.

"I always did believe in the system," Ian said. "I ain't giving up on the system."

When Judge Amano asked what Ian meant, his attorney, James Biven, said Ian couldn't say more because the case would be appealed. "I have advised my client not to make any other statements except that," Biven said. As Amano quizzed Biven about why he had given such advice, Ian's father made the first of several outbursts from his seat in the courthouse gallery.

"Protecting his client, for chrissake," Jerry Schweitzer said, interrupting the proceedings.

Amano asked Ian's father if he wished to step forward to be heard, but Mr. Schweitzer remained seated, calling the prosecutors "corrupt to the core."

As the sentencing hearing continued, Ian Schweitzer asked Amano to consider a stack of letters written by his supporters before imposing the sentence.

Amano said she had postponed Ian Schweitzer's sentencing hearing because many of the letters from Ian's supporters raised issues about his guilt or innocence. "I thought that might have been addressed by your brother's statements," Amano explained.

After a court recess, Jerry Schweitzer decided to address the court after all, and appealed to Amano for a light sentence for his son. "He's not the so-called mad dog that these people have portrayed him as," Jerry Schweitzer said. "He's my angel, and just because he doesn't have blue eyes and blond hair, he's still my angel. And he's not a mad dog, he's a good kid."

Amano denied a prosecution request that Ian's

kidnapping and sexual assault sentences be extended to life terms because—unlike Frank Pauline—Ian had no prior felony convictions. She sentenced Ian Schweitzer to life in prison with the possibility of parole for the murder conviction and an additional 20 years each for kidnapping and sexual assault. She said the three sentences had to be served consecutively. "Each and every one of those offenses represents your independent choice," Amano told Ian. "You made the decisions."

The Hawaii Paroling Authority would determine the actual time Ian had to serve. Lincoln Ashida said he would ask for 130 years.

After the hearing, Dana Ireland's parents said they were satisfied with Ian Schweitzer's sentence. "This whole damn nightmare is almost over," said John Ireland. "It's taken a long time to get there, but I think the prosecutors and the rest of them did a good job."

Two weeks and one day later, on May 9, 2000, Ian's younger brother, 24-year-old Shawn Schweitzer, appeared in court for his own sentencing.

During the hearing, Sandy Ireland said Shawn's inaction during the attack and murder of Dana Ireland and his silence afterward constituted "seriously unethical" behavior. "He is getting a second chance at life," Sandy said. "Something that my sister did not get."

Before Judge Amano imposed Shawn's sentence, he addressed the court. "I would like to apologize to the Ireland family," Shawn said, reading from a prepared statement. "I have had my own children. I know how a parent wants to do everything to protect their child. . . . I can think of nothing more painful than for a family to lose their child. . . . I know I will never be able to make it up to them."

Shawn spoke about wasted lives, including the life of Dana Ireland and the effect her untimely and tragic death had on her family. "My family's life is also forever changed," Shawn said. "No one seems to care about that. But I do."

Shawn apologized again for what had happened. "Try to imagine your worst nightmare come true. That's what happened to me. Only I could not wake up and make it go away. I accept responsibility, and my sentence."

After Shawn stopped speaking, Amano told him she had "kind of a hard time" with his portrayal of his family as victims. "Ms. Ireland is here. You, sir, should turn around and look at her to tell her you're sorry," Amano said. "If you are sorry, you need to say so . . . and not from a piece of paper."

Shawn Schweitzer continued to face forward. "I'm not the greatest speaker. I'm not very articulate with my words. But I am sorry."

Amano then grilled Schweitzer about what had happened the night Dana Ireland died. "What did you do?" she asked.

"I didn't help when I was supposed to," Shawn said.

"What should you have done?" Amano asked.

"I should have left the scene when it happened."

352 • Chris Loos and Rick Castberg

"Why didn't you?"

" 'Cause I was told to shut up and stay in the car."

Amano asked Shawn why he hadn't exited the car when Pauline and Ian Schweitzer got out after running over Ireland and her bicycle.

"I was scared," Shawn said. "I didn't know what to do."

"Do you know what to do now?" Amano asked. "You've had eight and a half years to think about it."

Shawn said he should have tried to get to a phone.

"Could you have said to your brother and Frank Pauline, 'Leave her alone?' " Amano asked.

"I did," Shawn said. "I told them to go get help."

"Today, would you step in and help?" Amano asked.

"I would try to stop the bleeding and help her till somebody came by," Schweitzer said.

Amano reminded Shawn that his brother drove Ireland to a second location before Pauline and Ian Schweitzer got out of the car with Ireland. "Could you have stopped them?" Amano asked.

"No," Shawn said.

"Why?"

" 'Cause I was too small."

"Do you realize that as a result of your actions you contributed to her death?" Amano asked.

"Yes," Shawn said.

"I don't ever want you to forget that," Amano said, before sentencing Shawn to five years probation. She also sentenced him to one year in jail but gave him credit for a year he had already spent behind bars, as agreed to in the plea bargain. She ordered Shawn to find full-time employment, school, or training or to perform 32 hours of community service per week.

"The idea is you're going to give back to the community for your crimes," Amano said. She also ordered Shawn to submit to random drug and alcohol testing and to undergo drug and alcohol assessments and a mental health assessment. She imposed a curfew from midnight to 6:00 A.M. unless Shawn was working or driving to or from work during those hours.

Despite a request from prosecutors that Shawn Schweitzer write a letter of apology to the Ireland family, Amano told him she wouldn't make that a requirement because she didn't want a letter that didn't come from the heart.

"If you want to write one, go ahead," Amano said. "If you don't—don't."

John Ireland, who wasn't in court for Shawn Schweitzer's sentencing, said he thought the sentence was "very, very lenient" but conceded that it probably was the best prosecutors could get under the circumstances. John said he would never have given up on getting justice for his slain daughter. "I would do it the same way if I had to do it again."

He said, however, that he regretted offering the reward for information leading to a conviction. "The reward didn't get anything," he said, adding that Sandy Ireland would work with police to determine how to divide the reward money.

After the sentencing, Lincoln Ashida seemed eager to justify the plea bargain by noting Shawn's young age at the time of the crime and his role as an observer. Even so, Ashida said he would have been comfortable taking Shawn to trial if the man hadn't confessed. Reporters quizzed Ashida about the DNA problem. Ashida said he thought that the DNA was Pauline's but that it was such a small and degraded sample that it gave a false reading. He vowed that his office would check with the lab for an explanation.

Shortly after Shawn's sentencing, the *Honolulu Star-Bulletin* conducted a poll. Eighty percent of the respondents didn't think the sentence was long enough. Twelve percent said it was fair and eight percent were unsure. In the same poll, 89 percent of those surveyed said Frank Pauline's minimum sentence of 180 years in prison was fair, while 85 percent said Ian Schweitzer's sentence of two consecutive life terms plus two consecutive 20-year terms was fair.

In August 2000 the Hawaii Paroling Authority decided that Ian Schweitzer wouldn't be eligible for parole until he'd served 130 years. The board ruled that Ian would serve 90 years for the murder and the full 20 years each for the kidnapping and sexual assault. Ian didn't appear at the hearing. It's unlikely he took any solace in the fact that Pauline's minimum term was 50 years longer.

Chapter 28

As time went by, Big Island residents talked less and less about the Dana Ireland case, but no one forgot it. "I don't think I'll ever have a day in my life that I don't think about that case," said Lincoln Ashida, three years after the trial. "It was the hardest case I ever tried. All the scrutiny, the public pressure, and the political pressure added to the stress. I cried some nights just with my wife. I love trial work but in the Pauline trial there was never a day of fun."

Lisa Kaneshiro said people talked to her about the case for years after her service as a juror. "This was a sad, sad case that touched everybody in our state," she said. "People truly cared. They still care." Most people were relieved with the verdicts but some still had their doubts. The prosecutors and police maintained that they had pursued and convicted the right people. The Schweitzer brothers' parents never let go of the idea that one son was falsely convicted by a jury and the other had made a deal to avoid his brother's fate. The defense DNA experts, shocked that hard evidence played such a small role in the trials, chalked it up to small-town incompetence.

On June 12, 2000, the *Tribune-Herald* published a prison interview with Frank Pauline, who continued to maintain his innocence. Pauline said he'd fabricated the story about the Schweitzer brothers' involvement because he hated them. "Right now I feel pity for them for what I did—and my animosity towards them was wrong," Pauline said. "I should have never took my hatred out and destroyed somebody else's life."

Pauline said the deal prosecutors made with Shawn Schweitzer was "so hilarious" because Shawn essentially repeated Pauline's original confession, substituting his own role as that of observer. Schweitzer's story couldn't be true, Pauline asserted, because Schweitzer said Pauline had raped Ireland, but the DNA found on Ireland's hospital sheet didn't match that of any of the three defendants. "The DNA, it speaks for itself," he said in the telephone interview from Halawa Prison on Oahu, adding that it proved that his own story was false. "When I made this story up, I came out and I told the cops that the Schweitzers, them wen' rape the girl," Pauline said. "Why doesn't the DNA match up with them?"

Pauline said he didn't resent Shawn Schweitzer's light sentence. "In a way, I'm happy for him, but I wish the brother would have got the same thing, too," Pauline said. "In fact, I wish they would have not got nothing. My lies is what wen' destroyed their lives. That was wrong on my part."

Pauline said police and prosecutors knew his story was false but jumped at the chance to pin the blame on him because of pressure from the Ireland family. "So they said, 'Okay, we'll take Pauline. Fuck him. He no good, anyway. He one punk; he was fucking around with drugs; he was one headache; he hurt a lot of people,'" Pauline said. "The truth is, I hurt a lot of people, you know what I mean? I ain't a good guy, but I never did kill nobody in my life."

Pauline said prosecutors obtained testimony to convict him by making deals with witnesses who testified at trial. "For instance, I cannot remember this guy's name. He took the stand. They told him, 'Can you point out Frank Pauline Jr.?' Then he point out one damn sheriff or one ACO. I told the prosecutors, 'Hey. Get pictures in the paper. You guys better tell you guys' witnesses, "Go look at the pictures," so they can point out the right guy next time. If they're going to lie, at least get this shit straight.' At least that's one thing I can say about me: When I made my story up, I got pretty much good facts together, you know what I mean? I got plenty stuff together for make my story sound pretty good. And apparently, it sound real good. Convinced plenty people."

Pauline said he eventually realized that by telling the jury he was a liar, the jurors assumed he had also lied on the stand. "It's a backfire, honestly, but

I nevah care," Pauline said. "You know why? I just wanted for tell the truth. That's all it was. I figure, truth going prevail. But in this case—nevah. . . .

"Sometimes I think I should have just took the stand and just lied. Maybe I would have won if I would have told one good lie, you know? But I just—I was tired already. I was sick. My whole family lying about me, saying this, that, saying all kind stuff about me. So I figure I come and I tell the truth, you know what I mean?"

Although Pauline said he made up the story because he loved his brother, he said his feelings for John Gonsalves had changed after the trial. "Honestly? I hate him," Pauline said. " 'Cause he promised me in the beginning that the worst I could get was maybe five or ten for lying, you know what I mean? So I figure, okay, I can handle that for help my brother. . . . But right now I don't even bother with him."

Pauline said the state should have prosecuted him for lying but not for Dana Ireland's slaying. "I get plenty animosity because of this and sometimes I feel like saying, 'You know what? These assholes like put me away for something I nevah do. Let the real guys stay out there and let 'em do 'em to someone else. Then maybe that going teach them a lesson,' " Pauline said. "That's how I feel, but yet that's wrong."

Pauline threatened to fire his attorney, Cliff Hunt, and hire a new lawyer to help overturn his conviction. "There was people who know who did 'em, who know where the vehicle is—and it was a truck, a small type pickup truck, that banged the girl," Pauline said. "So there was people that was waiting for Cliff to call 'em on the stand. And Cliff wouldn't listen to me and let 'em be called on the stand."

Pauline said he had faith he'd be vindicated. "I believe I get one guardian angel on my side that going help me." Pauline's assertion that he knew what kind of vehicle hit Dana Ireland added fuel to the theory that Pauline had fingered the Schweitzers out of spite. Those who knew Pauline's capabilities didn't believe that he was innocent. He seemed to know too much. But they did sometimes wonder if Pauline had named the Schweitzer brothers as his accomplices to protect someone else. Lots of other suspects had been cleared through DNA tests— with the same kind of DNA results that the Schweitzer brothers produced. Police had never managed to recover a shred of physical evidence against either of the Schweitzer brothers. All they had was the word of an admitted liar, jailhouse snitches, and an after-the-fact confession by Shawn Schweitzer, who had seen his brother sent to prison for life for maintaining his silence.

Edward Blake, who had first found the sperm on Dana Ireland's hospital sheet, remained distressed by the verdicts because of the DNA evidence. "It will never be solved until a name is put to that DNA profile," he said. Blake said the media were partly responsible for what happened by "whipping up" the public, thereby making Pauline and the Schweitzer brothers easy targets. "This is one of the more heinous crimes in Hawaii and it remains unsolved," Blake said. "If this is what we call justice, we might as well just throw away the justice system altogether and string people up on coconut trees."

Less than three weeks after Shawn Schweitzer's sentencing hearing, John Ireland sent this e-mail message to a friend in Hawaii:

I have wanted to talk to someone since Dana's murder trials have come to a conclusion. You seem to be one that may understand what I am trying to say. I have been fighting for years to see those responsible brought to court and that we finally know with some certainty what happened to Dana. Now that there is some justice and we know what happened to Dana, I feel like the old pro who has aged and lost his ability to play on the first team and has hung up his glove. I feel as though I have no purpose in life and have nothing to give to mankind. I am losing interest in crime victim rights legislation and since the conviction of those responsible for Dana's brutal death, I feel I have nothing more to fight for.

A few days later the friend called John to discuss his depression. John downplayed the e-mail message, saying the feeling had passed.

A month later, John Ireland suffered a series of strokes. He died on Halloween day, at age 76. He was buried next to Dana.

Although John is gone, his efforts won't be forgotten. Because of him, Hawaii has a sentencing provision that requires mandatory life sentences for criminals convicted of particularly heinous crimes. At his insistence, emergency telephones now stand in remote areas of the Big Island. George Mason University gives out an annual scholarship to siblings, spouses, or children of individuals murdered in Hawaii and Virginia. Across America, law enforcement officials who heard John's plea for compassion for the families of victims conduct their duties with a new perspective. The man left his mark.

Not long after John Ireland's death, Louise Ireland made a transformation. She'd spent years talking about nothing but the murder of her daughter. Now she was talking about normal things for a woman her age. "Isn't it just terrible about John?" she would ask. "I just don't know what I'll do." It was somehow comforting to hear Louise grieve the sudden loss of her husband because that's what 76-year-old widows are supposed to do. With time, the smile returned to her face, a sparkle returned to her blue eyes. She began to focus her thoughts on things other than the tragedy that had tormented her for 10 years.

Two weeks after John Ireland's death, the Hawaii Supreme Court announced that it would hear oral arguments on the appeal of Frank Pauline's conviction. Some people who cared about John were secretly glad he wouldn't have to endure another potential setback.

Legal observers thought the Supreme Court hearing was significant because Hawaii's highest court hears oral arguments in less than one percent of all cases appealed. In this case, Cliff Hunt was contending that Judge Amano had made seven errors that affected Pauline's right to a fair trial.

Arguments took place in Ali'iolani Hale, the Hawaii Supreme Court building in Honolulu, on November 17, 2000. The building, completed in 1874, was the site of an unsuccessful insurrection in 1899 by those opposed to changes made to the Hawaii constitution of 1887. In 1893 it had been taken over by people supporting the ultimately successful overthrow of the Hawaiian monarchy. The courtroom itself is notable for its extensive use of *koa*, a highly prized native hardwood.

The Hawaii Supreme Court justices had backgrounds as diverse as the community they served. The court consisted of Ronald Moon, a third-generation Korean American; Steven Levinson, a Jewish *haole* from Ohio; Paula Nakayama, a Japanese American; Mario R. Ramil, born in the Philippines; and Simeon Acoba Jr., a Hawaii-born Filipino.

Cliff Hunt and Charlene Iboshi each got a half hour to argue their positions to the court. That time included frequent interruptions by the justices. The issues that seemed to interest the justices most were whether the viewing of the Volkswagen by the jury and their experiment with the trunk were improper. Hunt contended—among other things—that Pauline's constitutional rights had been violated when the jury looked at Ian Schweitzer's yellow Volkswagen without the presence of Pauline or the attorneys.

Three of the five justices asked questions about that. "What difference would it have made if you'd been there?" Justice Levinson asked Hunt.

"You don't know," Hunt said. "It goes to the whole integrity of the process of the case."

"What would your position have been if the jury proposed moving the trunk?" Justice Acoba asked.

"We would have objected," Hunt said.

"Did you argue the victim's body could not fit into that trunk?" asked Chief Justice Moon.

"Yes," Hunt said.

Prosecutor Charlene Iboshi said she didn't think the experiment was wrong but said that if it was, it was a "harmless error" and not something that required the court to overturn the verdict. Iboshi explained that the jury had heard other evidence of Pauline's guilt. "He confessed four times to different people," she said. Iboshi argued that Pauline's presence during the viewing wasn't required because the procedure was "equivalent to sending evidence back to the jury room."

The justices also seemed curious as to why the Volkswagen wasn't formally received as evidence. "In order for an object to become evidence it has to be marked as an exhibit and moved into evidence," Justice Levinson said. "So why is it that this didn't happen?"

Iboshi responded that the attorneys—both prosecution and defense—had agreed with the judge's procedure for letting the jurors look at the car in the basement.

Hunt then argued that Judge Amano should have moved the trial off the Big Island because of pretrial publicity. "If there was ever a case that a trial court should have moved venue, this was the case."

Justice Ramil, noting that the case had received statewide publicity, asked Hunt where the trial should have been heard.

It could have been moved to another island or another state, Hunt said. In Big Island newspapers "it was virtually front-page news every time the case was reported." Furthermore, he said, community pressure for a conviction was stronger on the Big Island because that's where the crime took place. Any jurors who might have wanted to acquit Pauline "would have had to go back to their community and justify why they voted no," he said. "That was simply asking too much of the jurors to ignore that pressure."

Although Iboshi conceded that she couldn't recall any other Big Island case that had received as much publicity as the Ireland case, she said Judge Amano had taken "extraordinary measures" to ensure that Pauline got a panel of fair and impartial jurors. "We take offense to the position of Mr.

Hunt that Hilo is such a backwater place," she said.

Two other issues that Hunt appealed were that Amano didn't view the defense computer simulation videotape before ruling it inadmissible, and that she excluded it from the trial. Hunt said he had told the jury during his opening statement that James Campbell would testify that there was "no way" the Volkswagen could have been involved in the accident. Without the computer simulation, Hunt couldn't deliver on that promise.

Although Supreme Court observers say the justices' questions don't always reveal their opinions, Acoba and Levinson's inquiries about the videotape seemed to suggest that the two might have had opposing positions on the issue. Acoba asked Hunt why the judge objected if the simulation was based on the state's theory of the accident; Levinson noted that Campbell conceded some of his assumptions were not based on any established facts; Acoba countered by pointing out that Campbell's opinion would have been subject to cross-examination.

Another point under appeal was that the judge didn't directly question Pauline about whether he wanted the jury to consider the "lesser included" charges of manslaughter or assault. "There has to be a personal on-the-record colloquy," Hunt said.

But Levinson reminded Hunt that it was he who objected to giving the jury instruction about the lesser charges. "You were going all or nothing," Levinson said.

Hunt didn't make oral arguments about his final issue on appeal, Amano's denial of a motion for a new trial. In his written brief, Hunt asserted that Amano violated Pauline's rights by not allowing Hunt to ask the alternate juror if she discussed any evidence with other jurors before deliberations began.

At the conclusion of oral arguments, Hunt asked the justices to overturn Pauline's guilty verdict and set a new trial somewhere other than the Big Island.

Chief Justice Moon said the court would take the appeal under advisement.

More than two years later, the court issued a 59-page opinion and a two-page concurring opinion. It was on December 26, 2002—11 years and two days after Dana Ireland's attack—that the unanimous court said Pauline's conviction would stand.

The Court said Amano didn't make a mistake by denying Hunt's motion for a change of venue. And it said the news coverage of the case wasn't prejudicial to Pauline. "Though there was much public outrage over the crime itself," the opinion said, "the media accounts regarding Pauline were largely neutral, with some even presenting Pauline's views." Furthermore, said the court, Amano took precautions to make sure Pauline got impartial jurors

The Hawaii Supreme Court also said Amano wasn't required to view Campbell's tape and had a solid basis for excluding it from evidence. Likewise, the judge didn't have to consult Pauline before agreeing not to include the "lesser included" offenses of manslaughter or first-degree assault in the jury instructions. The court said such instructions must be supported by the evidence. In Pauline's case, said the court, "there is no rational basis to support the contention that the jury could have rationally acquitted Pauline of second-degree murder and convicted him of manslaughter or assault."

As for Hunt's motion for a mistrial, the Supreme Court said there had been no juror misconduct. Hunt had argued that the alternate juror, Teresa Miller, used the term "we" instead of "I" when voicing her opinions about the case after the presentation of evidence but before the verdict. The Supreme Court said it was clear that she was referring only to her own beliefs.

The Hawaii Supreme Court did say, however, that Judge Amano made some "procedural oversights" when the jury viewed the Volkswagen without Pauline. In analyzing the case, the court overturned a legal point established in a prior case that said a viewing doesn't constitute evidence. Having done that, the Supreme Court went on to establish procedural safeguards that must accompany any future jury viewing: First, the trial court has discretion in determining whether a viewing will take place at all. If it does, the defendant and attorneys have the right to be there. What's more, the judge must be present during the viewing, which has to be noted for the record.

Although Judge Amano should have followed

those procedures, the Supreme Court called the errors "harmless" and said they didn't interfere with Pauline's right to a fair trial.

Cliff Hunt said he would probably appeal the decision. After meeting with Pauline in prison to give him the bad news, Hunt publicly declared his belief in his client's innocence. "This guy didn't do it," he said. "Frank is devastated. He's just totally devastated."

Hunt said his motion to move the trial off the Big Island was appropriate for the Dana Ireland case. "Frank had no chance," he said. "He never had a chance in that community." He added that Judge Amano's decision to exclude Campbell's computer simulation took the "legs" out of his defense that Pauline had lied when he confessed. "The confession was bullshit," Hunt said. "If it happened the way he said, why wasn't his DNA there? Why wasn't the Schweitzers' DNA there?"

Hunt asked why prosecutors hadn't followed through with their promise to re-test the DNA. And if they believed there was a fourth person, he asked, why hadn't they made it a condition of Shawn Schweitzer's plea bargain to name that person? "There's no fourth person," he said. There's a single person walking around that community. The way this case is going to be solved is someday the guy who did it is going to confess before he dies."

Obviously, the lead detective who put the Dana Ireland case together didn't share Hunt's opinion about the Supreme Court's decision, "I'm absolutely, positively pleased beyond a doubt," said Steven Guillermo, who was now a lieutenant.

The prosecutors were happy, too. "We're very satisfied with the decision, the outcome for the Ireland family, the outcome for the community and for our office and law enforcement in general," said Charlene Iboshi. In response to Hunt's question about re-testing the DNA, she said her office had decided to hold off on that until technology improved. They didn't want to consume what little evidence was left.

Lincoln Ashida, now corporation counsel for Hawaii County, was relieved that the high note on which he'd left the prosecutor's office hadn't gone flat. "Until the Supreme Court rules and decides, there's always apprehension, no matter how good a case you have," he said.

Ashida said Judge Amano was careful at every step to protect the record. "Really, an appeal comes down to a Supreme Court scrutinizing what a judge did or didn't do," he said. "So I think, frankly, the judge is due some credit."

Sandy Ireland learned about the Supreme Court's opinion from a television newscast the day after Christmas. "It's been a long time, and it's sort of been weighing over my head," she said. "And it comes at a good time, too, 'cause Christmas is really hard for us."

Louise Ireland was a little confused about the significance of the opinion until someone explained that it meant Pauline would stay in jail. "I'm glad to hear that," she said. "I'm glad this whole trial business is coming to an end and that he did lose his appeal."

As usual, Louise had spent Christmas visiting Dana's grave, where she found a dozen red roses and a candle from Dana's former boyfriend, Jeff Stiles.

"He does it every year," Louise said. "I remember telling him, 'Don't you ever forget Dana.' And he said, 'I won't.' So maybe that's his way of making sure."

After much consideration, the Ireland family gave out the reward money with no fanfare and declined to discuss who got what.

From prison Frank Pauline sent a form letter to members of the media. In it he documented cases that had been reversed on appeal because of new DNA evidence exonerating the defendants. "I am writing this to make a point to the people who believed that I, Frank R. Pauline Jr., did commit the rape and murder of Dana Ireland on Christmas Eve 1991. Please read what I wrote and think about what went on in my trial. Also please keep in mind that DNA experts took tests that cleared myself and both of the Schweitzer brothers. This alone should have proved to the public that I lied about the death of Dana Ireland in order to help my brother John Gonsalves stay out of prison for his drug dealings."

What Pauline didn't realize was that his case differs in a significant way from those that were overturned because of DNA tests. In those cases, the DNA was new evidence, unknown to the juries who sat through the trials. In Pauline's case, the jury knew about the DNA and voted to convict him anyway. For that reason, Pauline had no new DNA evidence to present to another jury. He was legally guilty and would remain in prison barring an unlikely Supreme Court reversal on the other issues.

All the same, knowing Pauline is locked up does nothing to eliminate the lingering question that haunts young women as they ride their bikes past a stranger on a tropical country road: Whose DNA was it?

Authors' Notes and Acknowledgments

In writing this book, the authors examined news reports and official documents, attended the trials, and interviewed countless people. We used exact quotes whenever possible, but in some cases recreated dialogue from our own memories and from the observations of those we interviewed. In the case of early suspects and some witnesses, we have used pseudonyms. Otherwise all names are real.

This book would not have been possible without the cooperation of many people, especially John, Louise, and Sandy Ireland.

For enduring interviews that brought back painful memories, we also thank Dana's friends and relatives: Valerie Oliver Dexter, Mike Dickerson, Lowell Kilday, Robert Ossakow, Heather Preast, Jennifer Shepherd, Kelly Simpson, and Jeff Stiles.

Others who helped us include Hazel Allan, Ed Blake, Dan Boe, Nina Buchanan, Brenda Carreira, Pete Conol, Brian De Lima, Eileen DeWald, Marcie Greenwell, Fred Holschuh, Cliff Hunt, Charlene Iboshi, Lisa Kaneshiro, Harry Kim, Ira Leitel, Andy

Levin, Teresa Miller, Pat Pauline, Frank Pauline Jr., Billy Perreira, Martha Rodillas, Ida Smith, and Tom Yamauchi.

For their encouragement and assistance we thank Jim Alter, Jason Armstrong, Hunter Bishop, Tim Bryan, Hugh Clark, Donna Clayton, Rosemary Dimoff, David Fryxell, Iva Goldman, Nigel Hey, William Ing, Kay Kobata, Crystal Kua, Wanda Lee, Georgina Lindsey, Alice Lynd, Arlynn Nellhaus, Carleton Rehr, Marilyn Ribble, Pamela Shandel, Dave Smith, Ed Tanaka, Rod Thompson, and Patricia Walters.

For their invaluable insights and recollections, we are particularly grateful to Lincoln Ashida and Steve Guillermo.

For making this book a reality, we thank our agent, Robert Preskill, and our editor, Sarah Durand.

And finally, for their years of patience and tolerance, we salute our spouses Peter Loos and Joan Castberg.

True Crime Sagas
Ripped From Today's Headlines

MURDER IN GREENWICH
THE MARTHA MOXLEY CASE . . . SOLVED
by Marc Fuhrman
0-06-109692-X/ $7.99 US/ $10.99 Can

PERFECT MURDER, PERFECT TOWN
**THE UNCENSORED STORY OF THE JONBENET MURDER
AND THE GRAND JURY'S SEARCH FOR THE TRUTH**
by Lawrence Schiller
0-06-109696-2/ $7.99 US/ $10.99 Can

SON OF A GRIFTER
**THE TWISTED TALE OF SANTE AND KENNY KIMES,
THE MOST NOTORIOUS CON ARTISTS IN AMERICA**
by Kent Walker and Mark Schone
0-06-103169-0/ $7.99 US/ $10.99 Can

A WARRANT TO KILL
**A TRUE STORY OF OBSESSION,
LIES AND A KILLER COP**
by Kathryn Casey
0-380-78041-0/ $7.99 US/ $10.99 Can

DEADLY SECRETS
**FROM HIGH SCHOOL TO HIGH CRIME—
THE TRUE STORY OF TWO TEEN KILLERS**
by Reang Putsata
0-380-80087-X/ $6.99 US/ $9.99 Can

ESSENTIAL REFERENCE TOOLS
FROM HarperTorch

THE CONCISE
Roget's
INTERNATIONAL
THESAURUS®
REVISED & UPDATED
SIXTH EDITION

The world's number-one bestselling thesaurus of synonyms, antonyms, and related words

Edited by Barbara Ann Kipfer, Ph.D.
Robert L. Chapman, Ph.D., Consulting Editor

0-06-009479-6/$5.99 US/$7.99 Can

HARPER
COLLINS
NEWLY REVISED AND UPDATED
WEBSTER'S
DICTIONARY

A new, up-to-date, completely portable version of America's most well-known dictionary

0-06-055782-6/$5.99 US/$7.99 Can